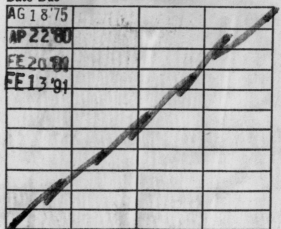

Iran

PAST AND PRESENT

IRAN

PAST AND PRESENT

BY DONALD N. WILBER

PRINCETON, NEW JERSEY

PRINCETON UNIVERSITY PRESS

1967

PREFACE

𝒯HE series of prefaces included in the first, second, third, fourth and fifth editions of this work are now replaced by this brief introduction to the sixth edition.

The purpose of the book remains—as stated in the first preface—to furnish definitive information about the past and present of this ancient land, and to present a factual picture of the country as a whole. Every effort has been made to achieve accuracy of facts, and to assemble the most recent background and statistical material. The author has benefited from the helpful suggestions of numerous reviewers to make specific amendments to the text and to round out the coverage of certain subjects.

This edition includes material on political, social, and economic developments in Iran through the year 1966. In addition, statistical material has been up-dated throughout the text.

The transliteration of proper names, place names, and descriptive terms from Arabic and Persian—two languages written in the Arabic script—presents problems. There is no single, standardized system for transliteration from Arabic and the exigencies of printing rule out the use of underlines, overlines, macrons, and the other symbols required for scholarly precision. However, the position of the Arabic characters *ayn* and *hamzah* has been indicated by the use of the apostrophe and a serious effort made to achieve internal consistency in transliteration.

December, 1966   Donald N. Wilber

CONTENTS

IRAN'S HERITAGE

MODERN IRAN

[vii]

CONTENTS

ILLUSTRATIONS

CREDITS FOR ILLUSTRATIONS

Iranian Information Center, 1, 3, 7, 8, 9, 10, 17, 19, 20, 21, 22
Arthur Upham Pope, 11
Donald N. Wilber, 2, 12, 13, 14, 15, 16, 18
Wilber Collections, 4, 5, 6

IRAN'S HERITAGE

I. PHYSICAL CHARACTERISTICS

Place Name

IRAN and Persia: the two names have been used to designate the same country, but are not true synonyms. When the Aryan peoples migrated from their original territory, somewhere within Asia to the upland plateau below the Caspian Sea, they called the new region Iran, which means "homeland of the Aryans." The great royal palace site of the Achaemenid dynasty, which originally ruled over the region northeast of the head of the Persian Gulf, was called Parsa, taken into the Greek language in the time of Alexander the Great as Persepolis. The powerful Achaemenid empire was called Iran, but the regional and palace name became transferred to the province within the empire as Pars or Fars, and hence the people of many other lands came to call the country Persia. In Sasanian times the official name of the empire of Iran was Iranshahr. Since 1935 when the Iranian government, for the sake of consistency, requested all foreign countries to use the official name of Iran, the correct designation has gained general usage. On the other hand the language of the country is Persian, *farsi* to the inhabitants, since it is the language of ancient Parsa, and it is written in Arabic characters.

Location

Iran's geographical position has made it the bridge for communication by land between Far Eastern Asia and the lands of the Mediterranean and Europe. Before the dawn of recorded history its mountain caves sheltered the hunters who were among the earliest people of the world to move down into the lower plains and to settle in villages, cultivate crops, and raise domestic animals. It also lay athwart the lines of movement of the early migrant tribes of central Asia, and became settled by many of these groups. Within historic times its rulers expanded their control far to the east and the west of the plateau and established the first great world empire. For hundreds of years the main trade routes between the Far East and the West crossed northern Iran, and later on, when sea routes became of equal importance, additional highways led up from ports along the Persian Gulf to the principal commercial centers both within the country and beyond its frontiers.

The vital role of the overland trade routes across Iran was seriously limited by the construction of the Suez Canal, and the decline of her importance as a channel of trade heralded a period of political and military weakness. At the same time her strategic location made her a bone of contention between great powers whose interests were diametrically opposed. Her present frontiers, established during the nineteenth century, were the result of a series of wars in which she was unable to hold her own against more powerful neighbors.

Iran today covers an area of 628,000 square miles, approximately as large as that part of the United States which lies east of the Mississippi River, exclusive of New England—a much smaller area than at any time in her long existence. In general, her previous frontiers were much farther to the east than at present and fairly close to her present western ones, the greater expansion toward the east having been the result both of the less broken topography in that direction and of the strong linguistic and ethnic relations between the people of that area and the Iranians of the plateau. In spite of its present restricted size the country is still known as the Empire of Iran, and its ruler is the *Shahinshah*, or "King of Kings," a title first used in Iran well over two thousand years ago.

Iran lies between the Caspian Sea and the Persian Gulf, and has common frontiers with Iraq, Turkey, Soviet Russia, Afghanistan and Pakistan. Along her perimeter dwell peoples of various languages or ethnic stocks whose area of settlement or of tribal movement overlaps the actual boundaries of the country.

Geology and Topography

The geological formations of the country have been fairly well studied, although not in a systematic fashion, by Persian and European specialists in this field, and small scale geological maps of Iran have been published. The more detailed studies of certain areas have been made in connection with the search for oil fields and for important mineral deposits.

The average traveler in Iran is made aware of its geological history by the lofty peaks, the ranks of jagged mountains springing abruptly from the fairly level plains, the vivid coloration of many formations, and the spectacular faulting or folding of the rocks. The traveler by air, who usually approaches Iran from the west or southwest, looks down on a series of mountain ranges which resemble the corrugated surface of a washboard. Each successive ridge is tilted from the vertical and higher than the one before until the general level of the high plateau is reached, but even there mountains rise on every side. From sufficient altitude the villages and tilled fields lose all identity, and the entire country seems to be barren and devoid of life.

The Zagros and the Elborz Ranges, which came into being in geological periods from the Paleozoic to the Pliocene, attain altitudes of over 11,000 feet. As mountains go they are rather young, as is shown by their sharp, broken profiles. The general configuration of these ranges and of the Iranian plateau seems to have been the result of prolonged pressure against the area of Iran from a Russian mass on the north and an African mass on the south. The fact that the southward pressure was the stronger is indicated by the steeper slopes of the Elborz as compared to the softer folds of the Zagros Range. The building of the mountain systems was of course complicated by vertical movements and by extensive faulting.

In several regions of the country the prominent cones of formerly active volcanoes are a dominant feature of the landscape. The principal volcanic peaks are Demavand, the highest peak in Iran, which figures in many ancient tales of heroes and demons, rising to 18,600 feet, in the north; Savalan, at 14,000 feet, Sahand at 12,138 feet, and Ararat (lesser Ararat is within Iran, but greater Ararat lies just over the frontier) in the northwest; and Bazman and Chihiltan at 13,262 feet, in the extreme southeast. Two of these cones still show some traces

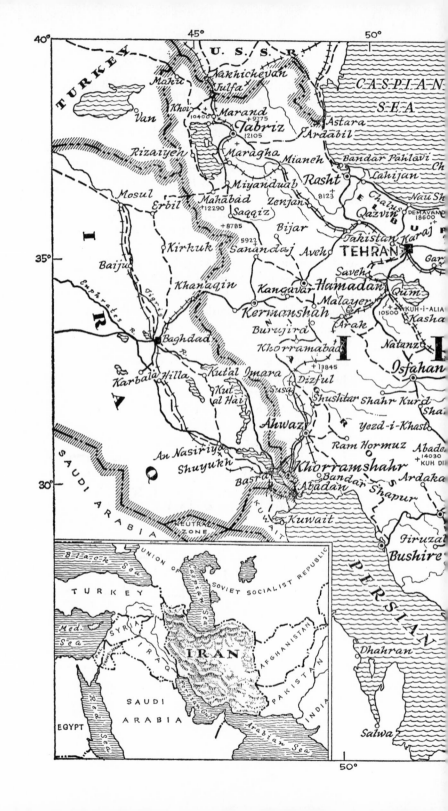

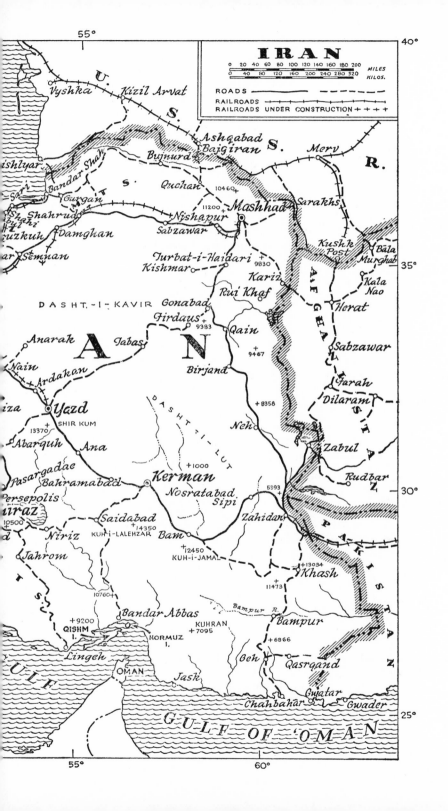

IRAN

MILES
0 20 40 60 80 100 120 140 160 180 200
KILOS.
0 40 80 120 160 200 240 280 320

ROADS ———
RAILROADS +++++++
RAILROADS UNDER CONSTRUCTION + + +

55°   40°
40°

U. S.
Vyshka   Kizil Arvat
S.
Ashqabad
Baigiran   Merv
Bujnurd   S.
R.
Quchan   10460+   Sarakhs
ishlyar
Bandar Shah   11200+   Mashhad
Gurgan   Nishapur   Kushk
Shahrud   Sabzawar   Post   Bala
uzkuh Damghan   Murghab   35°
ar Semnan   Turbat-i-Haidari   Kala
Kishmar   9830+   Kariz   Nao
Rui Khaf   A
DASHT-I-KAVIR Gonabad   F
Firdaus+   G   Herat
Anarak   A   Tabas   9383+   Qain   H
N   +   Sabzawar
Nain   9467   A
Ardakan   Birjand   Farah
iza   Dilaram
Yazd   D
A   +8358   N
SHIR KUM   S
13370+   H   Neh
Abarquh   Ana   T   Zabul
Pasargadae   -   I   Rudbar
Bahramabad   -   +1000   Z
ersepolis   L   5393   30°
iiraz   Kerman   U   +   Zahidan
10500   T   Nosratabad
d   Niriz   Sipi
Saidabad   +14350   Bam   +12450   +13034
KUH-i-LALEHZAR   KUH-i-JAMAL   Khash   P
Jahrom   +11473   A
10760+   Bampur R.   K
+9200   Bandar Abbas   KUHRAN   Bampur   I
QISHM   +7095   S
I.   KORMUZ   +6866   T
Lingeh   I.   Geh   Qasrqand   A
OMAN   Jask   Gwatar   N   25°
GULF   Chahbahar   Gwader

GULF OF OMAN

55°   60°   25°

of activity: all climbers who have made the ascent of Demavand have noted the presence of sulphur gases, and Chihiltan trails a smoky plume of sulphurous gas from its summit.

The oil fields of the south occur in a region of oval limestone domes, while the area south of Tehran is strewn with great salt plugs, a type of formation often associated with oil deposits.

Iran may be described in general terms as a high plateau some 4,000 feet above sea level, strewn with mountains. Specifically, there are four main topographical areas, each distinctive in character and extending beyond the frontiers of Iran:

1. The great Zagros and Elborz Ranges, stamping a huge V upon the surface of the country. The apex of the V forms in northwestern Iran and extends beyond into Turkey and the Russian Caucasus. The southern arm of the letter is represented by the Zagros Range, which runs southeast and roughly parallels the frontier of Iraq and the shore of the Persian Gulf, while the upper arm, the Elborz Range, looms like a great wall across the north of the country, breaking down into other ranges which run on into Afghanistan and Turkestan.

2. The area within the V begins as the high plateau with its own secondary mountain ranges and gradually levels off to become the empty deserts which continue into southern Afghanistan and Pakistan.

3. The region of Khuzistan, below the lower arm of the V, is a continuation of the low-lying plain of Iraq.

4. The Caspian Sea coast above the upper arm of the V is below sea level and forms a separate climatic zone.

The fact that each of these topographical formations extends beyond the frontiers of Iran does not mean that the country is easy of access, for its present boundaries are guarded by formidable natural barriers. The entire western frontier and the country inland from the Persian Gulf is protected by lofty ramparts of rock, where steep passes lead from sea level to a height of over 7,000 feet and down again to the plateau. Equally forbidding passes isolate the Caspian littoral from the rest of Iran, and along the northeastern and eastern frontiers the approaches are either through hilly country or across vast spaces of empty desert.

Drainage

There are four principal drainage basins, roughly corresponding to the topographical zones: The Caspian, the Lake Rezaieh, the Persian Gulf, and the great desert basins. The Persian Gulf basin is fed by three separate systems: the smaller streams of northwest Iran which eventually find their way into the Tigris River; the Karun and its tributaries, which empty into the head of the Persian Gulf; and the countless streams which indent the thousand-mile-long coast line of the Persian Gulf.

Most of the rivers and streams of Iran flow not into one of the three large bodies of water, but into the vast interior deserts where there are three subordinate drainage areas, separated from one another by lines of hills but having the same effect as that of a single basin. This feature of interior drainage has an important relation to the economic life of Iran.

The great majority of the inhabitants of Iran live along the lines of the V formed by the main mountain ranges. The mountains run in parallel files, enclosing long, narrow valleys walled at each end by mountainous cross barriers. The general pattern of mountains and valleys may be compared to a number of ladders laid down roughly parallel to each other, the uprights representing the lines of the mountains and the rungs the barriers across the ends of each valley. An average valley may be eight miles in width and from 25 to 40 miles long, flat bottomed, with rims rising directly and abruptly into the mountains above. Villages are more closely clustered along the rims than along the center line where may be found one of the highways which even in modern times have penetrated relatively few of the thousands of mountain valleys. Nomads spend the summers in the higher altitudes where the heavy snows and extreme cold of winter would make village life impossible, while farming communities abound in the valleys where the level ground is more suitable for cultivation. For centuries the farmers have led isolated, self-sufficient lives, and the barriers which separate them from the outer world have contributed to historical continuity, preservation of racial stocks, and comparative safety and independence in periods of foreign invasion.

Rivers

The more important rivers which flow into the Caspian are, from west to east: the Aras (Araxes), the Sefid Rud and its long tributary the Qizil Uzun, the Chalus, the Haraz, the Lar, the Gorgan, and the Atrek. None of them carry a great volume of water except in the spring. Their lower courses serve as spawning grounds for the sturgeon of the Caspian, productive of fine caviar, and these streams offer a reservoir of water power as yet untapped.

The largest river flowing into the Persian Gulf is the Karun, whose lower course is the confluence of the upper Karun and the Ab-i-Diz River. The Karun is navigable by small steamers as far as Ahwaz, some 70 miles from it mouth, and smaller boats can proceed even farther above the Ahwaz rapids. At Ahwaz the river is about one hundred yards wide, and is spanned by a handsome steel highway bridge and a railroad bridge.

Rivers which empty into the interior of the country are the Zayandeh Rud, which flows past Isfahan; the Jajirud, Karej, and Kand, near Tehran; the Qarasu, near Hamadan; the Hableh, east of Kashan; the Qum, flowing by the town of the same name; and the Kur, which runs past ancient Persepolis. Far to the east is the Helmand River, whose dammed-up waters, although nearly all of its course is within Afghanistan, are led through channels to irrigate a part of the province of Sistan.

These rivers are the principal perennial streams; most of the others run dry in the middle of the summer. Typical of the larger streams in this category is the Zayandeh Rud, whose waters nourish Isfahan and the score of adjacent farming communities. In the early spring this river is more than one hundred yards wide at Isfahan and nearly six feet deep, and since there are no controlling dams or barrages the flood water pours out to the desert areas and soaks away into the thirsty, barren ground. Later in the spring the communities upstream from Isfahan draw off its water to their fields, or flood paddies for cultivating rice, and as a result, in midsummer the river opposite Isfahan is little more than a trickle just adequate for the needs of the area while the villages still farther downstream are often without any water at all.

Seas and Lakes

The Caspian Sea, the largest landlocked body of water in the world, lies some 85 feet below sea level, is comparatively shallow, and for several centuries has been slowly shrinking in size. Its salt content is considerably less than that of the oceans, and though it abounds with fish its shelving coasts do not offer any good natural harbors, and sudden and violent storms make it dangerous for small boats.

Lake Rezaieh, formerly called Lake Urmiya, is about 80 miles long and 35 miles wide, or approximately the same size as the Great Salt Lake of Utah, and averages from five to six yards in depth with a maximum depth of eleven yards. Only a few minor streams flow into this landlocked body of water, which has resulted in a steady shrinking in the size of the lake and so high a concentration of salt that no fish can live in it. Its saline content, made up of salts and sulphates of magnesium, calcium, sodium, and potassium, is as high as 23%. Most maps shows a large island of Shahi well out toward the center of the lake, but within recent years the water has receded so far that during the summer months it is now possible to walk directly from the mainland to the shores of the "island."

Along the frontier between Iran and Afghanistan are several marshy lakes which expand and contract according to the season of the year. The largest of these, the Hamun-i-Sabari, is alive with wild fowl. Real fresh water lakes are exceedingly rare in Iran; there are probably not more than ten in all the country, all of them brackish and most not much bigger than ponds.

Deserts

The vast desert regions of Iran stretch across the plateau from the northwest, close to Tehran and Qum, for a distance of nearly 800 miles to the southeast and beyond the frontier. Approximately one-sixth of the total area of Iran is barren desert.

The two largest desert areas are known as the Dasht-i-Lut and the Dasht-i-Kavir, *dasht* meaning "plain," *lut* meaning "naked" or "barren," and *kavir* meaning "salt desert." These areas actually merge into each other, although they do display certain local variations. Some sections contain salt lakes which each year are swollen by the spring torrents from the interior rivers and in summer disappear beneath a hard salt crust. Other areas are stony wastes, wide stretches of saline soil or deserts heaped with sand dunes, and nearly all are crisscrossed by ranges of hills. At a few widely separated points copious springs flowing from the naked earth have created fertile oases, such as the charming village of Tabas, set in the midst of flowering gardens, orchards, and groves of date palms.

It is often said that the Dasht-i-Lut and the Dasht-i-Kavir are impassable except by the single road which runs from Yazd to Firdaus, but within recent years heavy trucks and military vehicles have traveled over long stretches of these deserts. Ruins of caravanserais and of villages found there are evidence that not too long ago the deserts were kinder to human existence, and some traces of a man-made "stone carpet" have been found where in earlier centuries caravans followed the desert trails. However, it is true that disaster dogged the caravans; many fell victim to exhaustion of water supplies in summer or to winter's sudden rains which could turn the surface into a slippery morass and always chance straying from the trail might mean, for men and camels, breaking through the salt crust to become hopelessly trapped in the mire beneath.

Climate

Rainfall in Iran, the result of atmospheric depressions moving eastward from the region of the Mediterranean Sea, is largely confined to the winter months from November to early April. Summer thunderstorms, so familiar to us, are quite rare, and the occasional rains in midsummer are limited to light showers.

Over most of the Iranian plateau the total annual rainfall is less than twelve inches, or about that of the state of Nevada. The extensive desert regions and the southeastern corner of the country receive less than five inches of rain a year. The northwest corner of the country often benefits by from 15 to 35 inches, and it is there that dry farming, the growing of unirrigated crops, is most widely carried on. However, even in areas receiving the minimum amount of precipitation the farmers will sow a limited amount of winter wheat with the knowledge that if the winter brings three or four good rains there will be a crop worth harvesting. Torrential downpours sometimes occur, and when this happens flash floods sweep down from the mountains to wash out roads, damage villages, and destroy crops.

The Caspian littoral presents quite a different picture, for there the annual rainfall is from forty to sixty inches and rain falls throughout the year, creating the extensive marshes and the dank jungle foliage which breed the fevers so common in this region.

Rain in the valleys means snow on the high mountains, and many of the higher peaks are crowned with snow until late in the summer. On the valley plains heavy snowfalls are comparatively rare, and in such towns as Tehran, Isfahan, and Kermanshah the snow usually melts away in a few days. Snow does not normally fall south of a line connecting Andimeshk, Shiraz, Yazd, and Qaen, and seldom along the Caspian coast. But the high passes of the main highways may be blocked for days or even weeks at a time in the late winter, and the Chalus road from Tehran to the Caspian Sea is usually closed for three months in the year. The amount of snow in the high mountains also controls the spring migrations of the nomadic tribes, whose flocks often cannot move through certain passes until May.

The Iranian plateau enjoys fairly mild winters and hot summers. For example, at Tehran there may be a period of several weeks in midsummer when the temperature reaches 100 degrees day after day, but the nights are relatively fresh and cool. The humidity in summer is only about 20%. In winter the temperature rarely reaches zero and usually is above the freezing mark in the middle of the day. The regions of Khorasan and Azerbaijan are cooler in summer and much colder in winter.

Much less tolerable conditions prevail at the head of the Persian Gulf, along the shores of the Gulf, and in the desert regions of the southeast. It is a question whether temperatures are higher at Abadan, Khorramshahr, and Ahwaz, or in the deserts. Both sections have recorded readings of 130 degrees, but the area at the head of the Persian Gulf is also plagued by a high humidity. The Caspian littoral ranges from warm to hot throughout the year, and in January, the height of the rainy season, the humidity averages 90% while in July it is about 75%.

In Iran the change from one season to the next is fairly abrupt. By March 21, the first day of the Iranian year, the fruit trees are in full bud and fresh green wheat covers the fields, and later, while the orchards are in bloom, wild flowers carpet the stony hills. Summer heat burns and kills the flowers. Autumn is not marked by a display of bright colors and the soft haze of Indian summer; instead there is a rapid transition from summer to winter.

Clear days are the rule in Iran, for the skies are cloudless for more than half the days of each year and only on about fifty are they stormy and overcast. Strong winds blow at certain periods and often fill the air with a haze of dust. In southeast Iran summer winds blow steadily over a period of weeks with a velocity that exceeds sixty miles an hour, and their force is utilized by windmills to grind flour from the local wheat harvest.

The cold of winter is more dreaded by the Persians than the heat of summer, for travel and transport may be forced to a halt and the farmer must conserve his limited supply of food.

Even more serious is the fact that the cold cannot be countered by a system of heating. All houses of any size are turned toward the south so that the welcome winter sun, which can be very warm, will shine directly into the main room of the house. All types of fuel are scarce and expensive, and in the villages and towns there is no way of heating the entire house. Families keep warm by using a *kursi,* which is a pan or brazier containing slow burning charcoal. The pan is placed on the floor with a circular table or frame about two feet above it, and on top of the table all the family quilts are draped to form a circle some three or four yards across. Members of the family may recline during the day, and sleep at night, under the quilts, with their bodies radiating like spokes from the hub of the charcoal pan and only their heads exposed to the cold air of the room.

II. HISTORY

Prehistoric Iran

ⓂAN's progress from the remote time of his emergence
as a species down to the present day may be shown on a scale
fifty inches long, of which each inch represents 10,000 years.
According to such a scale, man became a farmer at the 49¼
inch point, learned to write at 49½ inches, and at 49¾ inches
culture and civilization, such as that of the Achaemenid empire, was in existence. Most of the material which follows in
this chapter will deal with the final quarter inch on the scale
and with the long struggle of man against himself, against his
fellow men, and against nature. But some mention must be
made of the fascinating prehistoric period, the time before
written records were made.

The Paleolithic or Stone Age men of prehistoric times were
hunters. They fashioned rough weapons and implements, pursued the game upon which their lives depended, and took
shelter in caves. The population of any area was small, for it
bore a direct ratio to the number of wild animals in the region
and starvation was ever-threatening. Groups probably moved
within fairly well-defined areas, but the pressure of hunger led
to wider movement and there seems to have been considerable
intercourse over wide regions at very early periods. Development during the Stone Age was more rapid and earlier in the
Middle East than in Europe.

Three vital discoveries led to a marked change in mode of
life and probably in social organization. These were the introduction of cultivation, the use of metals, and community
life. It is probable that primitive people had long been gathering wild rice and wheat and roots, but the decisive step was
taken when cereals gathered in the fall were first stored and
sowed in the spring. This control over the means of subsistence
resulted in group movements from the higher mountains down
to the flat-bottomed valleys where level surfaces lay ready for
cultivation, a major change for which the topography created

[14]

both the means and the stimulus. The wild grains such as wild emmer, the ancestor of wheat, which still grows in Iran, were native not to the basins of the great rivers of the Near East but to the mountain slopes, and the challenge of and response to man's natural surroundings were stronger in the cool hills than on the hot plains. Planted fields soon surrounded compact settlements and animals were domesticated within them, and the new type of community life led to changes in the social relations between individuals and between groups.

Our knowledge of the earliest inhabitants of Iran is very fragmentary. Excavations in one cave at Behistun and in the caves called Belt and Hotu near Behshahr on the Caspian coast represent a splendid beginning. The initial finds indicate an active flint industry in the Middle Paleolithic period as well as skeletons and skulls of the Mesolithic period: this latter material has been dated to about 10,000 B.C. by the Carbon-14 method of analyzing pieces of charcoal from various levels of digging. The excavators themselves believe that these people were Nordic, of the same race as the Upper Paleolithic hunters of Europe.

About 6,000 B.C. the inhabitants of the area of Iran discovered agriculture, practiced animal husbandry, and made painted pottery and polished stone implements. The physical characteristics of these people are not known, although at a later date precise material comes from a rock-cut relief at Kurangun in southwestern Iran. Dated about 2,500 B.C., the scene contains the sharply cut profiles of some forty of the local people. Farming gave a more dependable food supply and it seems certain that the population expanded greatly and spread out over valleys and plains.

By the end of the Neolithic period, that of polished stone implements, large villages were scattered over the level plains. Each settlement was packed with closely crowded houses and there was no orderly system of streets and lanes. After 3,000 B.C. bronze weapons, implements, and other objects must have been made in vast quantities, judging by the mass of bronzes recovered in archeological excavations. Within Iran excavations of early sites have been carried on by French archeologists

at Susa, Nihavand, Sarpol, Asadabad, and near Kashan; by a
Swedish sponsored expedition at Gorgan; by the Oriental Institute of the University of Chicago near Persepolis; by the
University Museum of Philadelphia and the Kansas City Museum at Damghan; and by the Iranian Institute at Gorgan and
in Luristan. Notable work in the fields of excavation, exploration, and interpretation of the period of prehistory has been
done by Ernst Herzfeld, Sir Aurel Stein, and Carleton Coon.

The sites of early settlements appear as conspicuous mounds,
some nearly one hundred feet in height, of which there are
many thousand in Iran. The original settlements were founded
on the level plain or upon a slight natural rise. After heavy
rains the mud houses collapsed and new ones were built on
the smoothed debris, and rubbish was thrown out in the narrow
lanes so that their level was constantly being built up. Thus, in
the course of centuries the settlements rose higher and higher
above the plain. Occupation of a site would come to an end
when the area at the top of the artificial mound became too
small or when the population was wiped out by war or natural
calamities. Over the deserted site wind blew sand and earth,
and grass grew up to cover all traces of human habitation; but
heavy rains still wash pieces of pottery, seals, and other small
objects down to the base of the mound to reveal the presence
and approximate age of an ancient settlement.

Excavation work at a selected site begins at the top of the
mound where either a limited section or the entire area is slowly cleared. The technique of digging resembles the cutting
away of a series of horizontal slices. Within each slice the vertical position and location plan of every building and object is
carefully recorded, so that it is possible to detect marked
changes in construction and in types of pottery and other objects. Distinctive horizontal levels can be given a letter or number designation, and similarity of levels between different sites
used to establish common cultural traditions or to indicate
influences from one region toward another. This system of
comparative levels also permits the estimation of dates for
periods antedating written records.

The objects found at an ancient site include tools, implements for cultivation and weaving, seals, cult figurines, children's toys, and pottery. Pottery, found in large quantities at each site, yields definite information, and the designs offer a fertile field for speculation. The earliest pottery was handmade, but later the potter's wheel came into use. There is great variety in the size and shape of the vessels dug up, and many of them, so thin and fragile that they could not have been suitable for daily use, have been found in graves, suggesting that they were made to provide for the needs of the deceased in and beyond the grave. Vessels painted in red or black are decorated with geometrical patterns, lively animal figures, and, much more rarely, figures of human beings. The animals common to the region are depicted with amazing skill, and it is especially interesting to note that the village artists made sometimes very naturalistic and sometimes highly stylized pictures of the same beasts. They are always shown in profile, and represent the persistent memory image of the creator rather than a direct copy of the animal's form.

It seems possible that all the geometrical patterns used on the pottery had a symbolical meaning for the artists and the people of the time, representing man's halting efforts to grasp the significance of the world, his interest in his surroundings, and his awe of the forces of nature. Dependent as he was upon favorable weather for the crops upon which he subsisted, many of his designs symbolized natural forces involved in the weather or were a transference of the symbol to a similar animal form. For example, the moon, associated with rain, is symbolized by a crescent, and the crescent is then represented by the curving horns of the ibex. Others represented the sun, falling rain, a great pool, and a flourishing tree upon a mountain top. The symbols also signified evolving religious beliefs and myths which became so firmly entrenched in the minds of the people that they were handed down to be recorded finally in writing.

Pre-Achaemenid Iran

History is distinguished from prehistory by the existence of legible records of man's activity, and as history begins the area of Iran is dominated by military and cultural influences from Mesopotamia to the west. Although the highlands had led the way in the development of farming and in community life, the people of the Mesopotamian plains—the land of the two rivers—came into the ascendancy with the invention of writing, the codification of law, and the establishment of monumental architecture. At Susa, a civilization so dominated arose before 3,000 B.C., provided with its own records in a proto-Elamite script: this writing remains unread. North of Susa and the region of the Elamites were other groups dwelling on the slopes between the river plains and the mountains of the Iranian plateau. From Elam to the north were to be found the Kassites, the Lullubi, and the Guti: a ruler of the Guti, Annubanini, appears on a rock-cut relief near Sarpol on the ancient highway across the plateau.

The groups on or adjacent to the plateau waxed and waned in strength over the centuries, while Elam, centered at Susa, displayed the most continuity and advanced culture. The Kassites, however, enjoyed their centuries of glory, for in the eighteenth century B.C. they overran Babylon and controlled that area for nearly six hundred years. Then Elam reached its peak about 1150 B.C., with mastery over the Tigris valley, the shore of the Persian Gulf, and the Zagros range.

However, in the second millennium B.C. a fresh ethnic element came on the scene in the form of successive waves of Aryans. First to reach the plateau proper were the Indo-Iranians; about 1500 B.C. they moved from the region of the Oxus and the Iaxartes rivers south and west to the plateau and then still further west where they established the kingdom of Mitanni. Then, about 900 B.C., came the Iranians. These people had lived in settled communities, and after a fairly prolonged period of wandering and of nomadic life they established villages in Iran, which they named for their homeland. They spoke an Indo-European dialect, but comparatively little is known of their ethnic character. Apparently they completely supplanted the earlier residents of the plateau, although there is a slight possibility that one or more of the existing nomadic tribes of Iran stem from peoples indigenous to the area.

The Iranians included the groups of the Medes (Māda), Persians (Pārsa), Parthians, Bactrians, Soghdians, Sacians, and Scythians. The Medes settled in western Iran and at first, along with the Persians to the south, were dominated by the Assyrian Empire, so that knowledge of them derives almost entirely from Assyrian inscriptions. They soon grew strong enough to assert their independence and then to overthrow Assyria, but the details of these events are lacking since they were not entered in the Assyrian records. Ecbatana, modern Hamadan, was the Median capital. Cyaxares, king of the Medes from 625 until 585 B.C., completely destroyed the power of Assyria and extended his realm far into Asia Minor.

Fascinating descriptions of the Median capital of Ecbatana and of its fabulous palaces may be found in the works of the Greek historians, Herodotus and Polybius. However, the lack of standing architectural monuments of this period makes it necessary to speculate about the construction of towns, temples, and houses. Two sources of information are available. First, there are clear-cut pictures of towns and of buildings incised on the stone reliefs which were originally in the palace of Sargon at Khorsabad. The surviving written accounts of the eighth campaign of King Sargon of Assyria against northwestern Iran in 714 B.C. aid in the understanding of the reliefs. Villages protected by ditches and lofty walls of stone are shown. The temple of Khaldia at the village of Musasir is pictured with a façade of six columns and a gable roof. Another town displays structures of squared masonry in alternate courses of black and white stones.

The second source of information is the rock-cut tombs of the Median period. In such tombs as that at Sahna, the tomb called Dokkan-i-Davud at Sarpol, the tomb at Fakhriqa and the tomb called Dah u Dukhtar the standard treatment displays a columnar portico. The form is actually the copy of a house type, with members and elements common to wood construction executed in stone. Less conclusive evidence indicates that a tower-like house was also popular during the period.

The best known of the works of art which have survived from these long centuries are the so-called Luristan bronzes,

3. Persepolis. One of the monumental sculptured stairways leading to the *apadana*, or audience hall

back to Palestine. Cyrus, who died in 529 B.C., was not only a world conqueror and effective organizer, but the first to display that spirit of tolerance which is typical of the Iranian character.

His son Cambyses conquered Egypt, and later fell insane and died by his own hand near Ecbatana during a revolt led by a *magush* or priest named Gaumata. Gaumata, who falsely claimed to be a brother of Cambyses, held the throne for a brief time before he was put to death by the heads of the noble families. Darius, the leader of the avengers, who sprang from a different branch of the Achaemenid family, was made king in 521 B.C. First putting down a wave of rebellion throughout the empire, he crossed the Bosphorous in 512 B.C., subdued Thrace, and crossed the Danube, but withdrew without consolidating these gains. Aid given by the mainland states of Greece to revolting Greek colonies in Asia Minor aroused him again to action, and two campaigns against the mainland, in 492 and 490 B.C., ended in the Battle of Marathon and the Persian withdrawal to Asia Minor.

Xerxes I succeeded his father Darius in 485 B.C. With a force of 900,000 men, supported by a huge fleet, he led a Third Campaign against Greece which culminated in the capture and burning of Athens in 480 B.C. After the defeat of the Persian fleet in the Battle of Salamis and the loss of the Battle of Platea, he withdrew to Asia Minor. Although warfare continued for some time, the Achaemenids gradually worked out more friendly relations with the Greek states and colonies.

Artaxerxes I followed his father in 465 B.C. and reigned until 424 B.C. The first signs of the internal decay of the empire appeared in revolts in Egypt and other satrapies, and not until the accession of Artaxerxes III, who ruled from 359 until 338 B.C., were the earlier bounds of the empire reëstablished for a brief period. The empire finally came to an end under the timid Darius III.

Most of our knowledge of the history of Iran in Achaemenid times and the details of the political organization, the army, and the life of the people is derived from Greek historians, especially from Herodotus. The empire was divided into about twenty provinces or satrapies, each under a satrap or governor. The governors came from noble Persian families, and the post tended to become hereditary. The basic system of an absolute monarchy and a number of semi-independent governors which was established in this period continued in Iran until the end of the nineteenth century.

The army was divided into six corps of 60,000 each, each corps composed of six divisions of 10,000 men, the cavalry mounted on horses bred in Media and armed with the bow and the javelin. The ruler's personal bodyguard was composed of 10,000 members, known as the Immortals, who were drawn from the leading families of Persia proper. The provinces were linked by roads, of which the most vital was the "Royal Road" which ran from Susa up through Mesopotamia and Asia Minor to the city of Sardis, a distance of 1,500 miles. Messengers and travelers used a post system of relays of fresh horses stationed at the many inns along the routes. Agriculture flourished, and justice was fairly administered. Racial groups within the boundaries of the empire were allowed to retain their own religions, and often their ruling families were allowed to continue in power. The tribute in kind of early times was later developed into systematic taxation with the unit of payment the gold *daric*. Susa, Babylon, and Ecbatana were the important administrative centers and sites of royal residence, while Persepolis was the spiritual center of the empire.

The ruling aristocracy seems to have retained a chivalrous spirit, but its tribal background gradually gave way to "oriental" modes of life and manners of thought imported from the highly cultured region of Mesopotamia. Herodotus noted this tendency of the Persians toward assimilation of external influences when he wrote: "There is no nation which so readily adopts foreign customs as the Persians. As soon as they hear of any luxury they instantly make it their own." The prevailing belief of modern times that the Achaemenid Persians were barbarians in contrast to the civilized Greeks is false, for we know that Cyrus despised the commercial habits of the Greeks and it is apparent that in the fields of public administration, political organization, continuity of government, and tolerance of race and creed the Achaemenids far surpassed the Greek city states.

The documents of the Achaemenid rulers, cut into rock or baked in clay tablets, are in three languages current in the empire: Old Persian, Elamite, and Babylonian. Recent research suggests that the official records were kept in Old Persian written in the Aramaic script, while the Old Persian of the rock inscriptions was written in an alphabet made up of borrowed cuneiform signs. In simplest terms, Old Persian was a member of the Iranian language group; directly related to it was Median and also Avestan, the language of the earliest Zoroastrian texts.

The royal inscriptions are limited to recording briefly the family line and religious faith of the ruler, the names of the provinces, the suppression of revolts, and details about the construction of royal palaces. Characteristic of their purport is this excerpt from the long trilingual inscription of Darius on the rock cliff of Behistun: "I am Darius, the great king, king of kings, king of lands peopled by all races, for long king of this great earth, reaching even far away, son of Hystaspes, the Achaemenian, a Persian, son of a Persian, an Aryan, of Aryan descent."

The Achaemenid period saw the rise of a religion which aimed at replacing the pagan gods personifying natural forces and human passions with a universal system based on the un-ending conflict between good and evil. This was the faith preached by Zarathushtra, modern Zoroaster, who was born on the Iranian plateau and lived probably in the sixth century B.C. Concrete reflections of the faith appeared on monuments of the Achaemenids. The new doctrine recognized Ahura Mazda, from whose name the religion is often called Mazdaism, as the God of good, associated also with truth and light, and taught the immortality of the soul and the final judgment of humanity. Such concepts were too abstract to persist unchanged and were altered on the one hand by association with the older Iranian divinities and on the other by the ritualistic way of life of the Median clan of Magi who became the hereditary priesthood of the developing faith.

Among numerous architectural remains of the Achaemenid period are seven royal rock-cut tombs at Persepolis and at nearby Naqsh-i-Rustam. Cut high into a vertical rock face, they consist of one or more chambers behind exterior façades of a row of engaged columns supporting an entablature. The composition is that of a house façade copied in stone, of which there are earlier prototypes in Iran and in Asia Minor.

Pasargadae, in a well-watered valley, is the site of the tomb of Cyrus, a monumental replica in stone of a rectangular gable-roofed house, on a raised platform. Here also are the remains of several royal pavilions scattered through what was originally a wooded park, each unit consisting of a large rectangular hall with porticoes on one or more sides of the building and small, square rooms at the corners. These pavilions again copy a house form in stone and wood.

The site of Persepolis is the best known of the period. Projecting from the cliffs to overlook a wide fertile plain is a great rectangular terrace with masonry sustaining walls, whose construction was begun by Darius and continued by Xerxes and Artaxerxes III. A great double-flight stairway of stone leads up to the terrace. Back of the stairhead stands the portal of "all-lands" built by Xerxes, square in plan with four stone columns in the interior and four doors flanked by huge human-headed winged bulls. East of the portico and several yards above the terrace level, is the great *apadana* or audience hall, approached by a double stair whose sides are lined with two groups of figures cut in low relief on the stone masonry: one a long procession of the subject peoples of the empire bringing tribute offerings for the annual spring festival held at Persepolis; the other the Persian, Median, and Susian members of the royal guard. On each side of the main hall was once a portico with two rows of six columns and at each corner was a more solidly built square room. The vast interior hall, about 200 feet on each side, contained six rows of six columns 65 feet in height.

Just east of the apadana is the famous "hall of a hundred

columns" which was burned by Alexander the Great. The plan is like that of the apadana except that the great hall has ten rows of ten columns. Reliefs on the stone jambs of the portals show the king, probably Xerxes, holding royal audience or in successful conflict with mythological beasts which may represent the forces of evil.

Other important structures on the platform are a very small winter palace or *tachara* of Darius, the harem quarters of Darius and Xerxes which have been restored by the modern excavators of the site, the royal treasury, the *hadich* or palace of Xerxes, the palace of Artaxerxes III, and an unidentified building which may have been a queen's palace erected in the time of Darius.

The structures on the platform fall into three main groups: the portals, the audience halls, and the private quarters. Most of the structures were built close to each other with little attention to formal composition. Workmen and materials were brought to the site from all over the empire, and the style of the architectural details and the carved reliefs is a composite of the art of Egypt, Babylonia, and Asia Minor.

Excavations at the mound of Susa have laid bare the plan of a palace complex begun by Darius and continued by his successors. With large interior courts and long narrow rooms, certain sections of the palace were very like Assyro-Babylonian prototypes.

The composite and eclectic character of Achaemenid art is well reflected in carvings in stone of animals, human heads cast in bronze, statuettes in gold and silver of men clad in Persian dress, and small animal figures in bronze and precious metals. Animal forms in characteristic poses were cleverly used as handles for drinking vessels and bowls, giving evidence of both vigor and imagination. There are also gold and silver bowls ornamented with rosettes and lotus buds and flowers.

The jewelry of the period—armlets, bracelets, necklaces, and earrings—has come down to us in considerable quantity. It is best represented by the famous Oxus Treasury, a collection of gold and silver jewelry set with pearls, lapis lazuli, and colored stones, most of it now in the British Museum.

Achaemenid cylinder seals and seal stones, many bearing scenes of religious worship or wild animal hunts, have survived in large numbers. There are also gold and silver coins of imperial issue ranging in date from Darius I to Darius II, each bearing a portrait of the king, who is always armed with a bow and carries either a spear, a dagger, or arrows.

The excavations of the Oriental Institute of the University of Chicago and later of the Iranian government at Persepolis brought to light in the debris of the royal treasury many interesting objects, notable among which were the stone and alabaster plates and bowls brought back from Egypt by the victorious Achaemenid army.

Seleucid Period

It was the fate of the Achaemenid empire to be destroyed by another world conqueror, Alexander the Great—a conquest far-reaching in its effects, for it put an end to the integrity of the ancient east and oriented it toward the west.

Alexander, the son of Philip of Macedonia, was born in 356 B.C. In 336 B.C. he began to carry out his father's policies, first stabilizing the Greek mainland and then setting out toward Iran at the head of some 35,000 men. At Issus, just inland from the northeastern corner of the Syrian coast, Alexander's clever generalship put to rout an enormous Persian force commanded by Darius III, who fled when the tide of battle ran against him. Alexander then led his troops down the coast and into Egypt. Returning through Syria, he entered Mesopotamia and crossed the Euphrates and the Tigris. At Arbela he met and defeated a reformed Persian army which was ten times as large as his own. Again Darius III fled.

Alexander turned south to capture Babylon and went on to Susa and Persepolis where he seized intact the vast royal treasuries. Persepolis was burned, probably in revenge for the much earlier burning of Athens by the Achaemenid army. In the spring of 330 B.C. Alexander set out in pursuit of Darius

III, first to Ecbatana and then along the southern slopes of the Elborz Range where he came upon the body of the Achaemenid king, slain by his own followers.

Scarcely pausing to consolidate his vast new territories, as though driven by a restless urge to reach the world's end, the conqueror headed for lands completely unknown to the Greeks, even into the easternmost provinces of the Achaemenid empire. The journey of discovery also had the aspect of a scientific expedition, for a careful record was kept of the line of march and distances covered, and material collected on the new peoples, plant, and animal life was sent back to Greece. In Bactria, Alexander married Roxana or Roshanak, the daughter of a Bactrian noble. Beset by nomadic warriors, he turned southward and finally crossed the Indus, and at last his soldiers, after seven long years away from their Macedonian homeland, refused to go on. Alexander agreed to turn back. The army sailed down the Indus and then made a desperate march through the barren wastes inland along the entire length of the Persian Gulf to Persepolis. At Pasargadae the violated tomb of Cyrus caught his attention, and after ordering its contents found and restored he himself sealed the door with his signet to guarantee that the tomb was forever safe from molestation. It was robbed again as soon as he left the site.

At Susa he began to disclose his plan for a new world state which would unite Macedonian and Iranian elements on a basis of equality, Hellenization of the east having already begun with the establishment of Greek colonies. Alexander himself pointed the way toward a union of the peoples when he married the eldest daughter of Darius III and encouraged 10,000 of his troops to take Persian brides. Suddenly, when he was still less than thirty-three years old, he was smitten with fever at Babylon and died in 323 B.C.

The vast areas won by his resolution and skill fell into the hands of his army commanders, and soon became broken up into several major monarchies. The Seleucid monarchy, which embraced Iran, was at first centered at Seleucia on the lower Tigris, but the capital was later moved to Antioch in Syria.

The interests of Iran were neglected and the Seleucid hold was not secure. Soon appeared local dynasties, such as that of the Fratadara of Fars. The country was ripe for new rulers.

Parthian Period

The Parthians, also known to history as the Arsacids after their first rulers, were originally a nomadic Saka tribe which moved into an area east of the Caspian and then took over the region which had been the Parthava of the Achaemenid empire.

Arsaces I, 248–246 B.C., led a successful revolt against the Seleucid governor. Arsaces II, 246–211 B.C., established the independence of the new kingdom, and Arsaces III, 211–190 B.C., resisted the efforts of the Seleucids to reconquer it. The great leader Mithradates I, 171–138 B.C., extended Parthian rule over Bactria, Parsa, Babylonia, Susiana, and Media but allowed subject kings to retain their thrones. Crushed between the Romans and the Parthians, the Seleucid power was now broken. The Parthians then became involved in prolonged warfare against the Scythians on their eastern frontier, and migrations of the Saka about 130 B.C. caused serious difficulties which were ended by Mithradates II, 123–87 B.C., who consolidated and expanded the Parthian holdings until they stretched from within India to Armenia and took the title of "king of kings."

Under Phraates III, 70–57 B.C., began the series of wars with Rome along their common frontiers which continued intermittently for nearly three hundred years. Rome was determined to expand eastward and was interested also in the extensive commerce over the silk route whose entire western section was in Parthian hands. The fortunes of war swung east and west; Mark Antony suffered a decisive defeat at Phraata, south of Lake Urmiya; but Trajan's later expedition into Parthia was successful.

With the triumphs of Mithradates II, the Parthians came to consider themselves the political heirs of the Achaemenids. Their scanty cultural background was replaced by a veneer of borrowed culture which on the upper level was both Iranian and Hellenistic. One ruler called himself a Philhellene, Greek modes were adopted, and Greek at first was chosen as the official language. Actually most of the new Parthian cities, including Ctesiphon the capital, were erected in Mesopotamia, and Iran proper lay outside the main stream of commercial and artistic activity.

The Parthians spoke their own ancestral tongue, Parthian, a language which was directly related to Middle Persian. It was written in a script of Aramaic origin which employed ideograms. Long carved inscriptions and a number of texts in this script survive but the imperfections of the rudimentary alphabet make their decipherment extremely difficult.

In the first century A.D. the Parthians seem to have swung away from Hellenistic modes of thought. Symptomatic of the trend was their choice of Mazdaism as the official religion, whereby the Magi gained in power and prestige. Between A.D. 50 and 77 the first attempt was made to codify the Mazdaean traditions and the first redaction of the Avesta was prepared by order of a Parthian ruler. However, the Parthian tolerance toward all religions permitted Christianity to spread, in the second century A.D., throughout the western part of the empire.

Parthian architecture was not an original or important style. Nearly all the architectural remains of the period lie west of Persia proper and reflect Hellenistic and Mesopotamian influences tempered by traditions of local craftsmanship. Monuments above ground or excavated ruins survive at Dura-Europos on the Euphrates, at Hatra, Seleucia, Ashur, Nippur and Warqa in Mesopotamia, and at Phraata within Iran. These include palaces and houses, religious structures, and tombs, constructed of baked brick and stone. The only element of these structures that will be described is the *ivan*, the element which became an important feature of the later architecture of Iran—a long rectangular tunnel-vaulted hall with open façade and rear end closed by a wall. The Parthian ivans and other vaulted structures represent a transition from the post-and-lintel construction of the Achaemenid and Seleucid periods to the vaulted architecture of succeeding periods.

Parthian art was even more eclectic than the architecture and, indeed, the term Parthian art has little precise meaning. Objects found in different parts of the empire often have little in common. For example, in the Tehran museum are several small human heads carved in stone, one of them purely Hellenistic in style, one definitely Buddhistic, and the others Graeco-Bactrian. Probably, as was the case in the Achaemenid period, skilled artists were brought to the major cities of Parthia from every corner of the empire. In general, the art of the period uses Hellenistic forms regardless of the content originally associated with them, never managing to assimilate western influences and to recombine them in a fresh and original way.

Stucco, a material which was later to be highly developed in Iran, began to be used on buildings in friezes with incised geometrical and floral patterns. Terracotta, used for coffins and religious figurines, was even more popular, while pottery vessels coated with a green glaze anticipated later work in this field. Ornamental stone carving on architecture employed direct copies of Hellenistic motifs. Wall paintings of the period have survived: those at Dura-Europos have been studied in detail as have the paintings from Kuh-i-Khwaja in Sistan, which are Graeco-Bactrian in style, and apparently date from the first century A.D.

Sasanian Period

About A.D. 211 Ardashir organized a revolt in the province of Fars and in A.D. 224 his forces killed the last Parthian ruler in battle in Susiana. Ardashir soon controlled all of Iran except for the provinces of Armenia and Bactria. The name of his new dynasty, Sasanian, seems to come from an Old Persian title, *Sasan,* or "commanders," although it was later a family name. The Sasanians did trace their lineage back to the Achaemenids, through the Fratadara line of rulers who were independent until the province of Fars, or Pars, came under Parthian rule, after which they minted coins at Istakhr, near Persepolis, down to the time of Ardashir. Ardashir himself was a grandson of Sasan, a high priest of the temple of Anahita at Istakhr.

Ardashir, who made Mazdaism the state religion, came into immediate conflict with Rome, and exhausting wars with Rome and later with Byzantium continued throughout the entire Sasanian period. The forces of east and west were nearly always equally matched, although the first round went to the Sasanians with the defeat of Alexander Severus.

Shapur I, A.D. 241–271, the son of Ardashir and the second of three foremost kings of this dynasty, captured the Roman Emperor Valerian in battle and held him prisoner until his death. Armenia was the chief object of contention, changing hands many times in this and following periods.

There were some thirty Sasanian rulers. Narse, A.D. 293–302, was less successful against Rome, and under him the Tigris River became a fairly stable boundary between east and west. Shapur II, the great-great-great-grandson of Ardashir, came to the throne in A.D. 310 and during his long reign of sixty-nine years waged three separate wars with Rome. After his death internal strife broke out between the rulers and the nobles and clergy, over the authority of the kings. Three rulers were put to death by the nobles, and for nearly one hundred years successive kings were chosen from the Sasanian family by the high church officials and the great feudal lords.

Khusraw I, A.D. 531–579, the greatest ruler of the line, whom his subjects called "The Just," restored the full power of the monarchy. The empire was divided into four great administrative regions, and a fixed land tax based upon a comprehensive survey of the empire was levied. Irrigation projects were carried out and aid given to agriculture, and the country enjoyed real prosperity. Learning was encouraged by Khusraw. Himself able to read Greek, he had translations made from Greek and Sanskrit into Pahlavi. The legendary stories were collected. Christianity was viewed with tolerance.

Khusraw II, A.D. 589–628, at first was victorious against

Byzantium, but in the end the Emperor Heraclius inflicted such a decisive defeat at the battle of Nineveh in A.D. 627 that the Sasanian empire was thrown into anarchy. Yazdijird III, A.D. 632–651, struggled against the rising tide of Islam in vain and spent the last ten years of his life a hunted fugitive.

The Sasanian period witnessed the rebirth of a nationalistic Iran, strong and prosperous in her own right and unreceptive to foreign contacts and influences. The majesty of her "king of kings," which came directly from Ahura Mazda, demanded that the ruler should have practically no contact with his subjects. The remarkable internal stability of the empire was largely the result of the efficient and highly centralized administration of its group of ministers and large secretarial staff. The army was paid and controlled by the royal treasury.

The people were divided into four groups: clergy, warriors, secretaries, and commoners including farmers, merchants, and artisans. The first three of these groups made up the nobility of which there were four grades, each with its special titles and insignia. The highest grade was the *shahrdar*, the provincial governors of the Sasanian family, and the army was largely recruited from the fourth class of the nobility.

The center of the empire was, of course, the city of Shapur in the province of Fars, but two of the three capital cities, Ctesiphon and Gundeshapur, lay outside the boundaries of the home province.

The language of the Sasanian period continued to be Middle Persian written in the awkward and intricate Pahlavi script, but the language lost a good deal of its grammatical complexity and began to approach the final form of New Persian, or *farsi*. Among the secular writings were the Book of Great Deeds, the Book of Rank, the lost Book of the Kings, the Lands of Iran, and translations such as that of the fables of Kalila and Dimna. Certain lost works exist in later Arabic translations. In this period the Avesta was written down several times, and Shapur I recorded it in a special script which is known to us as *avestic*. This text was stated to be authoritative, but a new commentary was prepared under Khusraw I.

Mazdaism remained the strong state religion throughout the period. The church had a supreme head and a highly numerous clergy with two Magi resident in each village. The nucleus of the church organization was the sacred fire. Each village had its own fire, each large district a *vahram* fire, and there were three great national fires. The creed as codified in the Avesta was far removed from the abstract moral teachings of Zarathushtra. Ritual predominated, and there was a growing tendency to rank the deities of the sun and of fire with Ahura Mazda in a new trinity.

Other religions made some headway within the empire. Mani, described as a reformer who emphasized spiritual needs, and the alleged author of the Book of Shapur, preached during the reign of Shapur I and before many years his message reached the Roman empire. His teaching was tolerated by Shapur I and Hormuzd I, but in A.D. 276 Bahram I delivered him to the Mazdaean clergy to be put to death. Mazdak, a native of Khorasan, appeared as the dualist reformer of Zoroastrianism and advocated such specific precepts as non-violence, vegetarianism, and communism. The ruler Kavadh at first supported the new sect as a possible lever against the power of the clergy and the nobles, but the apostle and his followers were massacred in A.D. 528. However, the Mazdak sect persisted into Islamic times. Christians were frequently, often violently, persecuted in the first centuries of the Sasanian period, primarily because of the identification of the religion with the rival Roman Empire. After the end of the fifth century, when the Christians within the empire were members of the eastern Nestorian Church, they were treated with increased tolerance.

The architecture of the Sasanian period is represented by palaces and residences, fire temples, fortresses, dams and bridges, city plans, and special memorials. Quite a number of these buildings stand in fair condition, but the problem of dating them chronologically within the period is not yet solved.

At Firuzabad, Shapur, and Sarvistan in Fars, at Ctesiphon on the lower Tigris, and at Qasr-i-Shirin on the present frontier between Iran and Iraq are the remains of great palace complexes. The Firuzabad palace, believed to have been built in the time of Ardashir, is a rectangular building over 180 feet wide and more than 300 feet in length. In the center of the façade is a great ivan which leads into a square-domed throne chamber, and back of this chamber is an interior court surrounded by living quarters. All the rooms are covered either by domes or tunnel vaults.

At Ctesiphon the salient feature of the palace area is the great vaulted ivan called the Taq-i-Kisra which rises to a height of 90 feet and is 75 feet wide and 150 feet deep. Possibly built in the time of Shapur I, it was the great ceremonial room used for royal audiences. On its flanking façade walls is a poorly organized system of superimposed arcades which copy Hellenistic façade compositions. Later the Arabs tried in vain to pull it down, and in Islamic times builders tried to erect structures large enough to overshadow it. At Sarvistan, some sixty miles southeast of Shiraz, is a well-preserved palace which was probably built in the fifth century. The plan differs from that of Firuzabad: there are fewer and larger rooms and a number of entrances. Neighboring ruins suggest that the main palace was surrounded by gardens and other buildings. At Qasr-i-Shirin are the ruins of a huge complex covering an area an eighth of a mile wide and a quarter of a mile long, the main palace structure raised above the ground on a maze of tunnel-vaulted rooms. This work dates from the very end of the Sasanian period.

In recent years many fire temples have been discovered. It is probable that in some of them the sacred fire was kept in the main chamber and that in those which crown rocky heights it burned in the open air to be visible for many miles. The basic element of the fire temples is a square dome-crowned chamber which, whether an isolated unit or surrounded by a corridor, normally had a wide arched portal piercing each wall, the term for this plan type being carried over into the Islamic period as the *chahar taq* or "four arches." The dome over the chamber sprang from four arches or squinches which bridged the corner angles. It is noteworthy that the world of

Rome and Byzantium developed the form of the pendentive or spherical triangle to support a dome over a square plan, but the eastern and Islamic world has continued to use the squinch form down to the present day. The structural materials of the period were stone and fired brick and wall surfaces were frequently coated with plaster, as in palaces excavated at Damghan where incised plaster decoration was used extensively.

Architecture and the fine arts clearly reflect a strong reaction against earlier Hellenistic influences and even give evidence of a studied effort to re-use traditional native forms. Little conscious development of forms and motifs took place during the period. The reaction against the West persisted after the Arab conquests and had the final result of creating a great artistic and cultural gap between east and west.

An art form characteristic of the period was the carving of huge reliefs on rock faces, often near a spring-fed pool. Some twenty such carvings, most of them in Fars, bear representations showing the kings victorious over various enemies and the investiture of the king by Ahura Mazda who extends the ring and the scepter. The compositions are symmetrical, the figures are shown in profile, and naturalism is sacrificed to stiff formality and monumentality. These rock carvings are early in date while those in the grotto of Taq-i-Bustan near Kermanshah probably date from the end of the period.

Very well-known are the splendid silver dishes and bowls, many of which are now in Russia in the Hermitage Museum. Some show the king seated on his throne holding royal audience or enjoying the pleasures of the hunt, others show battle scenes, the investiture of the monarch, deities, vigorous animals, often in combat, and graceful birds. Vessels and ewers of bronze have also survived in quantity: notable among these are incense burners in the form of ducks or other birds. Many splendid Sasanian textiles are now found in museums and private collections, but it is not yet clear which of the many pieces assigned to this group were woven in Iran and which in the countries along the eastern shores of the Mediterranean. The pottery of the period is not particularly fine; a common type was glazed over patterns in low relief. Plaster decoration used on architectural surfaces consisted of border mouldings or plaques carved with floral or animal forms, or figures of animals.

The Arab Conquest of Iran

Early in the seventh century Khusraw II captured Damascus and Jerusalem and advanced to the very gates of Constantinople. Then the tide turned and the Byzantine Emperor Heraclius moved across Mesopotamia as far as Ctesiphon. At last Iran and Byzantium signed a peace of sheer exhaustion. Just then came the Arabs, overrunning Iran and bringing with them the Moslem religion. The centuries from the Arab conquest to the present day are generally known as the Islamic period of Iran; they cover almost exactly the same number of years as lay between the rise of Cyrus and the end of the Sasanian empire.

Arabia has always been the home of nomads, a Semitic people hostile to foreign invasion and influences, and in the opening years of the seventh century the peninsula was quiet. Medina and Mecca were small towns owing their limited prosperity to their positions along a main caravan route, and Mecca had been for some time the center of pagan cult worship and a place of pilgrimage. Upon the quiet scene appeared the Prophet Muhammad, born in 570. His great mission was not apparent until he had reached middle age, when the Qoran was revealed to him, and his religion gained momentum slowly. He made his exodus from Mecca to Medina in A.D. 622, the date which later became the Moslem year one, and attained complete control over the peninsula of Arabia only a few years before his death in A.D. 632.

His devoted friend and early follower, Abu Bekr, became the first *khalifa* (Caliph), or "Successor," and led a series of plundering raids into Mesopotamia and Syria, with such success that the nomadic warriors soon came into contact with the major forces of Byzantium and of the Sasanians. Heraclius was defeated in Palestine in A.D. 634, and in 636 a Sasanian army 120,000 strong was defeated in the four-day-long battle of

Qadisiyya. Ctesiphon fell, and the Arabs spread out onto the Iranian plateau. Another huge Sasanian army was utterly routed in 641 at Nihavand, the battle marking the end of the long Sasanian period. The Arabs overturned governments which were in a state of corruption and decay and the hope they held out to the great masses of the people of more equality and kinder treatment brought on a social and religious revolution. It is true, however, that there was no serious attempt at wholesale conversion to the Moslem religion other than the levying of a special poll-tax on non-Moslems.

Within Iran the conquest spread, spurred on by the Caliph 'Uthman's promises of the governorship of wealthy Khorasan to the first of his generals to reach the province. In A.D. 652 Iranian forces were defeated at Khwarazm on the Oxus River, and within a few years lands in distant Asia were under the Moslems. Bands of Arabs moved to Khorasan and settled there. The famous general Qutayba, who campaigned in the area from 704 until 715, was so zealous in promoting the Moslem faith that he quartered Arabs in every household of the captured towns and at Bokhara built a large mosque on the site of a fire temple.

For more than a century after the rise of Islam all the conquered lands gave unquestioning obedience to the authority of the Omayyad Caliphs, resident in Medina or Damascus. The areas were divided into provinces with a military governor and a head-tax collector in the highest station in each province. Details of administration, especially the complicated task of collecting taxes, were left in the hands of the officials of the regimes displaced by the Arabs. In Mesopotamia two tax registers were kept; one in Arabic for the new overlords, and one in Persian for the native population. Difficulties of communication meant that the more distant provinces were less firmly controlled by the central authority, so that Iran was not too severely treated. However, the coming of Islam did produce profound alterations in the political, economic, and social structure. The age-old Iranian ideas of divine right and autocratic control were challenged by a democratic spirit and by the internationalism of the new religion, while at the same time the cultural superiority of the Iranians and their pride in their institutions remained, to stamp the cultural and artistic future of Islamic Iran with a character quite different from that of any of the other Moslem countries.

In the eighth century strong feeling arose against the Omayyad Caliphs, and in A.D. 750 the reigning Caliph was defeated in battle. A new line of Caliphs known as the Abbasids took over the power, and in 763 founded a famous circular city at Baghdad which was to be their capital until 1258, when the Mongols sacked the city and ended the Abbasid line. Iranian soldiers had aided in the overthrow of the Omayyads, and in the new court Persians held high positions and Persian dress and manners prevailed.

The Rise of Local Dynasties in Iran

Khorasan, an area vastly larger than the present province of that name, became the most vital section of Iran. In 801 Tahir Dhu 'l-Yaminyan, the military commander for one of the sons of the Caliph Harun ar-Rashid, was made governor of Khorasan at his own request and established his capital at Nishapur. He was succeeded in the post by his two sons, a grandson and a great-grandson, each of whom paid a relatively small annual tribute to the Caliphs at Baghdad. The rulers of this local dynasty, known as the Taharids, who were celebrated as authors and poets, ruled from 820 until 873.

The next powerful figure to arise in Iran was Ya'qub ibn Layth as-Saffar, a coppersmith and highway robber who by 867 was master of Khorasan and Herat. Named governor of Khorasan by the Taharids, he soon overthrew that dynasty and brought within his rule Kerman, Fars, and Isfahan as well. Defeated in an attempt against Baghdad itself, he died in 879. His brother, 'Amr ibn Layth, moved into Transoxiana where the Samanid house had recently come into power, but was defeated and sent captive to Baghdad and there put to death in 902. Descendants of the line long held power in Sistan. In these brief years of Saffarid power occurred an event of cultural significance, when the secretary of Ya'qub composed the first poetry in Persian.

The Samanids, who had first been sub-governors under the Taharids, now gained complete mastery of eastern Iran and dominated the area for nearly one hundred years. Isma'il, the founder and outstanding figure of the dynasty, ruled from 892 until 907. A generous and intelligent person as well as a highly successful general, he was able in the peaceful latter years of his reign to devote much of his time to the building of Bokhara, his capital city. His tomb, which with other monuments built at this time is still standing, forms a perfect cube thirty-five feet on each side. It is crowned by a hemispherical dome, and interior and exterior surfaces of the monument are richly decorated, the exterior walls with elaborate brick bonding in checkerboard, herringbone, and open latticework patterns.

The Samanid dynasty reached its greatest power under Nasr ibn Ahmad, 913–943, when it reigned over Transoxiana, Khorasan, Sistan, Gorgan, Tabaristan, Ray, and Kerman. The court at Bokhara patronized men of learning. There Persian literature was born, under the hands of the poet Rudaki, and of Daqiqi, composer of epic poetry. The famous philosopher and scientist Abu 'Ali ibn Sina, known to the Western world as Avicenna, was active at this time. The Samanids rendered a very valuable service in arousing and reëstablishing Iranian national spirit, but the reversion to a feudal state led to the rise of powerful vassal lords and the final overthrow of the kingdom.

During the ninth century less important local rulers appeared in Iran. About 928 Mardavij ibn Ziyar assumed control of the Caspian littoral, an area known successively as Daylam and Tabaristan, the inhabitants of which had not been converted to Islam until about the middle of the ninth century. Members of the Ziyarid dynasty were Vashmgir, brother of Mardavij, and his sons Behistun and Qabus. Qabus was a poet and author, whose renowned tomb at the southeast corner of the Caspian Sea is the earliest monument with a dated inscription surviving in Islamic Iran. The inscription reads: "In the name of God, the merciful, the compassionate; this castle was built by the Amir Shams al-Ma'ali the Amir, son of the Amir, Qabus son of Vashmgir, who ordered it built during his lifetime in the lunar year 397 and the solar year 375" (1007 A.D.). The tomb, built of fired brick, is an enormous cylinder capped by a conical roof. The circular plan, broken by ten flanges, is 56 feet in diameter and the walls are 17 feet thick. The height from the ground to the tip of the cone is 160 feet. According to the historian Jannabi, the body of Qabus was enclosed in a glass coffin which was suspended by chains from the interior dome of the tower.

The region of Daylam is also important as the place of origin of the Buvayhid rulers. Mardavij ibn Ziyar had named 'Ali ibn Buvayh as a local governor, but 'Ali and his brothers Hasan and Ahmad soon acquired possession of central and western Iran. In 945 Ahmad entered Baghdad but left the Abbasid Caliphs, who awarded the brothers honorary positions and titles, in nominal spiritual control. The foremost ruler of the Buvayhids, whose centers were Isfahan and Ray, was 'Adud ad-dawla, who reigned from 949 until 983. After his death the kingdom tended to break up rapidly, and the western section was taken over by Mahmud of Ghazni although the eastern remained intact until the arrival of the Seljuqs.

There were nine men of the line of the Ghaznavids, whose power now arose in the east of Iran. Alptegin, the first of this Turkish line, had been sold as a slave to Isma'il the Samanid. He became governor of Khorasan, and about 960 proclaimed himself king of Ghazni. Mahmud, the seventh of the line, undertook to extend the limited kingdom of his predecessors, overthrowing the Samanids in 999 and absorbing the Ziyarids. In 1029 he pushed the Buvayhids west of the Iranian plateau so that his rule extended over Muhjara, Afghanistan, Transoxiana, Khorasan, Tabaristan, Sistan, and part of India. In Iran proper, only Kerman and Fars lay outside his rule.

Born of rude antecedents, Mahmud's early life was vigorous and destructive. The owls were said to have wished him long life because he left so many towns deserted and in ruins. While his subjects, executed for heresy and ruined by taxation, perished in vast numbers, his Indian campaigns yielded for him-

self and his army vast riches which were used to beautify
Ghazni and the provincial towns. In 1018 he ordered the construction of a mosque of granite and marble at Ghazni and in
connection with it a university and library.

Mahmud died in 1030 at the age of sixty. His son, Mas'ud,
erected a magnificent mausoleum for his father, and in such
awe and esteem was the memory of the great Sultan held that
the tomb was spared by 'Ala' ad-din, "the world incendiary,"
when he visited Ghazni one hundred years later. The tomb
now stands in a rude chamber covered by a clay dome. On a
rectangular base rests a triangular prism of marble carved
with an inscription giving the exact date, day and hour, of
Mahmud's death. In the same village two miles north of
Ghazni are two minarets built as towers of victory, on a stellar
plan and enriched with decorative brickwork, which are still
about 150 feet high, one bearing the name of Sultan Mahmud,
the other that of his grandson Mas'ud III.

Although Sultan Mahmud became the patron of all poets
and scholars, he was probably motivated less by sheer love of
learning than by a desire to enhance his personal prestige in
making his court the center of distinction and glory. All the
renowned men of learning were summoned to Ghazni and few
dared to refuse. One was the poet 'Unsuri, another the scientist
and historian, al-Biruni, who wrote his famous "Chronology
of Ancient Nations," a book on India, and other works—all in
Arabic. But Firdawsi outshone them all. Coming to the court
for the first time when he had already reached middle age, he
began to compose his great epic the *Shahnama*, or "Book of the
Kings," and kept at the task until it was complete in 60,000
rhyming couplets. The epic contains the saga of four ancient
dynasties, two of which are purely legendary and drawn from
the mythology of the Avesta. The other two are the Parthian
and the Sasanian, but here too the epic contains more of legend
than of accurate history. The lengthy work abounds in romantic and heroic tales, and was a source of inspiration to later
Persian poets as well as to such western authors as Matthew
Arnold, who retold one of the finest of the tales in his "Sohrab
and Rustum." The *Shahnama* was copied and recopied in all

later periods, and many copies were illuminated with miniatures by leading painters. It is written in a vigorous, direct Persian which contains relatively few Arabic words, and the language has changed so little since its composition nine hundred years ago that it can be read with ease by the people of present-day Iran. For centuries it has been recited, and even today thousands of uneducated people can repeat long passages of the poem.

Modern Persian literature reached full stature in this period, but it must be realized that many Persian authors of this time and later wrote in Arabic. The Arabic language with its entirely logical and highly evolved grammatical forms appealed to the Persian intellect, while the Arabic alphabet was far superior to the intricate Pahlavi script, so that Iranian men of learning knew Arabic as their second language. Many Arabic words came into Persian and, of course, the Arabic characters were now used for written Persian. Such notable figures as Sa'di and Ghazali wrote both in Persian and Arabic, and many authors whose native tongue was Arabic became so absorbed by Iranian culture and thought that their histories, poems and philosophical and mystical writings are in fact Persian literature, though in another tongue.

In the period from 641 until 1000 Iran was working out her own particular version of Islamic architecture. One of the fundamental precepts of Muhammad's religion was the necessity of prayer as stressed in the Qoran, and before long the true Moslem believer was required to recite five ritual prayers each day. The prayers could be said anywhere, provided that the believer's face was turned towards Mecca. Group prayers were recited at noon on Friday. The need for a special place for prayer appeared very early, and it is believed that the house of the Prophet Muhammad was used as the first *mosque* or "place of prostration." As the Arab conquests spread into far countries it became necessary to provide mosques for the soldiers. At first the mosque may have been any open space fenced in with a reed paling which could be transported when the army moved. A little later the area was determined by four arrows shot from a central point and a ditch dug around the space thus defined.

Still later, covered colonnades were erected around the open space or court. In each country the Arabs also took over existing structures for use as mosques: in Syria and Palestine churches were so used and at Ctesiphon the Taq-i-Kisra was converted into a mosque. When the Moslems began to build their own permanent mosque structures they adapted the architecture in vogue in each area and made use of the local craftsmen. The essential elements of the mosque were an open court with arcades on one or more sides and a covered sanctuary area within which was the *mihrab* or "prayer niche," so placed that worshippers would always face toward Mecca.

Within Iran a wealth of monuments of the Sasanian and earlier periods offered plan forms and constructional methods readily adaptable to the new religious architecture, and from documentary sources it is known that thousands of fine buildings were erected in the early Islamic period. Of these only a handful, and not the more renowned, have survived to the present day. Many earlier structures were converted into mosques; one precise account in an early history refers to an Achaemenid palace as having been so altered.

Of the extant monuments erected in Iran prior to the year 1000, the Tarik Khana at Damghan, a mosque which was probably built in the ninth century, consists of a square court surrounded by arcades which are several bays deeper on the side which sheltered the mihrab. The *Masjid-i-Jami* or "Congregational Mosque," at Nayriz, which may date from the tenth century, was built as a large ivan with the mihrab set into the rear wall of the hall. The tenth century Masjid-i-Jami at Nayin is similar in plan to the mosque at Damghan but has the added feature of walls, columns, and mihrab surfaces, decorated with plaster ornamentation in Arabic inscriptions and deeply cut geometric and floral patterns. Tomb towers still stand at Resget and Lajim and along the Caspian coast and at Damghan: that at Resget has inscriptions entirely in Arabic except for a last line in Pahlavi. These tomb towers established a type which was to persist for several centuries.

Among the art objects which have lasted until the present day pottery is well represented. The earliest pieces may well have been inspired by imitation of and rivalry with Chinese pottery brought to Iran over the long caravan routes, but in this period began the remarkable development of the pottery craft which was to make Persian ceramics the equal of that produced in any country at any period. A number of different types can be distinguished: the so-called Transoxiana pottery represented by flat dishes or bowls with geometrical or stylized floral patterns in black, purple, red, green, and yellow; Nishapur pottery of marked individuality but reminiscent of the Transoxiana ware; dishes decorated with splash glaze in imitation of Chinese types; bowls with designs in green and blue on a white glaze ground; and, early examples of the luster painted pottery which was later to be so highly developed.

The silver dishes of this period are in shape, technique, and subject matter direct successors of the Sasanian silver. A few fragments of fine textiles have survived. Wood carving is represented by the double doors of mosque and tomb, by Qoran reading stands, and by examples of the *minbar*, the pulpit which stands next to the mihrab in the mosque. Fragments of large scale wall paintings have also been found in archeological excavations.

Seljuq Period

Throughout almost countless centuries successive groups of hardy, warlike nomads had moved from central Asia toward the Iranian plateau, crossed the Oxus River, and had been turned south by opposing forces. Early in the eleventh century appeared a group of Turkish nomads more powerful than the others, to whom Mahmud of Ghazna allotted territory near Bokhara, later shifting them to Khorasan. Their chief, Tughril Beg, led them in revolt to crush the Ghaznavid power, and then fought his way across Iran to Baghdad. The reigning Caliph opened its gates to him in 1055 and, since the decadent Abbasid Caliphate had long lost its earlier power, was pleased to grant Tughril Beg the title of "King of East and West." Retiring to Ray where he established his capital, Tughril founded the Seljuq dynasty, whose main line was to rule for a hundred years from the Bosphorus to Chinese Turkestan; minor branches held on for a still longer period.

At the time of the advent of the Seljuqs into central and western Iran much of it was held by petty rulers ready to fly at one another's throats. The Seljuqs overthrew the local kingdoms, united Moslem Asia, and embraced Islam with great fervor. This period became one of the most momentous in the long history of Persian culture, for it was then that the rough, illiterate Turks first placed Persians in the highest official posts and then themselves developed into patrons of learning and the arts.

Tughril Beg's nephew and successor was Alp Arslan, who ruled from 1063 until 1072 with a brilliant Iranian, Nizam al-Mulk, as his *vazir* or prime minister. Of undoubted military ability, Alp Arslan waged many wars: moving westward, as have all the great warriors of Asia, he conquered Syria and defeated and captured the Byzantine Emperor Romanus Diogenes. Fatally wounded by one of his own prisoners, he remarked just before his death: "Yesterday, when I stood on a hill and the earth shook beneath me from the greatness of my army and the host of my soldiers, I said to myself, 'I am king of the World and none can prevail against me; wherefore God Almighty hath brought me low by one of the weakest of his creatures. I ask pardon of Him and repent of this my thought."

He was succeeded by his son Malik Shah, who reigned from 1072 until 1092. Two years after Malik Shah came to power he established the astronomical observatory in which 'Umar Khayyam and other men of science were employed to make the calculations for a new calendar, and adorned Isfahan, his capital, with many fine buildings and gardens. While the Sultan busied himself with wars, hunts, and royal audiences, Nizam al-Mulk remained vazir and held in his hands all the reins of government.

The real name of this famous vazir is almost forgotten. He was always known by the honorific title Nizam al-Mulk, Qavam ad-din, which means "Regulator of the State, Upholder of Religion." A superb administrator who retained the hereditary institutions of the country, he symbolized the imposition of the superior Iranian culture upon the Seljuqs. His practical experience was embodied in a still extant treatise entitled "On the History and Art of Government." In his unflagging efforts to promote religion and education he built a series of *nizamiyyas*, or schools, which were probably the first essentially civil, in contrast to religious, establishments of learning under Islam. The first of these was erected in Baghdad in A.D. 1065 and we know that there were similar colleges at Amul, Nishapur, Herat, Merv, Balkh, Damascus and other towns.

The Seljuqs belonged to the orthodox Sunni branch of Islam and took severe measures against the Shi'a branch, for the latter sect had become very strong in Iran as early as the Buvayhid period. The core of Shi'a resistance was the Isma'ili organization led by Hasan as-Sabbah, which has become known to the western world as "The Assassins." From their strong fortresses in northern Iran and farther west they dispatched agents to stir up civil disorder and to carry out political murders. One of their victims was Nizam al-Mulk.

Malik Shah's successors were unable to keep the kingdom intact and Syria and Asia Minor were soon lost. Moreover, the *atabegs*, the Turkish provincial governors, became so powerful that Iran began to split up into semi-independent units. The last ruler of the main Seljuq line was Sultan Sanjar, the third son of Malik Shah, who for twenty-two years before his accession to the throne in 1118 had been in control of Khorasan. Near the end of his life signs of internal disorder were overshadowed by threats from without, when the Qara-Khitay, a Turkish Mongol tribe, came from far China to defeat Sanjar in 1141 and occupy Transoxiana. In 1153 he was captured by the Ghuzz Turks and held captive for nearly two years, and before his death Nishapur was taken and burned.

Sanjar was buried at Merv, his favorite place of residence, in a tomb constructed during his lifetime which was originally connected with a now vanished mosque. The structure is a great square 77 feet on each exterior side with walls 19 feet thick. The four walls are crowned by galleries, and behind and above the galleries rises the bold profile of the great dome. Interior wall surfaces are covered with plain plaster, and the gallery vaults with decorated plaster on which incised lines imitate brick bonding patterns and trace delicate inscriptions against a floral background.

After the death of Sultan Sanjar the Khwarazmshahs speedily took over the Seljuq kingdom. Atsiz, the first of this line, who held power from 1128 until 1156, had acted as governor of Khorezmia (Khiva) under the Seljuqs but had been virtually independent of their control. His great grandson, Sultan Muhammad, 1200–1220, expanded the Khwarazmian kingdom to include all of Iran and was on the point of advancing on Baghdad when the Mongols made their appearance.

The Seljuq period is conspicuous for its great number of poets, philosophers, and learned men, foremost among whom was the philosopher and mystic theologian, al-Ghazali. Ghazali introduced into Moslem Sufism mystic Christian sentiment based on the concept of all-embracing love and at the same time brought Sufism within the bounds of orthodox Moslem belief, exerting an enormous influence upon all later Iranian thought. The greatest of the Persian mystic poets is Farid ad-din Attar whose works include three long poems on the theme of spiritual union with God, a source book on the lives and sayings of saints, and a collection of lyrics and odes. The works of Nizami are well illustrated by the *Khamseh* or "Quintet," comprising the four romantic epic poems: Khusraw and Shirin; Laila and Majnun; the "Seven Effigies" with its stories of Bahram Gur; the "Book of Alexander," legendary tales of Alexander the Great; and the ethical poem "The Treasure House of Secrets." The "Four Discourses" of Nizami-yi 'Aruzi is a series of anecdotes about leading figures of the time. Nasir-i-Khusraw was a famous poet and traveler who has left a very interesting and valuable account of his travels. 'Umar Khayyam, patronized by Alp Arslan and Malik Shah, was a philosopher, mathematician, and astronomer as well as a poet whose outlook is tinged with skepticism and pessimism.

A great deal of building activity was carried on during the Seljuq period and sections of several Iranian mosques date from these years. The mosques now introduce the standard plan of a central open court surrounded by arcades with an ivan on each side of the court and columned and vaulted prayer halls on both sides of each ivan. The small mosque at Zavara was constructed to this plan in a single building operation about 1135, but at most of the mosque sites only the traditional square chamber crowned by a dome was erected in this period and the ivans and arcades added later, to round out the composition. The square dome-chambers were also used for shrines and tombs: typical examples of the form are found at Sangbast, near Mashhad, in the great mosque and in the Haydariya mosque at Qazvin, in the mosque at Gulpaygan erected in the reign of Sultan Muhammad, and at Barsian. In the dome chamber of the Qazvin mosque is an interesting inscription which details the provisions made for financing the upkeep of these structures: "I have established as a trust for this edifice and the adjoining school three-quarters of the village of Havasabad, seventeen shares of the village of Juyran, all the orchard on the road to al-Jawsaq, all the vineyards at the end of the Abhar River . . . and all the shops in Qazvin. . . . I have embellished all this as a foundation, legal and eternal, according to conditions specified in the deeds, seeking thereby the favor of Allah. It is not legal for any governor or oppressor or usurper or anyone else to change or modify this trust. Should anyone attempt to do so, may the curse of Allah and the angels and all mankind be upon him."

The largest, most complex and most important architectural monument in Iran is the Congregational Mosque at Isfahan. Within the mosque are two splendid dome chambers, one erected in 1088 at the order of Taj ad-din, a political rival of Nizam al-Mulk, and the other built by Nizam himself in the same year. Tomb towers of the Seljuq period also survive. Especially noteworthy are the multiple-flanged tomb of Tughril Beg at Ray, three towers at Maragha, and two at

Nakhichevan. The Gunbad-i-Surkh at Maragha, dated 1147, has on its exterior walls double panels executed in a variety of bonding patterns in red brick. Other types of architectural decoration common to the period are strips of baked terracotta interlaced in geometrical patterns, and magnificent carved plaster mihrabs and inscription friezes.

The field of ceramics displayed an amazing development which was to culminate in the sometimes over-elaborate pottery of the succeeding Mongol period. Near the end of the Seljuq reign came dated luster pottery and architectural tiles as well as polychrome pottery from the workshops at Ray and Kashan. Such centers as Aghkand, Yastkand, and Amul turned out colorful glazed pieces on which the figures of animals and birds were incised or raised in low relief by cutting away the background areas. At Ray and Kashan subjects common to later miniature painting were used and many pieces show scenes from the *Shahnama*, horsemen and the hunt, nobility enthroned, or congenial groups in flowering gardens. A number of important centers turned out vast quantities of fine cotton, wool, and silk textiles; fragments of some fifty splendid silks recovered from Seljuq tombs at Ray show a consummate technical skill in the execution of inscription bands and human and animal figures. Metalwork of the period includes bronze mirrors whose backs are adorned with scenes in low relief. Many brass or bronze kettles, incense burners, jugs, candlesticks, trays, lamps, ewers, and pen boxes, and a smaller number of silver vessels and trays, are gathered in museums and private collections. Craftsmanship of the highest order appears in the engraved designs, which are often inlaid with silver or with both silver and gold.

Mongol Period

About the year 1160 occurred the birth of Temujin, who under the title of Genghiz Khan was destined to lead the Mongol hordes across the breadth of Asia. Rising from utter obscurity, Genghiz marshaled together the pastoral nomadic clans and swept south and east to overrun civilized China. In

1219 he turned west at the head of some 700,000 men, many of them mounted on wiry steeds. At the limits of the Khwarazmian kingdom he paused to send envoys to Sultan Muhammad. The latter scorned to treat with these unknown savages, and the result was the speedy destruction of his realm.

The Mongol army moved ahead to take Bokhara, Samarqand, Balkh, and Merv. Towns which offered resistance were besieged, stormed, burned, and frequently obliterated from the face of the land. Nishapur fell in 1221, its inhabitants and all living things, including cats and dogs, were slaughtered, and Sultan Muhammad was hunted across the country to the Caspian coast where he escaped in a small boat just a few paces ahead of his pursurers. In this first invasion and in the succeeding waves millions of the people of Iran were slain.

Genghiz Khan returned to the East when almost all of Iran had been overrun, and died there in 1227. The council which named his successor determined to send an army against the remnants of the Khwarazmian power, and the general Charmaghan led the Mongols as far as northwestern Iran and Iraq. In the next years the slaughter and plundering continued. In 1256 Hulagu carried out a mission against the Assassins, razing their fortresses and destroying their power. In 1258 he marched against Baghdad and after a siege lasting a month stormed the city. Thousands were slain, the palaces, mosques, and tombs of the Caliphs were burned, and a vast store of booty collected. The last of the Abbasid Caliphs was put to death and his line wiped out. In Palestine Hulagu was decisively defeated by the Egyptians: this was the first check administered to the Mongol forces.

He withdrew to Maragha in northwest Iran, and there the Mongols settled permanently in Iran. Hulagu took the title of *Il-Khan* or "khan of the tribe," the title which passed on to his successors and gave to the dynasty the name "Il Khans of Iran." Once the Mongols began to live in the country they were subject to manners, modes of dress, and religious beliefs foreign to their tribal mode of life. The force and continuity of Iranian civilization worked to alter their very character. The feudal system of government was retained, Persians were soon named to the highest administrative posts, and the Il Khan rulers became patrons of literature and the arts.

In 1267 Hulagu died and was succeeded by his son Abaqa, who ruled until 1282. The campaigns against Syria having met with failure, Abaqa revived the earlier idea of sending envoys to the courts of Europe and to the Pope. He proposed, as did several later rulers, a military alliance of East and West against the Moslem Egyptians. Such an alliance might have secured for the Christian nations the holy sites of Palestine, but they showed little serious interest in the plan. Takudar, a brother of Abaqa who succeeded him on the throne, now publicly professed the Moslem faith and took the name of Ahmad. Murdered in 1284, he was succeeded by Arghun, a son of Abaqa. During his reign the Nestorian Christians, long entrenched in northwestern Iran and Iraq, were especially favored, and their bishop rebuilt the church at Maragha. The reins of government were now entirely in the hands of capable Iranian officials. Upon Arghun's death in 1292 his brother Ghaikhatu reigned for four years and was then followed by Baidu who occupied the throne less than a year.

The accession to the throne in 1295 by Ghazan Khan, a great-grandson of Hulagu, ushered in a new golden age which was to continue during the reign of his successor Oljaitu. Ghazan Khan became a convert to Islam, and the spirit of religious tolerance which had marked the Il Khanid period began to wane. The court at Tabriz, the capital city, was entirely Moslem and Persian in character. Good government and general prosperity were the serious concerns of the ruler, with equitable taxes regularly collected, laws codified, and internal security established. Ten thousand men guarded the main roads along which numerous caravans passed in safety. Both Genoa and Venice had commercial envoys and colonies of merchants resident in Tabriz. In 1297 Ghazan ordered construction work begun in a suburb of Tabriz and in a few years his twelve-sided tomb structure, crowned by a great dome, was the center of a group of buildings set within gardens. The buildings included a monastery, a hospital, re-

ligious schools, an observatory, a library, a palace or administration building, and an academy of philosophy. Today the
site is marked by the mounds of masonry of his ruined tomb.

Near the end of his life, in a final attempt to conquer Syria
and Egypt, Ghazan Khan captured Aleppo but was defeated
by the Egyptians near Damascus. Ghazan stands out as a
figure of heroic proportions, but his great vazir, Rashid ad-
din, is a figure of equal interest. Rashid was a native Persian
who was first a practicing physician in the reign of Abaqa and
later court historian and principal administrator under Ghazan Khan and Oljaitu. Much of his energy went into the
writing of a universal history a part of which gave a detailed
account of the Mongols and the establishment of their kingdoms. Only the best and more reliable sources were used: the
official Mongol Chronicle was consulted, a Kashmir hermit
aided in composing the history of India, and two learned
Chinese dealt with the Chinese material. Rashid's information
about the political conditions in Europe was very accurate; he
knew far more about Europe than the Europeans then knew
of Asia, recording even the recondite fact that there were no
snakes in Ireland. When the work was completed in 1310
every precaution was taken to see that it should endure.
Many copies were sent to the libraries of large towns, the
manuscript was made available for copying, and several new
copies in different languages were turned out every year.

Outside Tabriz Rashid ad-din established a suburb named
"Quarter of Rashid," devoted to the promotion of the arts
and sciences, and soon theologians, jurists, traditionalists, re-
citers of the Qoran, students, and craftsmen of every trade
were lodged in 30,000 charming houses. Copies of the universal history were embellished with pictures, and contemporary records state that the manuscript painters were held in
high favor. Although some of this work continued to reflect
the formulae of the thirteenth century Baghdad school of
painting and unusually fine large sheets of paper were still
brought from Baghdad, the style was in close harmony with
the spirit and character of the court. In the miniatures the Il
Khan rulers and their wives wear Chinese headdress, and a

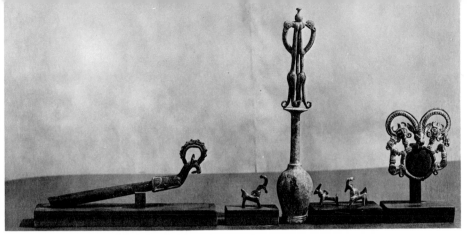

4. Luristan bronzes. Pre-Achaemenid metal work from western Iran

5. Persian ceramics. Left to right: tenth century bowl from Gorgan, twelfth century bowl from Ray, Safavid tile

6. Minor arts of the nineteenth century

7. Isfahan. The Imperial Mosque of the early seventeenth century

8. Qum. The Shrine of Fatima crowned with a gilded dome

strong Chinese influence is reflected in trees and flowers dashed in with the rapid strokes common to a brush technique and clouds given the twisted and voluted eastern forms.

Ghazan Khan died in 1304 and his brother Oljaitu reigned until his own death in 1316 at the age of thirty-six. As a child Oljaitu had been baptized a Christian, but he later embraced Islam and took the name Muhammad Khodabanda. He was much interested in the several Moslem sects and was successively a Hanefi, a Shi'a, and a Sunni. In 1306 Oljaitu ordered work begun on the city of Sultaniya, located on a wide plain fairly near Qazvin, which was to replace Tabriz as the capital of Il Khanid Iran. The ruler himself, Rashid ad-din, another vazir named Taj ad-din 'Ali Shah, and many courtiers vied with each other in financing the erection of palaces, public buildings, and entire quarters of the new city. Within its stone walls construction work was started on the mausoleum of Oljaitu which still stands in quite good condition: it is one of the finest monuments ever erected in Iran and would be a credit to any country or any style of architecture. The mausoleum is octagonal in plan. Its exterior walls are crowned by eight minarets forming a circle around the huge dome, which is sheathed with bright blue glazed bricks. The interior is a great octagonal hall 80 feet in diameter and about 170 feet high from the ground to the apex of the dome, with a small mortuary chapel on the south side. While construction work was being pushed forward Oljaitu conceived the idea of bringing the bodies of 'Ali and Husein, the Shi'a saints, from Iraq and turning his tomb into a shrine for their remains, and the decoration was carried out so that the name of 'Ali figured prominently in the inscriptions. Later on the plan was discarded, and the entire interior of the tomb was redecorated before the monument was completed and the new city dedicated in 1313. The bazaars of the new city soon became famous. In them could be found spices from India, turquoises from Khorasan, lapis lazuli and rubies from Badakhshan, pearls from the Persian Gulf, silk from the Caspian shores, indigo from Kerman, textiles from Yazd, cloth from Venice, Lombardy, Germany, and Flanders, brocades, oils, musk, Chinese rhubarb, sparrow hawks from Europe, horses and hounds from Arabia.

Abu Sa'id was enthroned as his father's successor at the age of twelve. Rashid ad-din lost his position and was finally put to death as the result of the plotting of his rival 'Ali Shah. Mongol power had now passed its peak in Iran, and it would have taken a greater figure than this ruler, who was a mere youth during most of his reign, to arrest the accelerating decline. The great nobles became increasingly unruly, and sections of the kingdom tended to break off from the main body. The south of Iran had been spared Mongol devastation because its rulers had made huge payments to the invaders, and now the Muzaffarid dynasty of Kerman spread its authority over Fars and most of western Iran. Abu Sa'id died in 1335. Ghazan Khan had slain many of the rival members of the Mongol families, and now the more remote claimants to the throne fought among themselves without decisive results. During most of the rest of the fourteenth century the country drew in upon itself and petty dynasties held fleeting power, of which the Muzaffarids were the strongest while the Sarbadarides held Khorasan and Damghan.

The period from the death of Hulagu to the end of the reign of Abu Sa'id was extraordinarily rich in literary production and at no other time were so many first-rate histories written in Persian. Considerable work was also done in the fields of medicine, botany, astronomy, and the natural sciences. Juwayni, one member of a remarkable family of Persian officials under the Mongols and himself governor of Baghdad for many years, completed his *Tarikh-i-Jahan Gusha* in 1260. This work contains the histories of Genghiz Khan, of the Khwarazmshahs and of the Assassins. Another Persian, 'Abdullah ibn Fazlullah, who is generally known as Wassaf, brought this work up to date in his history called the *Tarikh-i-Wassaf*. Rashid ad-din composed other important works in addition to his monumental history. Hamdullah Mustawfi of Qavzin, a protégé of Rashid ad-din, wrote a valuable cosmography, a general history of the world, and a metrical history of Islam in 75,000 verses.

A score of notable poets lived in this period, but the two foremost are Jalal ad-din Rumi and Saʿdi of Shiraz. Rumi, who died in 1273, was a great mystic and the founder of the Mawlawi order of "whirling" dervishes which remained strong in Asia Minor for many centuries. His long poem containing six books is called "The Mathnavi," the name of a narrative verse form in rhyming couplets, and is a work of first rank and the basic book of the Persian mystics. Rumi was a Sufi, and conceived many passages of the poem for the sole purpose of stressing moral and mystical verities.

Saʿdi is the brightest jewel of all Persian literature. Born in Shiraz, he spent his youth in study and then made a series of long voyages. At Tripoli he was taken prisoner by the Crusaders, but was finally ransomed by a friend and returned to spend the rest of his life in Shiraz, enjoying the respect of the local rulers and of Abaqa Khan until his death in 1291. His *Divan*, or "Collected Works," includes the *Gulistan*, or "Rose Garden"; the *Bustan*, or "Orchard"; and many other mystical and moral poems. The *Gulistan*, the classical model for all later Persian prose, is a series of anecdotes written in prose but containing poetic passages. The *Bustan* is entirely in verse and deals with justice and equality, modesty and simplicity, education, prayer and contemplation, and other subjects. Saʿdi, a Sufi, preached moderation as a primary virtue and recommended that we be content with our lot in this life and live as virtuously as possible in preparation for the eternal life.

Among the many men of science Nasir ad-din of Tus, who formerly had been in the service of the Assassins, won the admiration of Hulagu and was charged with the erection and management of an astronomical observatory at Maragha. The new structure soon housed many specially built instruments such as astrolabes, armillary spheres, and a terrestrial globe. A contemporary writer described him as "a man of vast learning in all branches of philosophy who controlled all the religious endowments in the lands under Mongol rule. He composed many works on logic, on the natural sciences and on metaphysics." He also wrote commentaries on Euclid, Plato, and Aristotle.

Building activity in Iran seems to have fallen off at the end of the twelfth century and scarcely any monuments of the early thirteenth century have survived to the present day. The Mongol invasions destroyed countless structures in the ruined towns and it was not until thirty years after their first appearance in Iran that monumental architectural construction began to revive. Hulagu built the Maragha observatory, a treasure house, his mausoleum, and other structures, but of them all only the foundation walls of the observatory remain. However, at least a hundred important structures built from the time of Hulagu to the death of Abu Sa'id still stand in Iran. Most of these are mosques, shrines, or tombs, but there are a few caravanserais and structures of other types.

The architectural style of these buildings is a direct continuation of that of the Seljuq monuments erected nearly a century before. The use of elaborate brick bonding as a decorative feature tended to die out but ornamental plaster reached a high development, and bold, exuberant patterns covered mihrabs, inscription bands, and the surfaces of walls and vaults. Much of the plaster was tinted in red, blue, white, green, and yellow. A new decorative technique appeared with the use of glazed tiles on both exteriors and interiors. At first small pieces of light and dark blue glazed tile were used, and then white and black were introduced until whole surfaces were covered with patterns made up of small, carefully fitted pieces of glazed tile. This technique, known as mosaic faience, was to become the hallmark of the architecture of the Timurid and Safavid periods.

Two of the three greatest monuments of the Il Khanid period, the mausoleums of Ghazan Khan and Oljaitu, have already been mentioned. The third was the mosque built at Tabriz by the vazir 'Ali Shah in the early fourteenth century. The vast complex included a large open court, a great pool with a central fountain, a monastery, a religious school, and the central element of the mosque. This latter feature was an enormous ivan hall a hundred feet in interior width. As first erected, it must have closely resembled the Sasanian palace, called the Taq-i-Kisra, at Ctesiphon. Today a massive section of the thirty-foot thick walls may still be seen. Other notable structures erected at Isfahan, Varamin, Natanz, and Bistam survive in good condition.

Few dated ceramic pieces survived the years of devastation between 1220 and 1242 but the larger number of extant examples dated after 1242 testifies to the revival of work in ceramics at Kashan, Ray, and other centers. The dated pieces from Kashan include great mihrabs assembled from several large pieces of luster tile, luster star tiles which were used with cross tiles in lining the lower interior wall surfaces of buildings, and fine luster or polychrome painted bowls, dishes, and jugs. The luster pieces have a red, golden, or brown transparent glaze obtained by covering the finished piece of pottery with a pigment of metallic copper or silver salts and then re-firing the piece so that a thin film of metal is deposited on the surface.

In general, the pottery is more ornate and combines a greater variety of techniques than was common in the Seljuq period. Characteristic of the Il Khanid period is the so-called Mina'i ware in which polychrome patterns were painted over the glazed pottery. Richest of all was the polychrome overglaze pottery on which parts of the design were gilded. Although certain distinctive pottery types have been assigned to the busy workshops at Kashan, Ray, and Sava, many other towns also produced fine ceramics. In recent years a great many pieces have been found in excavations along the southeastern corner of the Caspian Sea.

Some mention has already been made of the style of the illuminated manuscripts of the history of Rashid ad-din produced in his suburb outside Tabriz. Extant pages from an illustrated work of al-Biruni are dated 1307 and may have been painted at this same site. In this period also copies of the *Shahnama* were illuminated and the large pages formerly in the Demotte Collection, believed to have been painted in Tabriz. In these pages the Far Eastern influences are already less strong: compositions and details have been altered, the colors are stronger, and gold backgrounds are now in vogue. Other centers of miniature painting were probably at Shiraz and Herat. The splendid ornamented pages of a Qoran which was made for Oljaitu in Hamadan in 1313 are covered with geometrical and floral patterns very like the patterns used in contemporary architectural decoration, as are pages from Qorans written at Mosul and Maragha.

Textile weaving was carried on at Tabriz, Nishapur, Herat, Qum, Yazd, and other centers. About thirty fine silks, some of which show a definite Chinese influence, have been preserved in museums and private collections. Some make use of gilded or silvered thread, many are woven in narrow striped patterns, and still others covered with palmettes, lotuses and other floral forms. Some of these silks, one of which bears the name of Abu Sa'id, were found in Europe far from Iran.

The name of Abu Sa'id is also found on a magnificent brass basin inlaid with gold and silver. Other notable examples of the metalworkers' art continue the style of the Seljuq period. The wood carving of the period is known to us from a number of minbars and doors of mosques and shrines in which two main types of pattern were used: geometrical patterns of interesting polygons, and intertwined conventional plant forms.

Timurid Period

In the eastern reaches of Iran conditions had been unsettled for a considerable period of time. After the original Mongol invasion the lands of Transoxiana had been allotted to Chaghatay, the second son of Genghiz Khan, who there founded his own dynasty. Somewhat later the vast territory was split into two sections, Transoxiana proper and Turkestan, which carried on ceaseless warfare with each other until 1370 when Timur, then in the service of the ruler of Turkestan, managed to subdue the rival state.

Timur, or Tamerlane as he is known to the western world, was born near Samarqand in 1336, the great-grandson of the head of the Berlas tribe of Turks. Once master of Transoxiana, he turned his new strength toward the west. In 1380 he conquered Khorasan, Mazanderan, and Sistan; in 1384 Azerbaijan, Georgia, and western Iran; and in 1392 the whole of Fars. His campaigns were carried on with relatively small forces so that he sometimes met with reverses and his westward progress was slow. He moved on to Baghdad, and then into Syria where he took Aleppo and Damascus. His conquests, although less destructive than those of the Mongols, did work considerable havoc. One account of his exploits reads: "And as soon as they had surrendered and given up their arms, he drew the sword against them and billeted upon them all the armies of death. Then he laid the city waste, leaving in it not a tree or a wall and destroying it utterly, no mark or trace of it remaining." On the other hand, he frequently allowed the petty overlords, sultans, and amirs to retain their local power.

He also conquered much of Russian Turkestan and of India. In 1398 he returned to Samarqand, his capital, to organize the administration of his vast territories. The state which he established was essentially a Turkish kingdom but Iranian culture played the creative and dominant role, for Timur was a fervent Moslem.

A good deal is known about Timur's character, habits, and interests. According to one contemporary writer: "He was of great stature, of an extraordinarily large head and with long hair said to have been white from birth. He was of a serious and gloomy expression of countenance; an enemy to every kind of joke or jest, but especially to falsehood. He neither loved poets nor buffoons, but physicians, astronomers and lawyers. His favorite books were histories of wars and biographies of warriors. His learning was limited, being confined to the ability to read and write; three languages he could use—Turkish, Persian, and Mongolian." He seems to have loved the open air and, if the weather permitted, moved from one to another of his great gardens which girdled Samarqand. There he lived in tents or pavilions made of the most costly silks and brocades. The inherent cultural limitations of Timur did not affect his interest in the arts. He was passionately interested in architecture and gathered artisans and craftsmen at Samarqand to erect a series of structures each of which had to be higher and grander than the one before.

At Samarqand Timur erected for his favorite wife, a Chinese princess called Bibi Khanum, a vast religious school which took her name. Large sections of the original four-ivan structure still stand. At the center was a vast open court, surrounded by arcades and with a high minaret at each corner. Opposite the vaulted entrance is the square sanctuary chamber crowned with a dome set on a very high cylindrical drum. Timur also supervised the construction of his own tomb, which seems to have been completed just before his death in 1404. This tomb, known today as the Gur-i-Mir, has been preserved in good condition and is a fine example of characteristic Timurid style of construction on a monumental scale enriched by brilliant colored decoration. The tomb's exterior is octagonal and within is a square chamber with deep niches and portals on each of its four sides, decorated with extreme richness. The lower walls are lined with alabaster above which is a band of greenish jasper bearing a gilded inscription which recounts the deeds of Timur. Higher up, the walls are covered with paper pressed into patterns in relief which were painted with gold and blue and then varnished. Still higher are other encircling inscription bands with gilded letters against a blue ground. The interior surface of the shallow inner dome is also covered with decoration in blue and gold. Above it is a slightly bulbous dome, rising high above the lower chamber, and roofed with fluting patterned with light blue and dark blue glazed bricks with accents of tawny-colored brick.

When Timur died only a grandson and a son of his sister, among a host of his possible successors, were at Samarqand. His fourth son, Shah Rukh, was at Herat, and it was he who gained control of Herat, Khorasan, and Transoxiana after nearly a year of family feud and warfare. The third son, Miran Shah, gained control of western Iran including Tabriz and Baghdad but was soon engaged in conflict with his own sons. In 1408 the Qara-Qoyunlu, or the "Black Sheep," horde took advantage of the situation to seize Azerbaijan. In 1410 the Black Sheep chief Qara Yusuf took Baghdad and some years later his son acquired possession of the Isfahan region. Not until

1469 did the Aq-Qoyunlu, or the "White Sheep," sweep out their "black" rivals.

In the east Shah Rukh, from his capital city Herat, reigned over all of eastern Iran until 1447. He did defeat the Black Sheep at Tabriz and drive them into Armenia but in the end was forced to leave them in possession of the western region. Shah Rukh was one of the most cultured monarchs that Iran has ever known and made Herat the intellectual center of middle Asia. Prosperity grew under his intelligent government. Architects, painters, poets, scholars, and musicians were held in high esteem, and the artistic and literary movements of these years were to spread westward in later times and find final expression at Isfahan under the rule of Shah 'Abbas.

One of Shah Rukh's wives, Gawhar Shad, was the mother of his famous sons Ulugh Beg and Baysunghur and a great character in her own right. Her long and productive partnership with the architect Qavam ad-din of Shiraz, who was known as "one of the four great lights of the court," resulted in the construction of a number of splendid buildings. One of these is the perfectly preserved Mosque of Gawhar Shad within the area of the Shrine of Imam Reza at Mashhad, begun in 1405 and completed in 1417. The plan layout is conventional, with the usual arcades around an open court and four ivans at axial points, but the superlative feature is the glowing mosaic faience which sheathes all wall surfaces with patterns in dark blue, light blue, white, tan, yellow, black and green glaze. Immediately after the completion of the mosque Gawhar Shad ordered work begun at Herat on a group of great structures which once included a large *madrasa*, or religious school, a *musalla* which followed the normal mosque plan, and her own mausoleum. High minarets sprang from the corners of the buildings. Most of the ensemble was destroyed in 1885 but the mausoleum remains in fair condition: in it were buried her son Baysunghur and finally, after a life of more than eighty years, the queen herself. Qavam ad-din of Shiraz also built a fine madrasa at Khargird, west of Herat and just within the present eastern frontiers of Iran.

Shah Rukh was succeeded by his eldest son Ulugh Beg, whose reign was unfortunately very brief, lasting from 1447 until 1449. He was a great patron of Persian art and literature and was much interested also in the arts of China. But his ruling passion was the study of astronomy. He built an observatory which still stands at Samarqand and established tables of calculations which were finally printed in England in 1665. Baysunghur, a brother of Shah Rukh, died from acute alcoholism but not before he had achieved lasting fame in the fields of calligraphy, music, and painting. At Herat a large group of illuminators, bookbinders and copyists worked under his direct supervision.

Ulugh Beg was too humane, gentle, and kind for the times, and in the end was dethroned and killed by his own son. The kingdom fell into a state of anarchy which endured for several years. Finally, in 1469, Husein Bayqara came into possession of Khorasan and revitalized the early renaissance of culture and the arts at Herat. A contemporary wrote: "The whole habitable world had not such a town as Herat had become under Sultan Husein. . . . Khorasan, and Herat above all, was filled with learned and matchless men. Whatever work a man took up, he aimed and aspired to bring it to perfection." Among the group of luminaries at the court were men of both Persian and Turkish descent. There were the poets Jami and 'Ali Shir Nawa'i, the painters Bihzad and Shah Muzaffar, the calligrapher Sultan 'Ali, and the historians Mirkhwand and Khwandamir.

After the death of Husein Bayqara in 1506 the eastern Timurid kingdom fell into the hands of a Tartar horde whose racial origin was Mongol but whose cultural tradition was Turkish. This Tartar dynasty, the Shaybanids, continued to patronize the arts at Bokhara and Samarqand but was soon brought to an end by the rising power of the Persian Safavids.

Shams ad-din Muhammad Hafiz of Shiraz was the brightest of the great literary lights of the period. As a poor youth he had managed to attend school and learn the Qoran by heart: hence his literary name of Hafiz, or the "Memorizer." Hafiz lived in Shiraz and enjoyed the patronage of several local rulers until his death in 1389. A famous anecdote which describes a meeting in Shiraz between the humble poet and the conquering Timur is probably apocryphal. Timur is said to have chided Hafiz for his verse which reads:

> "If that unkindly Shiraz Turk would take my heart
> within her hand,
> I'd give Bokhara for the mole upon her cheek, or
> Samarqand."

stating that he had carried out his conquests to embellish those cities of Bokhara and Samarqand which Hafiz would give away for a trifle. Hafiz replied that it was through such prodigality that he had fallen on evil days. According to another version, which demands a transliteration of the Persian line, Hafiz answered that he did not actually write:

> Bi-khal-i-hinduwash bakhsham Samarqand o Bokhara-ra
> "I'd give Bokhara for the mole upon her cheek, or
> Samarqand."

but:

> Bi-khal-i-hinduwash bakhsham seh man qand o do
> khorma-ra
> "I'd give for the mole on her cheek three mans of
> sugar and two dates."

The *Divan* of Hafiz contains 693 separate poems of which 573 are odes, singing of spring, the rose, the nightingale, wine, youth, and eternal beauty. They breathe an ecstatic lyricism and blend the mystical and profane in passages of beautiful imagery, but through much of the work runs a vein of skepticism and indifference.

Jami, who was born in Khorasan and died in Herat in 1492, was at once a great poet, scholar, and mystic. It is believed that he composed forty-six major works in the fields of lyrical and romantic poetry, mysticism, Arabic grammar, composition of poetry and prose, music, the lives of the Sufi saints, and exegesis of the Qoran. During his life he was held in the highest esteem by his contemporaries and by rulers of distant kingdoms. His *mathnavi*, or romantic narrative poems, included seven long pieces, and his lyric works were collected in three Divans. No other writer of the period was preeminent in as many fields or so vividly expressed the mystical and pantheistic thought of Iran.

Of the other literary figures of the period only a few will be mentioned here. 'Ali Shir Nawa'i was the patron of such men as Jami and Bihzad and became equally famous as musician, painter and poet. Nizam ad-din Shami wrote a *Zafar Nama*, or "Book of Victory" which was the only account of Timur's conquests to be completed while Timur still lived. For its material the author, who had been involved in fighting at Baghdad and Aleppo, was given access to official records and documents. The much better known *Zafar Nama* of Sharaf ad-din 'Ali Yazdi, completed in 1424, is swollen with exaggerated praise of Timur, but is based largely upon the preceding work. Mirkhwand was the literary name of the author of the *Rawdat es-Safa*, a history of Iran from the period of the pre-Moslem kings down to 1506.

Many architectural masterpieces of the Timurid period, known to us from contemporary accounts, have vanished from the face of the earth. One such monument was the great mosque built by Timur at Samarqand, and only one section remains of the fabulous palace of Timur at Kesh which took twenty years to build. Standing monuments of the fifteenth century include the imposing shrine of Khwaja Abu Nasr Parsa at Balkh, the shrine of Khwaja 'Abdullah Ansari outside of Herat, the shrine at Turbat-i-Shaykh Jam and the tomb of Zayn ad-din at Tayabad, the latter two just within Iran's present eastern frontier.

Most of these structures, as well as those mentioned earlier, reflect an interest in large-scale architecture which is most evident in the great height of the principal ivan of each monument. Nearly every building of the period was gorgeously clad in multi-colored faience, and near the end of the period the glazed material was used on the interior as well as on the exterior surfaces. In western Iran is a structure whose decoration links the Timurid and the Safavid periods. This is the so-called Blue Mosque at Tabriz in which Jahan Shah, the most powerful ruler of the Black Sheep dynasty, was buried in 1467, two years after its completion. The main area of the building is rectangular in plan with a wide vaulted passageway around three sides of a large dome chamber which here took the place of the usual open court. Behind the dome chamber is a slightly smaller domed sanctuary. The exterior walls and entrance portal of the damaged structure have brilliant mosaic faience while on the interior the bright glaze is set against a background of reddish-buff brick.

Ceramic production seems to have been of minor importance in the Timurid period, but the marvelous development in book illustration is the major feature of fifteenth century art. The principal schools of painting were at Shiraz and Herat, the less important Shiraz school tending to continue the earlier traditions of painting at Baghdad and Tabriz. Herat painting reflects the influence of individual masters of conspicuous technical skill and replaces the rigid formalism of earlier periods with a studied naturalism. The work of this century represents the climax of development of Persian miniature painting. Compositions use a decorative rather than a realistic grouping of the figures. Details of architecture, costumes, and growing forms are executed precisely and elaborately. Although landscape is always treated as background for subject matter rather than as dominant motif, mountains, trees, and sky are painted with loving care. The subjects seem crystallized into static and unlifelike scenes, for the artists avoided true perspective, the use of shadows, and plastic moulding of figures, and the faces are usually void of emotion. The colors are very brilliant and pure and are applied in flat tones.

Bihzad, born about 1440 and still active under the Safavid ruler Shah Tahmasp, has always been considered the greatest Persian miniature painter and, of course, had a marked influence upon contemporary as well as later artists. Countless miniatures were once ascribed to his hand, but scholarly study has narrowed the field to a number of signed pages and a few other pictures which bear the unmistakable mark of his personal style. A copy of the *Bustan* of Saʿdi, now in the Royal Egyptian Library at Cairo, contains four miniatures each signed

"work of the slave Bihzad," and a fifth double-page frontis-
piece representing a banquet of Sultan Husein is certainly by
the master. A Nizami manuscript also has three small pictures
signed by Bihzad. A *Zafar Nama*, written in 1467 for Sultan
Husein Bayqara, contains six magnificent double-page paintings
of such scenes in the life of Timur as the king enthroned in a
garden, or supervising the construction of a mosque. These
paintings are unsigned but are generally assigned to Bihzad.

Bihzad must have had many pupils in Herat, and some of
the work of one of them, Qasim 'Ali, has survived. Other
pupils and painters who drew inspiration from his work moved
to Bokhara and set up flourishing workshops in that city. One
of these artists, Mahmud Muzahhib, painted a fine portrait of
'Ali Shir Nawa'i which is still in existence. The school of Herat
also attracted painters who were active before Bihzad reached
his prime or who were not under his direct influence. Among
the first group was Nasrullah Abu'l-Ma'ali, who illustrated
a manuscript of the fables of Kalila and Dimna which is now in
the Gulistan Palace at Tehran. There is also a copy of the
Shahnama with splendid pictures by an unknown hand. One of
the most charming miniatures ever painted in Iran is associated
with the Herat school and possibly with the painter Ghiyath
ad-din, who accompanied an embassy sent by Shah Rukh to the
court of China and kept a diary of his travels. The painting,
done on silk, shows the meeting of the Prince Humay of Iran
with the Princess Humayun of China, in a garden bursting with
fruit trees in blossom and a whole catalogue of exquisitely
drawn flowers.

Safavid Period

The Safavid period saw the reëstablishment of a truly native
Iranian dynasty after a lapse of eight centuries, and the resulting revival of national spirit and unity may be compared to the
movement which sprang up when the Sassanian dynasty arose
after the long Graeco-Parthian domination of the country. The
founder and first ruler of the Safavid dynasty, Shah Isma'il,
came into prominence as the leader of seven Turkish tribes of

Azerbaijan. These tribes, known collectively as the *Qizil Bash* or "Red Heads," could put 70,000 armed horsemen in the field. Isma'il himself was not a Turkish chief but had won respect as the descendant of a long line of religious leaders and the head of an order of dervishes. The progenitor of his line was Shaykh Safi ad-din of Ardabil, a Moslem saint, preacher, and worker of miracles, who lived from 1252 until 1334.

In 1500 Isma'il defeated the White Sheep and was crowned at Tabriz. By 1510 he had taken over Iraq, Fars, Kerman, Hamadan, and Khorasan, and his forces had penetrated as far east as Khiva. The Shi'a sect was proclaimed the state religion of Iran and ruthless force was used in converting reluctant Sunnis. The turn to Shi'ism fostered the bitter enmity of the Ottoman Turks, whose rulers at Constantinople now became the Caliphs of all Sunni Islam. Shi'a Iran now separated the Sunni mass of central Asia, India, and Afghanistan from the Sunnis of Turkey, Iraq, Egypt, and the other Moslem countries to the west of Iran. An early result of the religious friction was the invasion of Iran by the Ottoman ruler Selim I, who defeated Isma'il near Tabriz. This warfare continued for a long period, and the pressure on Iran from without was a powerful factor in uniting all Iran in loyalty to the Safavid rulers and the Shi'a faith.

The second Safavid, Shah Tahmasp, ruled from 1524 until 1576. He maintained the eastern frontiers but in the west suffered several defeats at the hands of the Turkish ruler Soleiman the Magnificent, who took over Iraq and penetrated as far as Tabriz and Isfahan. To escape the Turkish menace Tahmasp moved his capital from Tabriz to Qazvin, and there ruled over a cultivated court whose tone was one of refinement, sophistication, and grace. Tahmasp himself studied painting and became a skillful calligrapher.

After a short interval spaced by the brief reigns of Isma'il II, Muhammad Khodabanda, and Sultan Amir Hamza, the great Shah 'Abbas came to the throne in 1587. On the west the Ottomans were in control of all Azerbaijan and on the east the Uzbek Turks had invaded Khorasan and were in possession of Herat and Mashhad. Shah 'Abbas first signed a treaty which confirmed the Ottoman gains and then moved to drive the Uzbeks out of Khorasan. Free of that threat, he turned westward and, victorious over the Ottoman Turks, recovered Azerbaijan, Armenia, and Georgia. After 1598 the Persian forces had the advantage of the output of a cannon foundry started by the English Sherley brothers, but the Ottoman army remained the more powerful and in 1636, after the death of Shah 'Abbas, a treaty between the two powers settled the western frontiers of Iran until the nineteenth century.

Shah 'Abbas was the dominant figure of the Safavid line and the equal of any ruler in the long history of Iran. The years of his reign are well-documented, particularly in the accounts of the English travelers who visited his court. Sir Anthony Sherley wrote of him: "His person then is such as well-understanding Nature would fit for the end proposed for his being, excellently well shaped, of a most well proportioned stature, strong and active; his colour somewhat inclined to a man-like blacknesse, is also more blacke by the Sunnes burning: his furniture of mind infinitely royal, wise, valiant, liberall, temperate, merciful, and an exceeding lover of Justice, embracing royally other virtures, as farre from pride and vanitie, as from all unprincely signs or acts."

In 1598 'Abbas moved the capital to Isfahan; favored with every mark of royal concern, the city soon hummed with activity in the arts and crafts. The ruler pushed reforms in every field of public life. In place of an army composed of tribal forces led by tribal chiefs he created a regular, paid army which included the *Shah Sevens* or "Friends of the Shah," a force of 10,000 horsemen and 20,000 foot-soldiers. Roads, canals and caravanserais were constructed throughout Iran. In 1622 he allied Iran with a British naval force in the Persian Gulf to drive the Portuguese from the island of Hormuz, and encouraged British and Dutch merchants to trade at Bandar 'Abbas, making it the principal center for the export of silks. He established diplomatic relations with the European countries. Kurdish tribes were moved to Khorasan to form a living barrier against the Uzbeks, and a large colony of Armenian artisans were moved from Julfa in Azerbaijan to a new Julfa across the river from Isfahan. He was tolerant of non-Moslems, zealous for public security, severe in his impartial justice, and lavish in his charitable gifts. Besides making Isfahan the architectural wonder of the world he embellished Shiraz, Ardabil, and Tabriz with fine structures. He devoted special attention to the Shrine of Imam Reza at Mashhad, probably with the intent of keeping money within the country by making the shrine attractive to pilgrims who would otherwise journey to Mecca or to the holy Shi'a shrines in Iraq. He himself made several pilgrimages, one entirely on foot from Isfahan to Mashhad, and erected new sections of the shrine complex.

At Isfahan Shah 'Abbas undertook the construction of a new imperial city adjacent to the ancient town. The first stage of the work established the main lines of the general plan and saw the erection of the buildings essential for the domestic, civil, and religious requirements of the court. The second stage, beginning in 1611, elaborated the existing elements and duplicated the earlier structures in far larger and finer buildings. Today these splendid monuments remain in good condition, and Isfahan, of all the cities in the country, offers the visitor a complete picture of older Iran. Around the great Imperial Square were ranged a palace, the Imperial Mosque, a smaller mosque, and a monumental entrance to the covered bazaars. To the west of the square was a spacious garden area strewn with royal palaces and pavilions, pierced by a wide avenue which led across the river via a new bridge to garden palaces on the opposite side. The city, enclosed within mud brick walls, held some 600,000 people and 162 mosques, 48 religious colleges, 1802 caravanserais, and 273 public baths. Although many of the streets were narrow and winding, nearly every home had its garden court.

Unfortunately a less noble and perhaps less sagacious side of Shah 'Abbas came to the surface in his family relations. Through jealousy and fear of being supplanted in power he put to death some of his own sons, and neglected the education and administrative training of the others, and having personally undermined the future of the Safavid dynasty, was followed on the throne by a series of relatively inept rulers. An Iranian proverb runs: "When the great Prince ceased to exist, Iran ceased to prosper."

Shah 'Abbas was followed by Shah Safi, 1629–1642; Shah 'Abbas II, 1642–1667; and Shah Soleiman, 1667–1694; under whom Iran enjoyed years that were fairly free from war although the Ottoman Turks showed intermittent hostility. These rulers, though sometimes cruel and violent, did strive to increase the general prosperity of the country. Many travelers, merchants, and missionaries came from Europe to Isfahan and have left us fascinating accounts of the royal court and of life in village and town. But as the years went by the control of the empire passed more and more into the hands of the higher clergy.

During the reign of Shah Sultan Husein, from 1694 until 1722, one of the Afghan tribes, the Ghilzai, revolted at Kandahar and secured their independence. Then, at Herat the Abadi tribe followed their example, and in 1722 Mahmud ibn Mir Vays led the tribes against Kerman and on to Isfahan. Shah Husein then abdicated and himself crowned Mahmud as Shah of Iran, but the country soon broke up into separate areas. Mahmud and his successor Ashraf, 1725–1730, reigned over Isfahan, Fars, and Kerman. Czarist Russia occupied the western and southern shores of the Caspian, and the Ottoman Turks moved into western Iran until Ashraf, who was a Sunni believer, made an amicable arrangement with them.

Many philosophical treatises were written in the Safavid period by Mir Abul Qasim Findariski, Shaykh Baha'i, and Mullah Sadra and his numerous disciples, but the work had little originality and tended more toward a detailed reworking of Avicenna's earlier interpretations of the teaching of Aristotle. A severe clerical control forced all written thought to conform to orthodox doctrine. Sufism had finally lost its driving force and became repetitious and sterile. A number of mystical poets reiterated their belief that there was no real value in the world, in action, in courage and perseverance, and urged a placid submission to destiny and escape from the disillusionments and misfortunes of an active life into a personal world of fantasy.

In poetry and prose content became subordinated to form of expression. The chief delight lay in the use of ornate and elaborate language, and figures of speech were highly developed. A few of the devices used in this and later writing included homonyms, anagrams, palindromes (verses which could be read either forwards or backwards), adornment (the arrangement of verses in geometrical shapes), quadrilaterals (the arrangement of verses in a rectangle so that they could be read either horizontally or vertically), suppression (the deliberate avoidance of the use of a given letter of the alphabet), and enigmas (in which numerical dates are obtained from the sum total of the assigned numerical value of the letters in certain words). Rhetorical figures included hyperbole —the most highly prized of all the figures—simile and ambiguity.

Sustained architectural activity was a characteristic of the Safavid period. The great number of structures erected in this period which still stand in good condition includes scores of small shrines in hidden villages. Plan forms, structural methods, and materials used are all continuations of the work of earlier periods. The keynote of the period was color, and polychrome mosaic faience now clothed both interiors and exteriors of the principal monuments. The task of cutting and fitting and assembling many thousands of small glazed pieces which, on a single building, might take several years, finally proved to be so slow and so costly that it was superseded by a method of comparable effect. In this technique, called *haft rangi* or "seven colors," the details of a large decorative panel were painted with as many as seven different pigments on square tiles, and the colors then fired on the tiles in a single operation. The use of the double dome also characterized the period. Square chambers were covered by a shallow interior dome above which rose a high, more bulbous dome, with the open space between filled with an intricate supporting framework of timbers.

A particularly charming feature of the period was the setting of brightly colored buildings in pleasant gardens in reference to pools and streams. In such gardens were erected shrines of saintly men; a typical example is the tomb of Muhammad Mahruq at Nishapur, where the same garden shelters the remains of 'Umar Khayyam. Many palaces built by Shah 'Abbas and other rulers of the line were in the royal gardens. At Isfahan one may still see the palaces called Chihil Sutun, Talar Ashraf, and Hasht Bihisht, while others still stand along the Caspian coast at Amul and Ashraf. The rulers enjoyed living in the open air, as the following account testifies: "For thirtie dayes continually, the King made that Feast in a great Garden of more than two miles compasse under Tents, pitched by certaine small courses of running water, like divers Rivers, where every man that would come, was placed according to his degree, eyther under one or other Tent, provided for abundantly with Meate, Fruit and Wine, drinking as they would, some largely, some moderately without compulsion. A Royaltie and Splendor which I have not seene, nor shall see again but by the same King."

Carpet and textile weaving reached almost incredible perfection in the Safavid period. Great carpets woven in the royal workshops and destined for palaces or shrines were fabulously expensive to produce, and as we see them today hung on the walls of museums it is difficult to believe that such priceless objects were actually made to be walked upon. Nature and the flowering garden furnish the pattern themes. Some of the patterns most frequently employed were hunting scenes; entire gardens as seen from directly above; compositions of a central medallion surrounded by a field of floral scrolls, arabesques, and animals; fields of rows of flower-filled vases; compartmented flower-strewn fields; and, all-over foliage designs. The earliest preserved carpets of great distinction date from the opening of the sixteenth century, and the craft remained at its peak throughout the entire century. Three of the most famous are: the hunting carpet, more than 22 feet long and 11 feet wide, signed by Ghiyath ad-din of Jam and dated 1522, which is now in a museum at Milan; the very large medallion carpet with hanging mosque lamps which was ordered by Shah Tahmasp for the shrine of his ancestor Shaykh Safi at Ardabil and signed by Maqsud of Kashan in the year 1539; and the medallion and arabesque carpet, more than 26 feet long and 13 feet wide, woven in the first third of the sixteenth century and formerly in the collection of the Duke of Anhalt. Later in the century the workshops at Kashan wove a series of silk rugs; many small ones and three huge pieces have survived. Still more luxurious were the so-called Polonaise carpets whose patterns were interwoven with silver and gilded silver threads. Prayer carpets using the mihrab as the central theme were also woven in quantity in this period.

The textile weavers, working at Isfahan, Yazd, and less important centers, turned out silk twills, satins, velvets, silks using silver and gold thread in patterns only, and silks in which the entire background of the design is of metallic thread. Pieces from the period of Shah 'Abbas survive in quantity and are of first-rate technical skill. Ghiyath ad-din 'Ali of Yazd is the best known of the weavers who signed their work; he and his fellow workers at Yazd specializing in panels enclosing a single blooming plant set within an arched frame. A very popular theme was that of repeated floral sprays against solid grounds of salmon pink, deep blue, yellow, or green. Equally popular was the garden scene which often represented personages bearing a jug and a wine cup, cypress trees, flowering bushes, birds, animals, and a pool. Most of these stuffs were destined for costumes to be worn at the royal court, and a number of these Safavid costumes survive to the present day.

Shah 'Abbas assembled, in a building in the shrine complex at Ardabil, a very large collection of Chinese blue and white porcelain, and much of the pottery of the Safavid period followed Chinese models, using the delicate colors and refined designs of the Far East. Shah 'Abbas even went so far as to bring three hundred Chinese potters and their families to Iran to instruct the local craftsmen. Persian porcelain was produced in quantity but never rivaled the genuine Chinese work. Celadon ware, for example, was made in imitation of the Chinese type but the best of the Persian manufacture was a gray-green not true in tone to the master models. A typical Persian ware of the period is the so-called Kubachi pottery, many pieces of which carry a rapid, sketchy drawing of the human figure with the designs painted in blue, green, red, and tan on a cream slip and covered with a transparent glaze.

Afshar, Zand, and Qajar Periods

Nadir Quli was an Afshar tribesman, born at Mashhad, who rose from camel driver to robber baron with his headquarters the impregnable natural fortress of Kalat-i-Naderi in Khorasan. In 1726 he took service under Tahmasp Mirza, son of the Safavid ruler Shah Husein, and in 1729, in the vicinity of Isfahan, defeated the Afghans led by Ashraf and drove them from western Persia and from Khorasan and Herat. Nadir also recovered Armenia and Georgia from the Ottoman Turks, as recognized by the Treaty of Constantinople signed in 1736.

In 1731 Nadir deposed Tahmasp and ruled as regent for the latter's son, 'Abbas III, until the death of this last Safavid in 1736, when he ascended the throne of Iran as Nadir Shah, founder of the Afshar dynasty. As a political move aimed at ending the division of eastern Islam he proclaimed Sunnism the official belief of the country, but neither his proclamation nor his persecution of the Shi'a leaders had any lasting effect. The provinces of Iran were governed by members of his family. Believing that a plot against him had been inspired by his son Reza Quli Mirza he ordered Reza's eyes put out and his subsequent remorse drove him to acts of madness and cruelty. Discipline exercised over both the public and the soldiers of his army was very severe.

In 1736 he moved into Afghanistan, taking Kandahar, Ghazna, and Kabul; and then on to India where he entered Delhi and robbed the palaces and city of fabulous treasures which included the Peacock Throne. In 1740 he captured Bokhara and Khiva and the entire Uzbek region. He made a serious attempt to establish a fleet in the Persian Gulf, and in 1738 annexed the islands of Bahrein to Iran. In 1743 he marched against Iraq and seized Mosul and Basra. His reign represented a brief period of national power and prestige but the people of the country gained no benefit from his foreign conquests. His huge army lived off its own country as it marched from west to east and back again, and heavy taxes were levied on the inhabitants. In 1747, in the midst of provincial revolts, he was assassinated by one of his officers.

A blind son of Nadir, Shah Rukh, reigned over Khorasan from 1748 until 1796, but in this period the Afghans established their independence, and western Iran, torn by internal warfare, was taken over by the Zand and Qajar dynasties.

Karim Khan, chief of the nomadic Zand tribe in the region of Shiraz, became master of Isfahan, Shiraz, and most of southern Iran, and successfully repulsed the Qajars. He took the title of *vakil*, or "Regent," in the name of a weak Safavid descendant, and continued in power from 1750 until 1779. Shiraz, his capital, was embellished with palaces, garden pavilions, mosques, and a long vaulted bazaar, and the town still retains much of the architectural nature of this period. Karim Khan was a man of fine personal character and seems to have won the love and esteem of his people.

The Qajars were one of the seven Turkish tribes which had supported the rise of power of Shah Isma'il, the first Safavid ruler. Their fortunes had been at a low ebb under Nadir Shah, but after his death they became dominant in Mazanderan and made an abortive attempt to spread into southern Iran. They found their great leader in the person of Agha Muhammad Khan, a eunuch who progressed by way of violence and slaughter. Himself a Qajar noble, he united the branches of the tribe, rose to power in 1779, took Tehran, and became the first ruler of the Qajar dynasty, although not officially named as Shah of Iran until 1796. In the south Muhammad attacked the forces of Lutf 'Ali, the fifth of the Zand line to succeed Karim Khan. Lutf 'Ali sought refuge in Kerman but was finally captured and tortured to death while Muhammad punished Kerman by putting out the eyes of 20,000 of its inhabitants. By the time he himself was assassinated in 1797, Agha Muhammad Khan had gained control of the whole of Iran, including Georgia.

His nephew and successor Fath 'Ali Shah, who ruled from 1797 until 1834, was a man of quite different character. His reign ushered in a century in which Iran enjoyed comparative calm and peace while it suffered a moral and political decline.

Direct contact with the European powers began under Fath 'Ali Shah with a treaty of alliance, signed in 1807, between France and Iran. Napoleon expected this treaty to open the way for a French invasion of India by land, while Iran was to receive arms and military instruction to enable her to resist the expanding strength of Czarist Russia, which had annexed Georgia in 1801. However, Napoleon soon came to terms with Russia, and the hostilities which broke out between Russia and Iran were ended in 1813 by the Treaty of Gulistan confirming Russian possession of Georgia. In 1814 Iran and Great Britain signed a treaty of defensive alliance which, although it remained in force until 1857, was never of any value to Iran.

In 1826 Iran and Russia again went to war, and initial Persian successes were followed by a series of defeats culminating in the capture of Tabriz by the Russians. The Treaty of Turkoman Chai, signed in 1828, gave Russia the Persian districts of Erivan and Nakhichevan, exacted from Iran a large indemnity, reserved military navigation on the Caspian to Russian ships, and granted capitulations in favor of Russia. A later annex to the treaty gave Russia special economic and tariff rights.

From this time until well into the twentieth century Iran was to be torn between the conflicting interests of Russia and Great Britian. Russia was embarked on a course of expansion in Asia and had visions of a warm water port on the Persian Gulf, while Great Britain was faced with the need of controlling the Persian Gulf and all land areas adjacent to India, her great colonial prize.

Muhammad Shah, the grandson of Fath 'Ali Shah, ruled from 1834 until 1848. He did his utmost to improve the internal condition of the country, abolishing the practice of torture and forbidding the importation of slaves into Iran. During his reign Russia wooed Iranian friendship in order to have a free hand in consolidating her gains in the Caucasus and in Turkestan. Mumammad Shah, supported by Russia, made an attempt to reconquer Herat which was strongly opposed by Great Britain, who sent a British officer to organize the successful resistance of Herat.

The last of the imposing number of religious movements

which have been nurtured by Iran came into being during the reign of Muhammad Shah. It had its beginning in the meditations of Mirza 'Ali Muhammad, born at Shiraz in 1819, who spent his youth in religious study, first as an orthodox Shi'ite and later as the follower of a specialized branch of Sufism. As he reached maturity his teachings were welcomed by an increasing number of followers who hailed him as the *Bab* or "Door" between the world of flesh and the spirit, and he assumed the role of the "point of manifestation of the divine essence in the world." He preached universal peace, improvement of the position of women, removal of class distinctions, and a life led according to the spirit rather than the letter of religion, but his beliefs were entangled with a curious reliance on numerology.

The Bab was executed by the Iranian government at Tabriz in 1850 and about two years later some 40,000 of his followers were massacred. After the death of the Bab one of his ardent followers, Mirza Yahya, became the head of the sect and settled at Adrianople within the Turkish empire. There a schism rent the new faith, and upon the death of Mirza Yahya in 1912 the Babi branch became practically extinct. The leader of the opposing group, his half-brother Mirza Husein, took the title of Baha'ullah or "Divine Splendor" in 1863, and Babism gave way to Baha'ism. Baha'ullah soon combined the mystical Iranian elements of the faith with certain of the liberal ideas then current in Europe and promoted a universal, cosmopolitan religion without special rites or hierarchy. The center of the faith was established at Acre in Palestine and the work was carried on by 'Abbas Effendi, the son and successor of Baha'ullah. The movement has spread throughout the world, and one imposing temple has been erected at Wilmette, Illinois.

Nasr ad-din Shah, son of Muhammad Shah, ascended the throne in 1847 at the age of sixteen. His long reign was marked by friendly relations with Russia, whose influence within Iran became firmly entrenched. In 1856 the Persian army marched into Afghanistan and took Herat. Great Britain, who had fought against the ruler of Afghanistan from 1839 until 1841, demanded the immediate evacuation of Herat; the governor general of India declared war on Iran; and British troops were landed at the head of the Persian Gulf. Russia failed to support Iran and Nasr ad-din capitulated. By the Treaty of Paris, signed in 1857, Iran withdrew from Herat and recognized the independence of Afghanistan. The treaty also granted capitulations and special commercial privileges to Great Britian.

The rivalry between Russia and Great Britain in the Iranian theatre now took the form of economic penetration. Since the growing industrialization of the West demanded both access to raw materials and new markets for manufactured products, certain distant countries were marked for economic penetration, necessitating some degree of political intervention. Within Iran this policy found one application in a struggle for concessions. In 1872 a British banker, Baron Reuter, obtained an amazing concession from Nasir ad-din. Detailed in more than twenty articles, it gave Great Britain the right to construct railways and street car lines, to exploit minerals and oil for a period of seventy years, and to manage the customs service for twenty-four years. When Nasir ad-din made his first trip to Europe in the following year he was very coldly received in Russia and upon his return canceled the concession. However, in 1889 he placated Reuter with a concession for the creation of the Imperial Bank of Persia. In 1890 a British concern was given a tobacco monopoly, but the clerical leaders of the country supported a wave of general indignation by formally forbidding the use of tobacco within Iran until the monopoly was canceled. After 1863 Great Britain was also active in promoting the erection of telegraph lines across western Iran.

Russia was not idle. In 1879 Nasir ad-din agreed to the creation of a brigade of Persian Cossacks patterned on the Russian model and instructed and commanded by Russian officers, and forces were soon established at Tehran and other northern towns. The Discount Bank of Persia, a Russian institution, was opened at Tehran in 1891. In 1888 a Russian subject gained a comprehensive concession covering fishing rights in the Caspian. Meanwhile Russia was very active within the ancient domains of Iran: after 1865 her armies took Tashkent, Samarqand, Bokhara, and Khiva, and in 1882 Iran signed the Treaty of Akhal which gave Russia possession of the important city of Merv.

The American Legation at Tehran was opened in 1882, and between 1855 and 1900 at least fifteen foreign countries gained capitulation rights for their subjects residing in Iran.

Nasir ad-din did the best he could for his country, but circumstances were too strong to be effectively countered. He twice visited Europe and came back with the conviction that Iran needed only to adopt Western skills and methods to take her place in the modern world. He soon learned that this was not the case, for the concessions granted to foreign powers and subjects brought little advantage to Iran, while Tehran was crowded with adventurous strangers who hoped to make their fortunes at the expense of the gullible Persians. The Shah was, however, by no means a naive figure. While in Europe he had been unfavorably impressed by the military reviews and continual preparations for war made by each nation. After watching an impressive demonstration by an English fire department he wrote: "But, the wonder is in this, that on the one hand, they take such trouble for the salvation of men from death, when, on the other hand, in the armouries and workshops they contrive fresh engines for the quicker and more multitudinous slaughter of the human race. He whose invention destroys men more surely and expeditiously prides himself thereon, and obtains decorations of honor." Although the Shah made a serious attempt to improve the systems of justice and of public administration, his efforts were not crowned with lasting success and the country came increasingly under the influence of the clergy. In 1896 Nasir ad-din was assassinated.

His son, Muzaffar ad-din, reigned from 1896 until 1907. After a youth passed in idleness and the pursuit of pleasure at Tabriz, as sovereign he showed no more force or true concern for the affairs of state. His trips to Europe cost tremendous sums, often leaving the treasury almost without funds. Nobles and courtiers amassed fortunes while public officials failed to receive their salaries; a few landlords acquired tremendous holdings while the peasants were squeezed dry. Irrigation works fell into ruin, and the desert encroached on villages and fields.

At length the need for funds led Iran to secure from Russia, in 1900, a loan of 22,000,000 roubles at five per cent interest. Under the terms of the loan, part of the sum was to be used to pay off all other debts to foreigners and until the loan was repaid Iran could not borrow elsewhere without Russian consent. Payment was guaranteed by Iranian customs receipts. At the same time Iran renewed an earlier secret agreement not to grant any railway concession to foreigners without Russia's consent. Russia also began the construction of carriage roads in the north of Iran.

When the expenses of the Shah's visit to Europe in 1900 had been met, the debt to the Imperial Bank paid up, and other obligations settled, only 6,000,000 roubles of the Russian loan remained. Russia promptly made another loan of 10,000,000 roubles and Muzaffar ad-din as promptly left again for Europe. In 1901 Russia and Iran signed a customs agreement which provided for low tariffs on goods normally supplied by Russia and higher tariffs on goods furnished by other countries.

At last the time was ripe for change. Agitation for a Constitution seemed to spring up full blown but actually it had been strongly rooted in the contact of the younger, educated class with the liberal thought of the West. The merchants and some of the clergy and nobles also supported the Constitutional Movement in the expectation of financial or political advantage. In July 1906, the merchants and other dwellers of Tehran to the number of 10,000 flocked to the grounds of the British Legation where they were safe from arrest, and the clergy left the city, so that economic and public activity came to a standstill. The Shah then promised liberal reforms. Pressure was renewed, and in August 1906 he proclaimed the Constitution. The first Parliament was quickly formed and plunged into the task of dealing with the many problems incidental to establishing a new form of government.

In January 1907, Muzaffar ad-din died. His ambitious son,

Muhammad 'Ali Shah, hoped to take advantage of dissension within the ranks of the Constitutionalists to restore absolute royal power. The merchants had begun to lose interest in Parliament and no longer supplied adequate funds, and the clergy, having failed to win control of the new government, now turned against it. At this moment came the announcement of the Anglo-Russian agreement of 1907.

Great Britain had supported the Constitutionalists, who had demanded an end to Russian intrigue and influence at the Persian court. Russia had just emerged from a losing war with Japan. Great Britain sensed a new menace in a German plan to build a railroad across the Near East to the Persian Gulf, and proposed an agreement with Russia which would also serve as a means of defense against German ambitions. In 1907 Russia and Great Britain signed a treaty which contained provisions relating to Iran, Afghanistan, and Tibet. With regard to Iran, the contracting parties agreed to respect her integrity and independence and then proceeded to divide the country into zones of influence. Britain was to refrain from seeking any public or private interests in the Russian zone, which took in the entire northern part of the country and included the towns of Tabriz, Rasht, Tehran, Mashhad, and Isfahan. The zone reserved for English interests was much smaller, covering the southeastern corner of Iran. The area between the two zones, although not specifically defined in the agreement, was to be neutral. In actual fact it became a field of British activity and a barrier on the road to India.

Meanwhile the Shah, encouraged by Russian assurances of support, was ready to move against the Constitutionalists. In June 1908 the Persian Cossack brigade, commanded by the Russian Colonel Liakhoff, bombarded the Parliament building with several casualties, and the Shah proclaimed the dissolution of Parliament. The public response was swift and decisive. At Tabriz the revolutionists held the city until a Russian force entered and with considerable violence suppressed the so-called disorders. Revolutionary forces recruited at Rasht and Isfahan, the Isfahan force consisting of 5,000 Bakhtiaris led by one of their tribal chiefs, marched toward

Tehran. The Persian Cossack brigade was defeated outside of Tehran and in July 1909 the liberal troops entered the city. Muhammad 'Ali Shah first sought refuge in the Russian Legation and then fled to Russia, and the reinstated Parliament named his eleven-year-old son, Ahmad Shah, ruler of Iran. Russian troops remained in northern Iran.

The victorious revolutionaries soon fell into disagreement, and progress was slow until an American, Morgan Shuster, was engaged as Treasurer-General of Iran. With several American assistants, Shuster arrived in Tehran in 1911 and in a very short time had made considerable headway with a reorganization of the financial system, while his energy and obvious devotion to the best interests of the country won the people's hearts. Russia strenuously opposed his work, and in November 1911 presented Iran with an ultimatum demanding, among other things, that Shuster be dismissed. To put teeth into it Russian troops advanced as far as Qazvin, slaughtered many of the liberals at Tabriz, and at Mashhad bombarded the shrine of Iman Reza. The ultimatum was rejected by Parliament but accepted by the Cabinet, and Shuster left Iran to write his classic, *The Strangling of Persia.*

After the outbreak of World War I Iran declared her neutrality, but Tehran became a hotbed for intrigues of Russian, British, and German diplomats and agents. In the northwest of the country Turkey and Russia maneuvered for position, and a Turkish force advanced half the distance from Baghdad to Tehran before being defeated by the Russians. In 1916 Major Percy Sykes came from India to Bandar 'Abbas and recruited a force called the "South Persia Rifles," which gained control of the entire southern section of Iran and reached a strength of 5,000 men. In the vicinity of Shiraz a remarkable German agent named Wassmuss stirred up the tribes, while special German missions tried to cross Iran to win Afghanistan to their cause.

After the war Iran's claims were rejected by the Peace Conference, and she was confronted in 1919 with a treaty proposal drawn up by the British. Under its terms Great Britain once more pledged to respect the integrity and independence of

Persia, and agreed to furnish expert administrative advisors, to be paid by the Persian government, as well as military advisors and arms and equipment, also at Persia's expense. Persia would receive a loan, Great Britain would construct roads and railroads and the existing customs agreements would be restudied. The treaty would have placed Iran under complete British domination. Shah and Cabinet seemed ready to accept it, but popular feeling, encouraged by an American diplomatic protest, ran so high that it was never ratified in spite of strong British pressure. The entire country was now in a state of near anarchy. Bolshevik troops were in force along the Caspian littoral, and there was fighting between Soviet troops and a British expeditionary force.

Suddenly, in 1921, Iran and Soviet Russia concluded a treaty of friendship which represented a complete reversal of the Czarist policy toward Iran. Soviet Russia declared that all treaties and agreements formerly in effect between Iran and Russia were ended, as well as all agreements between Russia and a third power which were harmful to the best interests of Iran. She canceled all outstanding debts of Iran, voided all Russian concessions, and turned over to Iran such Russian assets on Iranian soil as the Discount Bank of Persia, the railroad from Julfa to Tabriz, the port of Enzeli (now Pahlavi), and roads and telegraph lines. She also denounced capitulations and gave Iran equal navigation rights on the Caspian Sea. One section of the treaty reflected the fears of the new Soviet government: neither state was to permit activity within its territory by groups or organizations which had designs against the other state. Each was to keep out of its country troops of a third power which threatened the security of the other. But if a third power should create such a threat within Iran, or attempt to turn Iran into a military base for action against Russia, and if Iran herself should be unable to cope with this danger, Russia reserved the right to send her troops into Iran in self-defense.

III. PATTERNS OF IRANIAN
CULTURE AND SOCIETY

Iran's civilization has its own distinctive character. One force which moulded it—a static one—was the geographical location of Iran as a land bridge between East and West, offering positive advantages to the growth of civilization and culture while at the same time inviting disaster. On the one hand, the lofty plateau was a point of convergence for travelers, traders, and men of learning and for intellectual and artistic currents, and during each successive period Iran was in rewarding contact with powerful civilizations which arose, in their turn, to the east or to the west of the plateau. On the other hand, the plateau region was from earliest times an attractive corridor for the westward sweep of migratory groups as well as a rich goal for booty-seeking conquerors. Invasions and conquests frequently devastated the country beyond apparent possibility of recovery, but after each bitter trial its culture re-emerged.

Iran met the challenge of its geographic position through its capacity for assimilation. This capacity for absorbing foreign blood and adapting foreign influences was due both to the topography of the land and to the vitality of its inhabitants. Peoples who entered Iran in mass migrations or as a victorious army tended to settle in an environment they found more attractive than their places of origin—the barren steppes to the northeast, the hot lowlands to the southwest, or the desert wastes of Arabia.

In the course of long centuries the total number of the newcomers far exceeded that of the original inhabitants of the plateau, but they were all absorbed by and became a part of Iranian civilization, a conversion favored by the low cultural development of the areas in which the newcomers usually originated, and by the force and attractiveness of the Iranian cultural modes. Probably the most striking example of this absorption is that of the Mongols, who entered the plateau

9. Muhammad Reza Pahlavi,
   Shahinshah of Iran

10. The audience hall of the Gulistan Palace at Tehran with the gem-
    encrusted thrones

11. Isfahan. The dome chamber, covered with glowing faience mosaic, of the Mosque of Shaykh Lutfullah, erected in the early seventeenth century

as barbarians reveling in slaughter and destruction and after two generations of settled existence became fervent admirers and advocates of every aspect of Iranian life.

Iran was always ready to receive and to recombine foreign ideas, influences, and specific artistic forms, a tendency which was apparent in prehistoric times and was specifically underlined by Herodotus when he wrote of the willingness of the Achaemenids to adopt foreign customs. The history of art and architecture is full of examples of this assimilative capacity. However, in the fields of artistic expression, of social organization, of religion, and of philosophy, elements admired merely because they were foreign and new were never slavishly copied. Instead, they were always restudied, reworked, and reexpressed in a characteristic fashion.

The history of Iranian culture exhibits a remarkable persistence and continuity which in itself is certainly not peculiar to Iran, but the specific enduring elements which produced it and the manner in which they were expressed are distinctive: pride in the past; type of social structure; character of artistic expression; the search for the meaning and purpose of life; and the Iranian outlook and attitude toward the surrounding world.

We may speak of Iran's pride in the past and of its continued awareness of the value of its cultural heritage, but we cannot speak of the inhabitants of the plateau as "patriotic" Iranians; they never thought of themselves as "Iranians" or as loyal supporters of some such pregnant symbol as "the homeland" or "the divine ruler." The closest approach to such a state of mind came in the early Safavid period when religious unity in Shi'ism, military unity against foreign armies, cultural unity in a period of intellectual activity, and personal loyalty to the Safavid dynasty served to establish a common bond throughout the empire. On the other hand, a sense of deep pride in the glorious past of the country has always persisted, and has helped to bolster self-respect as each successive historical period seemed to bring a decrease in the power and prestige of the nation. Fate had so arranged matters that Iran's earliest historical period, the Achaemenid, had seen the establishment of the first world empire, and that later periods emulated but could not surpass the splendor of the past.

Examples of this high regard for the past and of efforts to establish identification with it are very numerous. The Parthian rulers thought of themselves as the political heirs of the Achaemenids, and the Sasanian dynasty proudly traced its lineage to the Achaemenid kings. Firdawsi, in assembling all the oral and written material on Iran's early glories, set up a standard for later hero worship. Just a few years ago Reza Shah went back to these national traditions for the name of his new dynasty, and when family names came into general use in Iran many of those chosen were names of the ancient kings and heroes of the country.

Iran's social structure was built around the rule of an absolute monarch supported by feudal lords, who as early as the Achaemenid period were named governors in control of vast areas, and in this and later periods their power tended to become hereditary and therefore confined to relatively few families. The loyalty of the feudal lords was always a somewhat precarious quality, and at every period the monarch was faced with the task of retaining their military support while keeping them from growing too powerful. The situation of the common people was much the same at any period. Bound to the soil, living and cultivating the land in the same way for centuries, their condition was fairly easy when the monarchy was strong enough to spread the benefits of irrigation and of public safety, but very unfavorable when political weakness led to economic chaos. The thousands of villages in which they lived were remote from the main roads and were little affected by the recurrent invasions, and it may well be that the isolation of the villages was a major factor in the preservation and continuity of Iranian civilization. At every period men came from these remote villages to rise to positions of influence and power; the most important ruler of modern times, Reza Shah, was born in a small village on the northern flank of the Elborz Range.

The authority of the provincial governors and of the feudal

landowners remained strong until fairly recent times. The final subordination of local autonomy to centralized power was certainly an important factor in the economic decline of the country, since under this centralization tax collection in the provinces was farmed out and all revenues were delivered to the Shah with little or nothing returned to the provinces.

However, life under autocratic rulers never stifled the individuality of the Iranians. Human life itself had little apparent value when thousands or hundreds of thousands of people might be killed in a single invasion, but the self-respect of the people themselves was never destroyed. However humble his status, the Iranian was rarely servile or passive under insult. Society was not fixed within a rigid caste system, and there was no limit to the level to which an individual endowed with wit, courage, and energy might rise.

Artistic expression in Iran had its own marked and continuous character. Iranian art has always been decorative and, normally, non-representational. It is, of course, unfair to allow western prejudice in favor of representational art to result in an unfavorable judgment of decorative art. Decorative and abstract art carries its own forceful meaning through the use of symbols rather than of pictures, and Iran early developed a vocabulary of forms and patterns which had permanent meaning and validity for its people. The earlier works of art established standard compositions which endured with little change for centuries, although they were sometimes reworked as new artistic media came into popularity. Iranian art was always characterized by precision, clarity, and lucidity; for example, in ceramic production interest in a display of technical skill resulted in great variety but never worked, as it did in the Far East, toward the creation of shapes which deny the quality of clay. Iranian ornament, however colorful and elaborate it might be, was always based upon a clearly visible foundation pattern and never became involved in the restless and confused exuberance common to post-Renaissance ornament in Europe and to later Indian decoration.

Iranian art shows a steady stylistic development of the type common to Western art, but it went forward at a much slower rate and was not marked by abrupt changes in style. There was no real gap between pre-Islamic and Islamic art in Iran, and the Moslem prohibition against the representations of living forms, although it was not always observed, only favored the natural predilection for decorative art. Artistic motifs from early times carry over into work of the Islamic periods, and in the realm of architecture the plans of the Sasanian palaces and temples reappear in the mosques. Early forms and methods of construction carry on almost unchanged, for the Iranian builders were seldom intrigued by the unusual and new and rarely experimented with the elements of building construction.

Iranians have always been deeply concerned with the aim and purpose of life. In most general terms, the constant ideal has been that of human conduct according to the principle of "good thoughts, good words and good deeds." Mazdaism, one of the world's first philosophic and comprehensive religious systems, set the pattern for later theological thinking and preached a practical morality which summoned each individual to fight for truth against darkness and lies. Manicheism retained the principle of opposing forces of good and evil, of light and dark, and, uniting aspects of Mazdaism, Christianity, Buddhism, and Judaism, found its climax in the belief that man must redeem his own soul by rigorous denial of the fleshy appetites. Mazdakism, while retaining the concept of the conflict between light and dark, went even farther than Manicheism toward defining perfect good. In order to put an end to such evils as hatred, discord, and war, their natural causes, the desires for women and wealth, must be neutralized. Hence, women and property were to be held in common in a classless society of equal individuals.

Even the shattering blow of the Arab conquest of Iran could not divert the course of such speculation, for the Iranians opposed the material power of the Arabs and the enforced domination of the Moslem religion by the persistent force of their own traditions. Iran, in developing Shi'ism as a sect of Islam and mysticism as an expression of spiritual longing, maintained the continuity of its own thought within the forms of orthodoxy. In the Shi'a concept of the Mahdi, the twelfth direct descendant of 'Ali who was to appear at the end of the world to destroy evil and establish the final triumph of good, the Iranians departed from orthodox belief, which regarded Muhammad as the last and greatest of the prophets, and revived the essence of their ancient myths of the hero who, believed dead, returns in glory. 'Ali, believed by the Iranians to have married a Sasanian princess, and his successors, the Twelve Imams, were especially revered in Iran. The Imams, representatives of the forces of good and light, struggled with Shaytan (Satan) who assumed the role of the pre-Islamic Ahriman.

From a defensible point of view the so-called Arab philosophy is actually Iranian and at times runs counter to Moslem tradition. A majority of the more noted "Arab" philosophers either were of Iranian origin or were inspired by Iranian teachers, and mistaken attributions have arisen from the fact that many of the Iranians active in this field wrote in Arabic. Philosophical activity began with the study and interpretation of the Greek philosophers and continued with attempts to reconcile Greek thought with Moslem doctrine, but it finally entered such fields of Iranian and eastern origin as mysticism, illuminative philosophy, and moral philosophy.

Islamic mysticism had its highest development in Iran. The Iranians seem to have a natural predilection for spiritual intuition—modern Iranian observers have stated that all Persians are mystics at heart—which was, in this case, strengthened by the appeal of fine intellects. The mystical tenets of Sufism, which was so popular in Iran, ranked it as a heretic doctrine of Islam until Ghazali brought Sufism into the breast of the orthodox Moslem faith by transforming it from a doctrine to an attitude toward life—an attitude of humble faith, boundless love, and pure morals. Ghazali's writings were a source of inspiration to later generations, although his principles lost some of their lofty purity in transmission. Thus, the outlook of Khayyam is obscured by a layer of fatalism, passiveness, and skepticism, and the works of Hafiz have a double character—both mystic and profane. Sa'di alone of the later figures stresses the finest sentiments of moral philosophy, expressed in lessons of practical morality.

Ghazali and his immediate spiritual heirs attained a level of speculative thought which was never equaled at later periods when the flow of life was interrupted by the invasions of the Mongols, of Timur, and of the Afghans. They were followed by a host of mystical poets, masters of this craft so beloved in Iran, who seemed to reflect the state of the times when they underlined the lack of any true values to be found in the external world and in such qualities as courage, industry, and perseverance. They wrote of the need to yield to destiny and of the satisfaction of personal escape from harsh reality into a private realm of dreams, and taught that attachment to the material things of this world prevents man from ascending to that highest level of moral and spiritual perfection which is the goal of life. Such teachings and such an attitude became part and parcel of the outlook of generations of Iranians and still have a pervading force.

Modern Iran must decide whether it as a nation can compete in a world which places so high a value on material possessions, and still retain this outlook. It is now an integral part of a larger world in which national survival depends upon adopting the techniques, methods, and attitudes of the most successful nations. The Iranian character itself must be, and is being, modified. The bustle and urgency of business and trade pervades the urban atmosphere, and the urge toward material accomplishment and the acquisition of possessions becomes increasingly strong. With the accelerated tempo of life has come a practical interest in efficiency, precision, and the avoidance of delay, but in the larger view it appears that features rooted within the cultural pattern make it difficult for the Persian to feel in harmony with the modern world or even with his own fellows. Conspicuous examples of this difficulty are given in the following paragraphs.

Always marked individualists, the Persians seem reluctant to enter into group cooperation or to accept collective responsibility. The Persian is not a joiner nor does he find it natural to work with others toward a mutually desired goal. This is not due to any lack of initiative but because his primary concern is for his own family. Whereas in many countries a feeling of belonging and of group association is fostered at the higher educational levels, at neither the Iranian secondary or college levels are student organizations emphasized. Practical reflections of the dominance of individualism may be found in the political scene. Basic to any modern political party are such factors as continuity, definite program, suitable organization, regular contributors, and devoted workers, but such a party has failed to emerge in Iran, except for the foreign-inspired and -directed Tudeh party. Even Reza Shah when he was in a position of absolute authority, found it impossible to establish a "government" party within or without the Parliament. The Parliament continues to function without crystallizing into one or more stable blocs or factions; instead there are shifting alliances and an absence of a feeling of urgency, compulsion, and responsibility. As Dr. Mossadeq said: "In our Parliament each deputy has his own personal opinion and this is why bills, even the simplest, cannot be passed rapidly by this body." The political scene also lacks pressure groups or other organizations reflecting special interests, while the relative ineffectiveness of the labor unions is in part due to the lack of active participation by the majority of the workers.

Individualism finds current expression in the drive for the accumulation of wealth. Aware of his position in a society in disequilibrium the Persian feels that he must pursue self-interest and this he does in a fashion that brings into relief the least attractive aspects of human character. Speculations in land or in commodity markets in the expectation of quick, large gains are favored over capital investments. The accumulation of wealth is considered a key to prestige and influence and to marriage with established families; it often provides the means for the individual to emigrate to a more stable, easygoing society.

Somewhat related to exaggerated individualism is the feature of negativism, expressed in the form of destructive criticism. It would be quite easy to demonstrate that the Persians of today are active and alert in finding fault with situations of all kinds, but are much less ready with constructive criticism. As many as 200 newspapers have appeared ephemerally at Tehran to attack groups, classes, institutions, and individuals. Parliament reflects the same disinclination to stand for something positive, since the uniform pattern is severely critical. It may be said that this failure to stand for something positive and constructive is one of the greatest handicaps in the way of establishing long range internal stability in Iran.

This attitude of destructive criticism may be supplemented by a certain vagueness and lack of rationality. As a practical example, these factors frequently appear on the political scene: the policy of negative equilibrium which has been discussed on another page reflects an unwillingness to face up to the facts of the situation. By some of its adherents it was interpreted to mean that Iran could avoid all the problems which go with the exploitation of oil resources simply by building its future upon an oilless economy. It is possible to suggest that the attitude of mind which combines negative, vague, and unrational feelings may be the unconscious reflection of a feeling of frustration and helplessness caused by the impact of the currently superior military power, economic strength, and mechanical skill of the western world. It would seem that efforts to cultivate a positive constructive attitude toward the future of Iran will require a complete revision of the system of education so that a grounding in the techniques of a mechanized life may be associated with the sound, basic currents of the Iranian cultural tradition.

Current trends and events may work to modify the Iranian character, which is itself an image of the cultural tradition of the country. For example, for hundreds of years writers on Iran have emphasized the prevailing atmosphere of tolerance, of friendliness, and of overwhelming hospitality, and such concern for the individual have been admired in other countries where a democratic outlook was common. However, recent political agitation has been most harmful in weakening or undermining such admirable qualities. Thus, the Tudeh party has attempted to create and foster dissension, distrust, and hostility between social classes, between the people and officials, between teachers and students, and even between neighbors. At one recent period one had only to walk the streets of Tehran to be aware of how indifferent, jostling, rude elements were permeating the population, and this was true not only with regard to a local feeling toward foreigners. Among themselves the Iranians have never been advocates of physical violence, being much more addicted to argument and invective. Hence, those riots, the fights between opposition elements, and even the street fights between individuals which appeared to be becoming endemic were damaging the Iranian character. It may be added that the atmosphere of emotionalism built up by elements other than the Tudeh party was also conducive to unrestrained expression rather than to tolerance and respect for the opinions of others. With a return to relative stability this disruptive drift away from the national character has been halted, but only true, constructive national progress can insure continuity in Iranian character and life.

Only now is Iran beginning to develop its own sociologists and social psychologists. As the trained researchers study the behavior patterns and motivations of their fellows certain basic hypotheses and theses regarding this society will emerge: tested by experience there will arise practical suggestions as how to reorient and stabilize this culture which has endured so long with such consistency and such strength.

MODERN IRAN

Note: With reference to dates and statistics given in this section, two notes of explanation are necessary. Dates given in Christian years are approximations of the Iranian year; that is, the Iranian year 1330 is given as 1951, although this year began on March 21, 1951, and ended on March 20, 1952. Figures given as tons are metric tons; a metric ton equals 2,205 pounds.

IV. THE PAHLAVI PERIOD

On February 21, 1921, just five days before the Irano-Soviet Treaty of Friendship was signed at Moscow, the weak and vacillating government in Tehran was overthrown by a combination of political pressure within the capital and military pressure by the troops who had marched to the city from Qazvin. The leader of these troops was Colonel Reza Khan.

Reza Khan was born at Savad Kuh in the Caspian province of Mazanderan on March 16, 1878. His father and grandfather had been officers in the old Persian army. In young manhood he himself had joined the Persian Cossack Brigade and advanced to high command through sheer ability and force of character. Tall of stature and with a forceful, rugged profile, he was a strict disciplinarian. Without formal education, with a limited experience outside of military matters and a restricted knowledge of the world beyond Iran, he was, nevertheless, a man of purpose and vision.

For the first one hundred days after the occupation of Tehran the new government was headed by Sayyid Zia ad-din Tabatabai, son of a cleric and himself a crusading journalist. In trying to force acceptance of certain measures and reforms he clashed with Reza Khan, now commander-in-chief of the armed forces and Minister of War, and was compelled to resign as Prime Minister and to leave Iran. Reza Khan himself remained Minister of War in several successive cabinets until 1923, when he became Prime Minister. A few months later Ahmad Shah, the last ruler of the Qajar dynasty, left Iran, never to return.

In 1925 a special Constituent Assembly chose Reza Khan as Shah of Iran, and the first ruler of the new Pahlavi dynasty was crowned in the spring of 1926. Reza Shah felt more keenly than any of his compatriots the tragic contrast between Iran's glorious past and her present impotent state, and was resolved to rouse the country from her lethargy and to foster national unity and pride. Iran was to throw off all foreign intervention and influence and to win full independence and the respect of other nations. She was to be industrialized, and her social and economic institutions reformed, along Western lines, a program similar in working details to that of neighboring Turkey. Under it remarkable progress was made during the next few years.

In the field of foreign affairs Reza Shah terminated the system of capitulations, negotiated customs autonomy, and put an end to the practice of seeking loans abroad. British interference in Iranian affairs was no longer apparent; the right of currency issue was taken away from the British-owned Imperial Bank of Iran, and the contract with the Anglo-Iranian Oil Company was canceled and replaced with one more advantageous to Iran.

Reza Shah displayed implacable hostility to local manifestations of communism and jailed both socialistically inclined and Soviet-inspired labor leaders, writers, and teachers. In 1931 the Majlis enacted a bill which was designed to deal with individuals spreading foreign ideology. It provided prison terms for those advocating forcible overthrow of the political, economic and social order, for those endeavoring to separate territory from Iran, and for those trying to weaken those patriotic feelings which related to the independence and unity of the country. At the same time the ruler realized the value of maintaining close commercial and economic ties with Soviet Russia. In 1927 five pacts, and in 1935 several more, were concluded between Russia and Iran, covering fishing rights in the Caspian, the return to Iran of installations at the Caspian port of Pahlavi, commercial relations, customs tariffs, and guarantees of mutual neutrality and security.

Reza Shah created a large army, provided with modern weapons, which soon brought every corner of the land under the control of the highly centralized government. An age-old social order was sacrificed to the new progressive regime. Nobles lost power and prestige, and the use of titles was abolished. The merchants lost freedom of enterprise as they were drawn into the governmental system of monopolies and of controls over industry, commerce, and trade. The tight grip of the Moslem clergy over many phases of public life was a challenge to the position of the new ruler, who took steps to break down their power and prestige. The clergy lost direct control of much of its vast trust funds; religious law gave way to civil and criminal codes; licenses were required for the wearing of clerical garb; civil marriage and divorce registers were established; the position of women was improved; non-Moslem foreigners were permitted to visit the splendid mosques of the country; religious passion plays were suppressed; dervishes were forbidden to appear in towns; and religious teaching gave way to state schools. The object of direct attack was not religion itself, as in certain other countries engaged in a reworking of their social structure, but rather those forms and expressions which were clearly outmoded in a revitalized Iran.

In spite of the strong hand of the central government, the regime had to deal with plots and uprisings: a minimum of information on these subjects reached the public. In 1929, 1930, and 1931 there were strikes by industrial labor at Abadan, Tabriz, and Isfahan, and in 1930 there was an uprising of Kurdish peasants in Khorasan. Tribal revolts broke out among the Kurds of Azerbaijan in 1937 and in 1939. On several occasions alleged plots against Reza Shah led by army officers or members of the government were discovered and those involved harshly punished. In the cause of extending and promoting internal order the regime devoted special attention to breaking the power of tribal leaders. Chiefs of the Qashqa'i, the Mamasanis, and the Lurs were imprisoned at Tehran and some were put to death. However, as late as 1936 the Qashqa'i were in revolt against the central authority. Reza Shah was particularly aggressive in the case of the Bakhtiari leaders. In 1934 at least 32 of these leaders were put on trial at Tehran, and as a result four were executed, four given life imprisonment, and sixteen prison terms.

Although foreign specialists were employed to guide the program of industrialization and the reform of finance and administration, after 1930 foreigners were no longer given posts of authority but were employed as technicians and engineers. For Reza Shah evinced a mounting antipathy toward other countries, a feeling born of both resentment of foreign criticism and of extreme patriotism, and fostered also by the repercussions upon Iran of the world-wide economic depression.

Faced by the great depression and a shortage of foreign exchange, Reza Shah's government assumed control of economy and trade. To handle items of import or export monopolistic firms were created in most of which the state owned all or a large percentage of the stock. The prices of imported goods were fixed above prevailing world levels, and the government drained off substantial profits. Barter agreements were put into effect between Iran and Germany and Soviet Russia.

Profits from monopolies and income from normal and special taxes furnished the funds for the establishment of state-owned industry, and remarkable progress was made in the construction of factories. Transportation facilities were greatly expanded through the construction of the Trans-Iranian Railway, the building of thousands of miles of new roads, and the importation of trucks and passenger cars. On the other hand, agriculture and irrigation were neglected, so that the farming population received little direct benefit from the new industry and suffered a decline in its standard of living.

Unfortunately Reza Shah's self-dedication to the advancement of Iran was complicated by his increasing interest in accumulating a vast personal fortune and by his unwillingness to delegate authority. Large sums of money and titles to villages, farm land, and forest came into his hands. In the realm of administration he exercised stern personal control, and Parliament, losing all spirit of initiative, passed every measure proposed by the government. At his orders the army used severe measures in suppressing disorder among the nomadic tribes. Government officials avoided assumption of initiative or responsibility, and presented only optimistic and favorable reports of the internal situation and of relations with foreign countries, for blunderers were as harshly punished as were the personal opponents of the ruler. Freedom of speech and of the press were nonexistent, and the government set up an office for guiding public opinion. The opportunity to develop capable administrators and public leaders among the rising educated generation was neglected. In general there was a weakening of moral stamina and a pervading atmosphere of resignation and helplessness.

On the outbreak of World War II Iran declared her neutrality and attempted to carry on normal relations with all the powers. Imports of machinery, construction materials, and manufactured items were vital to the industrial program and economic life of the country. Circumstances strongly favored the maintenance of good relations with Germany in particular, for by 1938 that country had attained first place in Iran's foreign trade, facilitated by barter and special payment arrangements. Moreover, Reza Shah had a deep-rooted antipathy toward communism and toward the possible spread of the doctrine within Iran.

After Germany declared war on Soviet Russia in June 1941, Russia and Great Britain, newly allied, were immediately aware of the strategic importance of Iran, since a German drive into the country by way of the Caucasus would tend to menace the Soviet rear. It was also important as a protected supply route to Russia, and the British navy was dependent upon the output of the oil fields near the head of the Persian Gulf. Germany, equally aware of Iran's importance, stepped up its plans to provide a friendly, receptive atmosphere for the German armies when they penetrated Iran. The colony of German businessmen at Tehran—several hundred strong—was well disciplined and had considerable success in convincing the Persian elite that Germany was winning the war. From 1940 German secret agents, such as Franz Mayer and Berthold Schultze, had been active in organizing fifth columns and centers of support among the tribes of the southwest and at Isfahan and Tehran. The sum total of German activity provoked from Great Britain and Soviet Russia a demand that immediate steps be taken to amend a situation which was incompatible with Iranian neutrality. Reza Shah failed to comply effectively with the protests, probably because he was misinformed as to their seriousness and probably also because he believed that the Allies would not resort to direct action. On the other hand, the Allies may have been convinced of the impossibility of arranging cooperative action with so forceful a personality.

On August 26, 1941, Russian forces entered Iran from the northwest and British troops marched across the Iraq frontier and also landed at the head of the Persian Gulf. British ships staged a surprise attack upon the Iran naval forces at Khorramshahr, sinking every vessel with a considerable loss of life. The Iranian army put up a token resistance which was called off in three days. Reza Shah pondered the best interests of his country and of the Pahlavi dynasty, and abdicated the throne. Taken in British charge, he went first to Mauritius and later to South Africa where he died in 1944. Since 1941 a flood of articles and several books have been published in Tehran dealing with the reign of Reza Shah. Foreigners must base their final judgment of him upon this source material, but it is already clear that he was one of the great figures of all Persian history and that almost single-handed he brought Iran abreast of the modern world.

Muhammad Reza succeeded his father on the throne of Iran. Foroughi, a philosopher, author, and respected elder statesman, became Prime Minister and devoted his entire attention to the conclusion of a friendly working agreement with the Allies which would favor the prosecution of the war against Germany. On January 29, 1942, the Tripartite Treaty of Alliance was signed between Iran, Great Britain, and Soviet Russia. In the first article of the treaty the two Allied powers undertook to respect the territorial integrity, sovereignty, and political independence of Iran. The Allies agreed to use their best endeavors to safeguard the economic existence of the Iranian people against privations and difficulties arising as a result of the war. Other articles specified the facilities to be granted the Allies for the struggle against Germany, but stated that the presence of Allied forces on Iranian soil did not constitute a military occupation, and that all such forces would be withdrawn from Iranian territory not later than six months after all hostilities between the Allied Powers and Germany and her associates had been terminated.

Military supplies destined for Russia began to arrive at the head of the Persian Gulf early in 1942, to move up over the Trans-Iranian railway and the motor roads leading north. In December 1942 the first American troops arrived in Iran; a force, known as the Persian Gulf Command, which eventually numbered 30,000 men. The Americans operated the rail line from the Gulf to Tehran and maintained a truck convoy system from the Gulf to the north of Iran where the supplies were turned over to the Russians. The truck line transported 400,000 tons of war materials, while the railroad carried over four million tons of supplies, for Soviet Russia and Iran. Working together as an efficient and cooperative team, the Allies moved over five million tons of war materials across Iran and into the hands of the Russian army.

By the spring of 1942 diplomatic relations with Germany, Italy, and Japan had been severed and their nationals expelled from Iran. On September 9, 1943, Iran declared war on Germany, and announced her adherence to the Declaration of the United Nations.

At the end of November 1943 Roosevelt, Churchill, and Stalin arrived in Iran for the Tehran Conference. Of vital moment for the Iranians was the Tehran Declaration, in which the Allied leaders recognized the aid given by Iran in the war, agreed to continue economic assistance to Iran, stated that economic problems confronting Iran at the end of the war would be given full consideration by the proper international conferences or agencies, and expressed their desire for the maintenance of the independence, sovereignty, and territorial integrity of Iran.

The impact of the war upon Iran was severe. Food was short and goods of every type very scarce, inflation sent prices soaring, and large amounts of currency issued to meet Allied expenditures within the country added to the inflationary trend. Successive short-lived cabinets were too concerned with daily emergencies to be able to consider the fundamental problems resulting from the swift changeover from the autocratic reign of Reza Shah to the more democratic form of government. Reza Shah had failed to establish a majority party within Parliament, and the members of the Parliament elected in 1943 failed, due to lack of unity and purpose, to give sustained support to successive cabinets. Prime Ministers followed each other at frequent intervals. Successive cabinets were charged with favoring the interests of foreign nations, with being too conservative, or with being too radical.

In 1944 American and British oil companies made overtures for concessions in southeastern Iran, and in October of the same year Soviet Russia requested an oil concession in the north of the country. Parliament's answer was to pass, in December 1944, a bill prohibiting any Iranian official from concluding an agreement with any foreign power or interest regarding any concession. Iranian leaders decided that decisions vital to the interest of the nation should be made only after the end of the war, and in October 1945 Parliament passed a bill which postponed elections for the next session of that body until six months after all foreign troops had left the country.

The new political parties were extremely vocal. In the province of Azerbaijan the radical *Tudeh*, or "Masses," party was nominally replaced by the so-called Democratic Party of Azerbaijan. This group, whose field of activity was occupied by Soviet troops, vigorously denounced the policies of the central government and attacked Iranian army garrisons and police posts throughout the province. The area was in open disorder, and in November 1945 government reinforcements were sent from Tehran, only to be halted by Soviet forces stationed at Sharifabad, to the west of Tehran. In December the Democratic Party of Azerbaijan, announced the establishment of an autonomous state of Azerbaijan. In January 1946 the Iranian government notified the Security Council of the United Nations of alleged interference by Soviet Russia, through the medium of its officials and armed forces, in the internal affairs of Iran. The Council unanimously adopted a resolution stating that Iran and Russia should inform the

Security Council of the results of their negotiations on this matter, and retained the right to request information on the progress of the negotiations.

In February 1946 Ahmad Qavam became Prime Minister of Iran and went at once by plane to Moscow for negotiations. He was in that city on March 2, the date previously agreed upon by the Allied powers for the complete evacuation of their troops from Iran. The Americans had left earlier, and the British forces moved out by the final date, but Soviet Russia announced that the evacuation of its forces from some areas of northeastern Iran would begin on March 2, while troops in other areas would remain pending clarification of the situation. On March 18 Iran protested to the Security Council that the USSR was maintaining troops in Iran territory contrary to the Tripartite Treaty, and that the agents, officials, and armed forces of the USSR continued to interfere in the internal affairs of Iran. The question was discussed by the Council. Near the end of the month talks between Ahmad Qavam and members of the Soviet Embassy at Tehran resulted in an exchange of notes, made public on April 4, which provided for the withdrawal of all Soviet forces from Iran within a period of six weeks; for the presentation to the next session of Parliament of a proposal for the formation of a joint Irano-Soviet oil company which would exploit the oil resources of the northern provinces of Iran; and for the peaceful internal settlement of differences between the central government and the revolutionary movement in Azerbaijan. The agreement regarding the withdrawal of Soviet troops was reported to the Security Council, which adopted a resolution to defer further proceedings in the Iranian question until May 6, at which time both the USSR and Iran were to report to the Council whether the withdrawal of all Soviet troops had been completed. On May 22 the Council suspended discussion of the Iranian question. The Soviet troops finally evacuated Iran.

Prime Minister Qavam then turned his attention to internal affairs and prepared to deal with the open conflict between the right and left wing political parties, with tribal unrest, with the problem of Azerbaijan, and with basic reforms. The session of Parliament had come to an end, and he was free to work unhampered by Parliamentary pressures until the next elections.

Sayyid Zia ad-din Tabatabai, head of the National Will party, was arrested, and his party vanished from the political scene. The Prime Minister announced the formation of his personally sponsored party, the Democrats of Iran. In the summer of 1946 he accepted the collaboration of the Tudeh party, and three of its founders, who were generally regarded as Communists, were taken into his cabinet. In September the penetration of Tudeh elements into southern Iran and dissatisfaction with the too conciliatory attitude of the government with regard to the Tudeh leaders and the Azerbaijan regime, culminated in open revolt by southern tribes. Close cooperation between the Qashqa'i, Mamasani, Hayat Daudi, and Tangestani tribes resulted in the seizure of the towns of Kazerun, Bushire, and Bandar Dailam. The government realized that it would lose support in other parts of the country as well unless it displayed a harder, nationalistic attitude. The cabinet was re-formed without the members of the Tudeh party, and the Democrats of Iran began to dominate the political picture.

Long-drawn-out negotiations were held with the leaders of the so-called government of Azerbaijan and general points of agreement reached. In October the Shah issued a royal decree providing for elections for the new Parliament, and the Prime Minister announced that the elections would be held throughout the country as soon as the security forces of the nation were everywhere in position to supervise the voting. The insurgent government of Azerbaijan now went back on its agreement to allow such supervision. Therefore, early in December 1946 the central government dispatched troops to Azerbaijan. Tabriz, the capital of the province, was quickly entered, the Azerbaijan regime collapsed at once, and some of its leaders fled across the Russian frontier.

Discussions were also carried on with the tribal heads of the Kurds, Bakhtiari, and the Qashqa'i. With the Qashqa'i an

agreement was reached which was to form a pattern for relations with the other tribes. On the one hand the tribe was
to turn over arms to the government, and on the other the
tribe was to have proportional representation in Parliament
and enjoy better educational, medical, and transportation
facilities, and local officials were to be named from among
residents of the area.

The Parliamentary elections began early in 1947. The Tudeh party, whose power and influence had markedly declined,
decided not to participate in the elections. By the summer of
1947 nearly all the returns had been tabulated, and of the
members chosen all but a handful belonged to the Democrats
of Iran party. Qavam, who had remained in power for a considerably longer period than any of his immediate predecessors and during that period faced and dealt with pressing problems, seemed ready to establish long-range plans for the future
of Iran, counting on the support of a friendly Parliament.

In the spring and early summer of 1947 specialists of the
Morrison-Knudsen International Company conducted field
work in Iran. This American firm had been retained by the
Iranian government to make studies and specific recommenda-
tions for improvements in the fields of agriculture, fuel and
power, transportation, communications, irrigation, and industry.

The XVth Parliament was convened on July 17, 1947, and
on August 30 chose Qavam as Prime Minister. On October
22 Qavam presented that body with a report on the negotiations leading to the April 1946 agreement for the establishment of a joint Irano-Soviet oil company. Parliament at once
passed, by a vote of 100 to 2, a bill containing several clauses.
These voided the 1946 agreement as contrary to a law of 1944
forbidding such negotiations by government officials; provided that experts were to survey the oil resources of Iran
during the next five years and that if oil were located in the
north in commercial quantities the government could enter
into negotiations for the sale of such oil to the USSR; stated
that in the future no concessions would be granted to foreigners or to companies in which foreigners had any interests;

and, directed the government to study concessions granted to foreign companies, especially the southern oil concession, with a view to increasing the benefits derived by Iran from such concessions.

After this date opposition to Qavam grew among the Democrats of Iran, in Parliament, and within his own cabinet, and on December 10 Qavam resigned after failing to win a vote of confidence from the Parliament. On December 21 Ebrahim Hakimi was chosen Prime Minister. Hakimi's cabinet displayed only limited activity in dealing with current problems and longer range reforms.

On February 10, 1948, Parliament approved a bill which provided for the purchase of $10,000,000 worth of American surplus military equipment, a proposal designed to modernize the equipment of Iran's security forces. In general the XVth Parliament failed to face up to its responsibilities and during the first year of its term passed only a handful of bills. The tenor of debate and the terms of certain of the bills did reflect an aggressive chauvinism. The desirability of revising the Anglo-Iranian Oil Company contract was discussed; a trade bill which prohibited foreign merchants in Iran from importing goods was passed; and, a proposed bill instructed the government to restore Iranian sovereignty over the island of Bahrein in the Persian Gulf—Bahrein being within the concession area of the Arabian-American Oil Company and held by a local ruler who has exclusive treaty relations with the British. Groups within Iran which believed that legislative procedure must be accelerated favored granting broader powers to the Shah and in May a bill was introduced which would provide for the establishment of the Senate, a body provided for by the Constitution.

In June 1948 a new cabinet headed by Abdol Husein Hajir, later murdered by a religious fanatic in the fall of 1949, came into office. In July Muhammad Reza Shah visited England and in November his divorce from Queen Fawzia was announced. In November the cabinet of Hajir fell and Muhammad Saed became Prime Minister. The relative calm of the year 1948 was marked by rising unemployment, by signs of reviving Tudeh party strength, and by a series of Soviet notes which charged that Iran was permitting the United States to establish military bases in Iran.

On February 4, 1949, an unsuccessful attempt was made to assassinate the Shah. The immediate reaction was of importance. On the one hand, the Tudeh party, held to be responsible for the outrage, was banned and those of its leaders who did not flee the country were tried and sent to prison. On the other, elements of the nation rallied around the Shah. The Parliament displayed a burst of activity before the session ended in July and approved the formation of the Senate and the program of the Seven Year Development Plan. On November 16 the Shah arrived in the United States for a state visit, and by the time of his departure at the end of the year he had made many public appearances, speaking in fluent English of his country's aims and needs.

The Shah appeared resolved to press for social and economic reforms: in opening the sessions of the XVIth Majlis and the Ist Senate he demanded that corrupt individuals and practices be purged from public life. In private meetings he urged deputies and government officials to render full support to efforts to improve conditions within the country. In this field the Shah and members of the royal family were already active through the Imperial Organization for Social Services, an institution set up to expend the revenues from crown properties in a program of public health.

In the field of economic progress attention was focused upon the Seven Year Development Plan with Overseas Consultants, Incorporated, a group of eleven leading American engineering firms, engaged to carry forward the investigations begun by Morrison-Knudsen International Company. By August 1949 its specialists had completed their field surveys and published a five-volume report on the methods to be followed in implementing economic and social development. The Iranian Majlis authorized the establishment of a Plan Organization to manage the execution of projects expected to cost some $650,000,000. Overseas Consultants characterized the plan as "the largest industrial program in one country in history" and one which was to revamp the entire structure of Iran "from the bottom up."

The Iranian budget for 1949 had been supplemented by a special development budget, designed to yield $42,800,000 and including in its receipts 70% of the oil royalties for that year. Beginning in 1950 the entire amount of the royalties received from the operations of the Anglo-Iranian Oil Company were assigned by law to the financing of the Plan Organization and it was hoped that additional sums would come from foreign sources. Adequate funds were not forthcoming, Overseas Consultants were released at the end of 1950, and projects were maintained on a much reduced scale.

Two caretaker cabinets appeared to mark time throughout the first half of the year. In May 1950 the United States announced that arms would be sent to Iran in recognition of the adherence of that country to the principles of the Mutual Defense Aid Program. On June 26 General Ali Razmara became Prime Minister. Razmara had behind him a long and active military career, culminating in the post of Chief of Staff, and he was noted for shrewdness, ability to make decisions, and devotion to work. He had unlimited confidence in his own abilities and stated privately that unless he could accomplish certain basic reforms within two months he would resign. He did neither. Lack of legislative support halted his initial plans for instituting local self-government, funds were lacking to push the development plan, and the oil issue soon crowded everything else into the background. Political opposition soon appeared: a week after Razmara came into office Tehran witnessed a hostile demonstration sparked by the National Front—then composed of twelve Majlis deputies grouped around Muhammad Mossadeq—and the evervocal Ayatollah Sayyid Abol Qasem Kashani came out against Razmara.

Razmara approached the oil issue by requesting the Majlis to take definite action of some kind on the still unratified Gass-Golshayan agreement of July 1949, an agreement which would have about doubled the royalty payments made by the Anglo-Iranian Oil Company. At first his position on this agreement was a neutral one, then he asked for favorable action, and finally he withdrew the proposed agreement from the Majlis after its Oil Committee had voted unanimously against acceptance.

Several events of more than passing interest marked the closing months of 1950. In September the Imperial Anti-Corruption Commission—formed in response to an earlier request of the ruler—turned in a report which gave rise to violent protest and recrimination. The report consisted of three long lists: List A, of honest and essential governmental employees; List B, of honest officials whose services could be dispensed with; and List C, of corrupt government officials who should be dismissed. Almost everyone thought the right names were on the wrong lists and this noble attempt to separate the sheep from the goats was quickly abandoned. In October the United States announced that the first Point IV program to be carried out in any country would be initiated in Iran.

As the year neared its end Razmara appeared to despair—as had certain of his predecessors—of obtaining substantial financial aid from the United States and, after declaring a policy of neutrality, moved to renew dormant trade negotiations with the USSR. These culminated in November in an agreement for the barter exchange of goods valued at $20,000,000.

Early in 1951 the Shah announced that he would split up the imperial estates and sell them to landless farmers at low prices and on payments over a long period. In February 1951 the ruler married Soraya Esfandiari, a young woman whose father was a leader of the Bakhtiari tribe and whose mother was a German.

In March events took a violent turn. On the third of that month Razmara appeared before the Majlis to present a report prepared by his government which stressed the fact that Iran still lacked the number of skilled technicians required to operate the oil industry and he went on to indicate that the time was not ripe for the nationalization of the industry. On the seventh he was shot and killed while attending a ceremony in a mosque. His assassin, Khalil Tahmesbi, a member of the militant religious group called the *Fedayan-i-Islam*, or Devotees of Islam, was arrested, and two days later his organization threatened to kill the Shah and other leading figures if he were not released.

On March 11 Hosein 'Ala, long a respected and experienced diplomat and public official, took over as Prime Minister to head a government whose task was soon complicated by the fact that the Majlis seemed resolved to act independently of the government. On March 15 the Majlis passed the bill providing for the nationalization of the Anglo-Iranian Oil Company, and on March 20 the Senate approved the same bill. Demonstrations and rioting broke out, with the Tudeh party demanding the immediate seizure of the oil installations and the early recovery of the islands of Bahrein. Three British nationals were killed in rioting at Abadan and the United Kingdom reacted to this disturbing situation by announcing that it was "ready to act as we see fit to protect British lives and property." The National Front deputies reproached 'Ala for his alleged unwillingness to implement nationalization and, as the public followed their lead, his position became untenable. He resigned on April 27.

Following a unanimous vote by the Majlis for the immediate seizure of the oil industry, on April 29 Dr. Muhammad Mossadeq was named as Prime Minister. A spate of words has been devoted to Mossadeq by the world press since that date, but comparatively little attention has been given to his background or to the question of just how he happened to rise to preeminence. Dr. Mossadeq had been active as government official, deputy, and cabinet minister in the years immediately following World War I. In the Majlis he outspokenly criticized the actions of General Reza Khan, soon to become Reza Shah Pahlavi, and paid for this rashness by a period of detention and then years of enforced residence in a quiet village. After the Allied occupation of Iran in 1941 he reappeared at Tehran and was chosen from the capital as a deputy to the XIVth Majlis, owing his election in part to his reputation for sincerity, deeply felt convictions, and personal honesty. In this Majlis he made a number of long speeches which hammered away at a single theme: that Iran must free itself from foreign influence and foreign domination. In a notable speech begun on October 29, 1944, and carried over for two days, he dealt at length with the history of oil concessions in Iran, and made a classic attack upon the position of the Anglo-Iranian Oil Company. Near the end of this speech he stated: "The Iranian nation wants a political equilibrium which will be in the interests of this country and that will be a "negative equilibrium." While not precisely defining "negative equilibrium," he implied that in the past Iran had survived the pressure of competing great powers by first giving something to one and then something else to another: this was positive equilibrium. He advocated the opposite course, the course of granting no favors or concessions to any powers and hence giving none of them grounds for complaining that his interests had been ignored at the expense of those of a rival. In December 1944 Mossadeq was instrumental in drafting a bill passed by the Majlis which prohibited any official from concluding an agreement with any foreign interest or power regarding a concession in Iran. Again, in October 1947 Mossadeq led the Majlis in the passage of a bill which rejected the proposal of the government that a joint Irano-Soviet oil company be set up to exploit the oil of northern Iran. The same bill contained an article directing the government to study the southern oil concession (of the Anglo-Iranian Oil Company) with a view to increasing the benefits derived by Iran. In this article was the germ of the nationalization law, and in steadily pushing for the complete elimination of foreign participation in Iranian enterprise Mossadeq was transformed from a rather uninspiring reciter of facts and figures into a leader of public opinion. It is of interest to note that Mossadeq rose to prominence as the advocate of negative action rather than as the promoter of a constructive, progressive program.

The day after Mossadeq came to power the Anglo-Iranian Oil Company suggested that the oil industry should be divided between two companies; with an Iranian company to manage production at the fields and the Anglo-Iranian Oil

Company to operate the refinery and distribute the products. This proposal drew little attention, and on May 3 Mossadeq said that his government would use the profits from the nationalized oil industry to strengthen the local economy and to give comfort and ease to the people. In this same statement he promised an early reform of the laws governing national and local elections. His government then refused the request of the A.I.O.C. that the oil dispute be submitted for arbitration as provided for by the terms of the 1933 concession agreement, on the grounds that Iran's own courts had competence in this situation.

During the next few months so many events of considerable importance occurred that not all of them can be included in a brief recapitulation. Early in May Mossadeq made an initial display of his talents for showmanship when he sought "refuge" from potential opposition within the Majlis building, donned pajamas, and went to bed. His National Front now began to assume a more definite form. The Iran Party supplied members of his cabinet and of his immediate entourage, and the newly formed Toiler's Party, headed by Mozaffar Baghai, attempted to attract the workers to the National Front.

Near the end of May the United Kingdom announced that paratroopers had been ordered to Cyprus and on the 26th the A.I.O.C. asked the International Court of Justice to appoint an arbitrator in the oil dispute. However, on the following day the British stated that they were prepared to consider some form of nationalization. On June 11 an A.I.O.C. negotiating mission, headed by the Deputy Chairman of the company, arrived in Tehran, but left after ten days of fruitless talks. On June 24 A.I.O.C. tankers stopped loading oil at Abadan.

In the middle of July, W. Averell Harriman arrived at Tehran as President Truman's personal representative and strove to find a common ground for renewed negotiations. As a result, an official British mission headed by Richard Stokes, Lord Privy Seal and Minister of Materials, came to Iran early in August with an offer which detailed the earlier suggestion for an Iranian operating company and a British purchasing organization. According to this plan, the purchasing organization would be permitted to obtain the oil products at a price discount. Following rejection of this plan, on September 10 the United Kingdom withdrew Iran's special sterling exchange facilities, which had permitted Iran to exchange sterling credits for dollars, and also banned the export of essential commodities and materials to Iran. At Abadan the refinery had shut down at the end of July and the last British technicians left the country early in October.

Near the end of September the United Kingdom submitted a resolution to the Security Council which asked that Iran be instructed to abide by the July 5 provisional ruling of the International Court, which had ordered the maintenance of the *status quo* pending a final settlement. Dr. Mossadeq flew to New York to defend Iran's action before the Security Council. On October 19 the Council, considering a revised resolution, voted to postpone consideration of the case until the International Court had ruled upon its competence in the matter. Dr. Mossadeq and his party remained in this country into November: Mossadeq requested a loan of $120,000,000 and President Truman wrote him that this application would be given careful consideration.

In the final month of 1951 the International Bank offered to act as a friendly intermediary, suggesting that it operate the oil refinery with the aid of British technicians and sell the oil at a discount to the A.I.O.C. The initial approach was welcomed by Iran, but obstacles to an agreement arose.

As 1952 opened the International Bank renewed its efforts and the points of difference appeared to narrow to three: the price at which oil should be sold, whether British technicians should be employed within Iran, and whether the Bank would act on behalf of Iran or as a neutral agency. In January balloting for the XVIIth Majlis got under way. It was to continue for several months, with the government permanently suspending elections after only 80 of the required number of 136 deputies had been chosen. Most of these 80 were elected as supporters of the National Front. Near the end of January the Iranian government ordered the closing of all British consulates in Iran. At the middle of February Hosein Fatemi, editor of the National Front paper *Bakhtar Emruz* and later Foreign Minister, was severely wounded by a shot fired by a fledgling member of the Devotees of Iran.

In March an International Bank mission to Tehran was unable to resolve the points of difference referred to above, and in the same month the Department of State refused Mossadeq's request for $120,000,000 on the grounds that Iran had the potential of obtaining ample revenues from its oil resources. Near the end of May Dr. Mossadeq went to The Hague to be present when Iranian representatives argued that the International Court was not competent to intervene in the oil dispute. Even before his return to Tehran the Iranian government revived another delicate international issue by sending to Iraq and the United Kingdom notes which set forth Iranian claims to sovereignty over the Bahrein Islands.

On July 5 Dr. Mossadeq took the customary action by resigning as Prime Minister just prior to the opening of the constricted XVIIth Majlis. On the 13th he was again chosen to head the government, but stated that he would be unable to cope with the problems confronting the country unless he was granted full powers for six months—powers which would enable his cabinet to enact laws before their approval by the Majlis—and unless he also assumed the post of Minister of War. The Shah declined to accept this second condition and on the 17th Ahmad Qavam, who had last headed the government in 1947, was selected as Prime Minister by the Majlis. On the 19th and 20th National Front elements took to the streets in protest against this appointment and, eagerly joined by the Tudeh party, carried disorder to the point where the government seemed powerless to establish control. As a result, Qavam resigned and on the 22nd Mossadeq was again Prime Minister and also Minister of War, although he soon changed the name of the latter post to that of Minister of National Defense. Just as he came back into office the International Court ruled that it had no jurisdiction in the oil

12. Typical mountain landscape north of Tehran

13. The outskirts of a typical farming village with its irrigation channel

14. One of hundreds of the sturdy old brick bridges of Iran: the bridge at Qaflan Kuh

15. Mashhad. A stalactite-filled vault in the Mosque of Gawhar Shad

dispute. Mossadeq was quickly awarded full powers by the Majlis and his government sent a note to the United Kingdom demanding the sum of £49,000,000. The amount was claimed as due under the terms of the Gass-Golshayan agreement and did appear as a "contingency fund" on the books of the A.I.O.C., although the Majlis had never ratified the agreement itself.

Throughout August the oil issue continued to dominate the local situation. W. Alton Jones, President of the Cities Service Company, came to Iran upon Dr. Mossadeq's invitation in order to survey the ability of Iran to operate the oil industry and to make suggestions as to how the oil could be moved into the world market. His interviews with the press first brought home to Iranian officials the fact that expanded production in other Middle Eastern fields had filled the temporary shortage created by the stoppage of oil exports from Iran.

On August 30 Truman and Churchill sent a joint note to Iran which outlined still another broad formula for the settlement of the dispute. After lengthy preliminary statements, Mossadeq sent his formal rejection of this proposal on September 24. In his reply he offered a ten-day period of grace in which the British might accept four articles relating to the joint submission of the dispute to the International Court. These articles suggested that Iran was increasing its counterclaims against the A.I.O.C. On October 5 the British Foreign Office and the Department of State sent notes intended to clarify the original statement of August 30. On October 7 Dr. Mossadeq suggested to the United Kingdom that the A.I.O.C. make an immediate payment of £20,000,000 to Iran and then send a mission to Iran for negotiations which could be concluded within three weeks. Following the conclusion of negotiations Iran would expect to receive the balance of £49,000,000. On the 14th the British rejected this suggestion and on the 16th Mossadeq addressed the Iranian people by radio, with a long review of the dispute. Two points in his speech were of particular interest: that Iran was compelled to sever diplomatic relations with the United Kingdom, and that the Iranian government "proposes to insure a balanced budget based upon its existing income." This last statement represented a marked shift of position from that of his speech of April 26, 1951, in which he forecast a huge income from oil in these words: "The nation is losing 300,000 pounds (sterling) daily through the delay in nationalization." Relations were severed by Iran on October 22 and soon the last members of the British Embassy left the country.

Near the end of 1952 the National Front government appeared less intent upon reaching an oil agreement and more concerned with bargain price sales to independent purchasers. In these months efforts were made to strengthen the position of the government with respect to potential opposition. In the military field, a number of ranking officers were retired and the Guards Division at Tehran split into independent units. In the political field, a bill passed by the Majlis ordered the dissolution of the Senate scarcely two weeks after the session of the latter body had been inaugurated by the Shah. In November bills provided for the confiscation of the property of Ahmad Qavam and for his prosecution as being responsible for the rioting in July. Another new bill was limited to these words: "Considering that the treason of Hajji Ali Razmara toward the Iranian people is a proven fact, if it is recognized as true that Khalil Tahmesbi was his assassin, this individual will be pardoned and freed by the present law."

In January 1953 Mossadeq won an overwhelming vote for an extension of his plenary powers, although several of his more powerful supporters abstained. In February the government stiffened its control by a severe law regulating the press, by another penalizing strikes against the government and by arresting and detaining General Zahedi for several weeks. In the aftermath of the excitement of nationalization of oil Iran refused to renew and extend the expiring 25-year-old Iran-Soviet fisheries concession. Under this concession a joint company, dominated by its Russian members, had drained off profits from the fishing along the Iranian coast of the Caspian

Sea and had turned its monopoly on the export of caviar to the advantage of the USSR.

Since Mossadeq first began to nibble away at the position and prestige of the Shah by such actions as that of assuming the post of Minister of Defense, some sort of a showdown with the supporters of the throne was bound to follow. On February 28—when it appeared that Dr. Mossadeq was forcing the Shah to leave the country for some weeks—supporters of the ruler stormed Mossadeq's residence, forcing him to flee over the garden wall and to seek refuge in the Parliament. While this attack only hardened the Prime Minister's convictions, it may have heartened possible opposition.

On March 12 a special committee of Majlis deputies, chosen to report on rumors of dissension between the Imperial Court and the head of the government, stated that such dissension did not exist and added that according to the constitution the ministers of the government, rather than the Shah, were responsible for the conduct of affairs. Supporters of the Shah felt that the report might be used to remove the army entirely from the ruler's influence, but in spite of Mossadeq's insistence the Majlis failed to act upon the report. At the same time the Tudeh party benefited by the lack of interference on the part of the government—as exemplified by the March ruling of a Tehran court that its members could not be prosecuted for activity against the constitutional monarchy and in favor of communist doctrines—to muster its strength, and in a test of this strength sacked the Point IV headquarters at Shiraz on April 14. On April 23 Minister of Court 'Ala resigned and an ardent backer of Mossadeq was moved into the post.

Throughout the first half of the year the oil issue was quiescent with no negotiations in progress and only a rare call at Abadan by a small Italian or Japanese tanker. On June 29 President Eisenhower answered a letter written to him by Prime Minister Mossadeq a month earlier, the first letter having called the President's attention to the existence of a dangerous situation in Iran. Eisenhower made it clear that, failing the settlement of the oil issue, the "United States is not presently in a position to extend more aid to Iran or to purchase Iranian Oil." However, the letter added that the current technical assistance and military aid would be continued. On July 1 Mossadeq had one of his followers elected as president of the Majlis in place of Kashani who was now denouncing him, and by this date had adopted an increasing number of authoritarian devices as the opposition became more widespread. In fact, the situation at the end of June should be reviewed before examining the events leading to his downfall.

By this time he was no longer regarded by foreign correspondents as a curious figure—a pajama-clad weeper—but as a master in gauging and directing public opinion. Within several of the social strata his popularity remained high, but many of the most influential followers had fallen away because he had offended them or failed to deliver anticipated rewards for this support. Exercising his plenary powers Mossadeq had resorted to a number of types of control: extension of martial law; appointment of military commanders personally loyal to him; imposition of a stringent public security law; prohibition of strikes by government employees and public service workers; suspension of the Senate; suspension of elections for the Majlis; the decree of a very strict press law and the arrest of newspaper editors; dissolution of the Supreme Court; arbitrary retirement of government officials; and the restrictions on movements of citizens and foreigners within the oil producing area. While some such actions had been taken under previous Prime Ministers, this activity seemed contrary to the nature of the man who long insisted that elections must be completely free and who had sternly opposed the imposition of martial law and of restrictive press laws. On the other hand, the National Front regarded Mossadeq as the emotional symbol of a regenerated Iran. For long years Iran had been a buffer between the strenuous rivalries of the British and Russian empires, and even when these pressures had eased the country was still unable to regain the proud position it had held in earlier centuries. As a result, bitter antipathies were nourished: their intensity could not be imagined by anyone unfamiliar with the local scene. By sweeping the British—oil company, diplomats, and business-men—from Iran, Mossadeq engendered a spirit of national self-confidence, long lacking in Iran. However, the passage of time tended to make him a prisoner of the extreme nation-alist elements, for they opposed any actions toward an oil settlement which seemed a withdrawal from the most advanced position taken by Iran.

By the end of June 1953 many groups and individuals had withdrawn from the National front. Makki, the hero of na-tionalization who had turned the valve shutting off the flow of oil at Abadan, had deserted Mossadeq as had Dr. Baghai, leader of the Toilers' party. The neo-Nazi Sumka party was in opposition as were elements of the ultra-national Pan-Iranist party. Kashani and a number of other religious leaders of varying degrees of sanctity now condemned Mossadeq at every turn. In spite of the press restrictions a majority of the Tehran papers attacked Dr. Mossadeq, while within the Majlis more and more deputies spoke against his government. Lack of confidence among the merchants was reflected in the fact that the free rate of the rial rose from 75 to the dollar in 1951 to 130 rials in July 1953.

To maintain control Dr. Mossadeq seemed to feel that two actions were necessary. In the first of these he turned from negative equilibrium in search of positive equilibrium: on the one hand he exploited every possible occasion to con-vince the Iranian public that the United States supported his government, while on the other he warned American officials that unless financial aid were forthcoming Iran might fall to the communists. By the second action he intended to make himself the sole spokesman of the "national movement." For some months government had been by plenary decree with the Majlis inactive, either because supporters of Mossadeq stayed away to prevent a quorum or because his opponents resorted to the same tactics. Mossadeq resolved to get rid of the Majlis and as an initial step arranged for more than 35 National Front deputies to resign—thus removing the possibility of any quorum. Then on July 25 a decree was issued providing for a referendum on the question of whether the XVIIth Majlis should be dissolved or retained. Voting in conspicuously separate booths, some 2,043,389 were said to have voted for dissolution and only 1,207 for retention. Now Dr. Mossadeq was faced with the difficulties relative to a new election. The previous elections had brought in a Majlis which he had welcomed as being 80 per cent representative of the will of the people and then later had denounced. Should he now permit the populace to vote freely, the Tudeh party might elect deputies who would oppose him at every turn. The huge turnout for a Tudeh demonstration on July 20 was a sign of the times. However, a decision on the elections was spared him for on August 15 a political storm broke over Tehran.

On August 13 the Shah, in residence at his palace at Ramsar on the Caspian, had signed firmans dismissing Mossadeq and naming General Zahedi as Prime Minister. Late on the evening of the 15th a detachment of Imperial Guards seized Hosein Fatemi, Minister of Foreign Affairs, and two other leaders of the National Front. Colonel Nassiri, of the Imperial Guards, went to Mossadeq's residence at one in the morning on August 16 and presented him personally with the firman of dismissal and obtained a receipt, before he and his small group were arrested.

During the night there was other activity by military units but by dawn Fatemi and his friends had been released and a broadcast statement by the government spoke of the failure of a military coup d'état. Mossadeq met with his cabinet in emergency session, but said nothing to anyone about the firman. During the day he issued a decree dissolving the Majlis. That afternoon a mass meeting arranged by the National Front received word that the Shah and his wife had gone to Baghdad by air and the fervent orators, including Fatemi, were hailed with cries of "Down with the dynasty," and "Death to the Shah" from elements of the Iran party, the Third Force, and the Tudeh party. Participants left the meeting to stream along the streets, smashing showcases and windows housing pictures of the Shah.

On August 17 Fatemi released the text of his instructions to the Iranian embassy in Iraq to avoid contact with the person who had fled, but by that time the Shah had been welcomed by the government of Iraq. In his own paper, *Bakhtar Emruz*, Fatemi poured out abuse against the ruler, comparing him with a snake and stating that "the people of this country want to see this traitor hanged." At Tehran crowds shouting "Mossadeq is victorious" pulled down statues of the ruler and his father, Reza Shah, while the underground central committee of the Tudeh party called for the uprooting of the monarchy and the establishment of a democratic republic.

On the 18th the atmosphere altered slightly as another side of the story began to unfold. Opposition papers managed to appear: they printed reproductions of the firman naming General Zahedi as Prime Minister, statements of the Shah at Baghdad, and an interview from the hidden Zahedi that he was the legal Prime Minister and that the so-called coup d'état was a device thought up by Mossadeq to divert public opinion. Members of the government and the National Movement met during the day to discuss the formation of a regency council, while within the city street names were changed from Reza Shah to Republic and from Pahlavi to People. The Shah flew on to Rome. However, during that afternoon appeared the first pro-Shah demonstrations, while both nationalist elements and the armed forces pitched in to break up Tudeh demonstrations—apparently the nationalists were beginning to feel that the communists would be the chief gainers from excesses and disorder.

Early on the morning of August 19 a ground swell began to roll up from south Tehran—the older section of the town —as a number of groups armed with crude weapons converged upon the official and business center of the capital. Confronted by armed forces, their shouts of "Long live the Shah" won over soldiers and police. Tanks joined the swelling columns, as did unarmed soldiers from the barracks. By noon the offices of all the newspapers which attacked the monarchy had been ransacked as had the headquarters of the groups supporting Dr. Mossadeq. Other groups of mixed civilian and military members stormed the ministerial buildings. A long column wound its way north of the town to take over Radio Tehran and at two in the afternoon this station announced that General Zahedi headed a new government. At this same time the major fighting of the day broke out at Mossadeq's residence, but it was not until near the end of the afternoon that he once more fled over the garden wall. Before dark Zahedi had been heard over Radio Tehran and quiet reigned. Broadcasts from the provincial stations offered loyalty to the Shah and the new government. Within the next few days Dr. Mossadeq, members of his former cabinet, officials, editors and many members of the Tudeh party were placed under arrest, but Hosein Fatemi remained in hiding—aided by the Tudeh party—for seven months.

On August 22 the Shah returned to a tumultuous welcome and spoke of the necessity for the government to concentrate all its attention upon social reforms. By this time it was perfectly clear that a spontaneous uprising of the masses, including thousands who were not normally involved in parties or politics, had occurred. The insults of Fatemi, the destruction of the statues of the ruler and his father, and the shouts in favor of a republic had an effect quite opposite from that intended for they had aroused fears as to the future of the country and the wisdom of casting aside long established, national traditions. The Tudeh party had completely misjudged the popular temper, its erstwhile supporters melted away, and it was powerless to react against the changed situation. In the few days of uncertainty General Fazlollah Zahedi, who was boldly critical of Mossadeq, served as the rallying point. Conspicuously active in the Iranian army for years, in 1941 he was arrested by British forces in Iran, charged with supporting pro-German activity, and sent into exile for several years. After his return to Iran he became head of the Tehran police, then a Senator, then Minister of Interior in the 1951 cabinet of 'Ala, and then in the same post in the first months of Mossadeq's regime. Openly opposing Mossadeq from 1952, in May, June, and much of July 1953 he found political sanctuary in the Parliament buildings and dispassionately attacked the methods—not the aims—of Mossadeq. The government which he now headed was to prove unspectacular, but more stable than any in recent years.

American concern for Iran and its government appeared on September 5 when President Eisenhower and General Zahedi exchanged messages confirming that the United States had made some $45,000,000 available to Iran as immediate economic aid to assist in stabilization and to establish the basis for economic development, and again in December when Vice President Nixon visited Tehran.

On November 9 Dr. Mossadeq and his chief of staff, General Riahi, went on trial before a military court faced with charges which included having failed to obey imperial firmans and with having plotted to overthrow the constitutional monarchy. The trial went on day after day, its record covering hundreds of pages. Many incidents of the time of turmoil were now disclosed, such as the fact that the oath to the Shah had been suppressed within the armed forces and the action taken by Mossadeq to prepare for a second referendum which would determine the prerogatives of the regency council. On December 21 Mossadeq was sentenced to three years in prison and Riahi to two years.

In the closing months of the year the Zahedi government displayed its determination to try to reach a settlement of the oil issue. Zahedi spoke of the effective bankruptcy of the treasury, and appointed Dr. Ali Amini, Minister of Finance, as chief negotiator for Iran. In October Herbert Hoover, Jr., made the first of several trips to Iran, this one to lay the groundwork for talks between Iran and the British. On December 5 the government resumed diplomatic relations with the United Kingdom.

The year 1954 witnessed prolonged and intensive activity directed toward the settlement of the oil problem. On February 1 the Anglo-Iranian Oil Company announced that it was meeting with seven other large oil companies with interests in the Middle East to discuss ways of resolving the difficulties which prevented Iranian oil from returning to the world markets and about this same time the American government stated that should five American oil firms join a consortium they would not be liable for anti-trust prosecution. Technical experts representing the eight companies flew out to survey the condition of the fields and refineries in Iran.

Elections for the XVIIIth Majlis and the IInd Senate began in January and were conducted with far greater expedition than usual, for by mid-March a sufficient number of deputies had been chosen so that the Majlis could open with the required quorum. All of these deputies had asserted their loyalty to the Shah, and their number included no known supporters of the National Front. On April 10 the oil consortium was formally established at London and representatives left for Iran. Negotiations went forward, stalled on complex issues, and then were resumed over the next months. The major problem was that of how any agreement could be fitted within the rather rigid terms of the Nationalization Law. In the end, persistence and good will won out and on August 5 the Iranian delegation and the International Consortium announced full agreement in principle, subject to putting the agreement into legal form and having it ratified by all parties concerned. The companies making up the consortium were the Anglo-Iranian Oil Company (which name was changed to The British Petroleum Company Ltd. in December 1954), Gulf Oil Corporation, Socony-Vacuum Company, Standard Oil of California, Standard Oil of New Jersey, The Texas Company, The French Petrol Company, and Royal Dutch Shell, and it was their belief that in the first three full years of operation under this agreement Iran would derive a total direct income of £150,000,000. The legal form of the agreement, nearly 50 pages long and extremely technical throughout its many articles, was presented to the Majlis for ratification on September 21 by General Zahedi and Ali Amini. After full discussion, on October 21 some 113 deputies voted in favor with 5 opposing the agreement and soon thereafter it was also ratified by the Senate. Tankers began to load at Abadan at once, while on November 2 the United States announced that it would put the sum of $127,300,000 at the disposal of the Iranian government: $85,000,000 as a loan and the rest as free assistance, the purpose being to permit Iran to pursue its development program pending adequate receipts from oil revenues. Public opinion, tired of delay and uncertainty, generally welcomed the settlement. At Tehran hopes were high with Abol Hasan Ebtahaj, long the dynamic head of the National Bank of Iran and later with the International Bank at Washington, newly returned to head the Plan Organization.

Throughout the year internal stability was high and the government—employing the means common to recent years of continuing martial law and strict control over the press—met with little opposition. Elements of the Iran party, the Third Force, and the Pan-Iranists regrouped into a rather ineffective "National Resistance Movement," dedicated to the return of Dr. Mossadeq to power. While Zahedi had declared himself to be the executor of the national movement, he had not won over the intellectual and middle class supporters of Dr. Mossadeq. Elements of the faculty and student body at Tehran University and other institutions also continued faithful to Mossadeq as did many Iranians pursuing their studies abroad, who described the recent regime as the "republican" period in Iran. The Tudeh party struggled to analyze its own errors, to regroup its dependable elements, and to try to attract all opponents of the government into a popular front: the larger subject of the policy and activity of the party is discussed in a following chapter. On September 20 military authorities at Tehran made the first detailed announcement of the discovery of an extensive penetration of the armed forces by the Tudeh party and hundreds of officers and men were arrested. A flood of confessions provided material for establishing the five different sections of the party within the armed forces as well as defining their activities which ranged from advocating the overthrow of the constitutional monarchy, to sabotage, and to training for partisan warfare against the government. Those arrested were tried in groups and more than a score of officers were executed. As an immediate reaction the government proposed a bill carrying stiff penalties for members of organizations which were collectivist in nature, which were against the Moslem religion, or which attacked the constitutional monarchy.

In December the Shah left Iran for his second visit to the United States. During the preceding months his statements on social reform, in favor of the oil agreement, and in condemnation of the communist infiltration of the armed forces had been warmly received.

In April 1955 General Zahedi resigned as Prime Minister, with the general feeling that his energy and courage had not been successfully applied to domestic reforms. Immediately Husein 'Ala took his place and included in his cabinet as Minister of Finance 'Ali Amini who had played the leading role in the earlier oil negotiations. On October 11 Iran adhered to the Baghdad Pact, initiated in February 1955 by Turkey, Iraq, Pakistan, and the United Kingdom. November 17 Prime Minister 'Ala was slightly injured by a would-be assassin; on this occasion the government took rapid and stern action. A by-product was a fresh investigation into the murder of General Razmara: Ayatollah Kashani was arrested and questioned and in the end the actual assassin was brought to justice.

In February 1956 the oil consortium announced satisfactory progress in an atmosphere of full cooperation during its first year of operations in Iran. In March, at the beginning of the Persian year, the Shah pardoned a number of former Tudeh party members and former collaborators of Dr. Mossadeq. At the end of March the Development and Resources Corporation of New York signed a five-year agreement with the Plan Organization covering the agricultural and economic development of the southwestern region of Khuzistan. In May the Shah made a state visit to Turkey, and after his return opened the XIXth Majlis, speaking of the necessity of strengthening the armed forces, making rapid progress in economic development, and putting the oil revenues to the most effective use. In June the Shah and Queen Soraya paid a state visit to Moscow: the ruler, in conversations with the

Soviet leaders, defended Iran's membership in defensive alliances.

Early in January 1957 Iran subscribed to the Eisenhower Doctrine with official enthusiasm. In the same month the publication of a lengthy report of hearings before a committee of the House of Representatives brought to light severe criticism of the manner in which American economic aid had been dispensed in Iran: in rebuttal the Department of State asserted that this aid had stabilized the financial and political structures of the country. In April the Shah named Dr. Manuchehr Eqbal as Prime Minister. While Eqbal was to remain in the post for a record 1,245 days, his appointment marked a period in which the ruler took charge of the operation of the government—Eqbal did not hesitate to inform the Majlis that he was the servant of the Shah. In the political arena the ruler put into force his concept of rival and competitive political parties: Eqbal headed the Melliyun party and Asadullah Alam the Mardum party. Sessions of the Baghdad Pact nations were held at Karachi in June. The United States, previously a member of the Economic Committee, joined the Military Committee, although it continued to refrain from taking up full membership: in the meetings emphasis was placed upon the construction of telecommunications and highway and rail links between the member countries. Later in the year the Parliament passed a bill providing for the establishment of a National Security Organization—known as Savak after the initials of its name in Persian—which was to centralize the control of political subversion and of counterespionage activity. It was headed by General Timur Bakhtiar.

In March 1958 the Shah, responsive to the advice of a council of elder statesmen, wrote to childless Soraya, then in Europe, and obtained her consent to a divorce. The following month the ruler announced that the entire resources of the crown, with the exception of the lands which were under distribution, had been turned over to the Pahlavi Foundation, and that the income would be used in the fields of health and education and for charity. The revolution of July in Iraq had an immediate impact upon the government of Iran. The Shah began to advocate an over-all program of land reform, stating that the regime in Iraq had been overthrown because it failed to undertake the distribution of land. In addition, he set up an Imperial Investigation Commission which was to receive complaints from the public against public officials and to see that proper action was taken. This general concern carried over into the opening months of 1959 when the Parliament passed two bills designed to provide the material required for the prosecution of appointed and elected officials engaged in illegal or corrupt practices; such officials were required to submit statements of personal and family assets.

In February Abol Hasan Ebtahaj, long the managing director of the Plan Organization, resigned when that organization lost its autonomy. Early in the year Iraq withdrew from the Baghdad Pact, and the remaining members announced that its name had been changed to that of the Central Treaty Organization (CENTO). On March 5 Iran and the United States signed a bilateral agreement that provides for American aid in case of aggression against Iran: this agreement was bitterly attacked by the Soviet Union. On December 14 President Eisenhower visited Tehran and praised the contributions of Iran to regional stability. Finally, on December 21 the Shah was married to 21-year-old Farah Diba.

The event of 1960 which drew the most attention was the elections for the XXth Majlis, held in August after weeks of hectic campaigning in which Dr. 'Ali Amini came to the fore as spokesman for the independent candidates. When the results were announced, some two-thirds of the new deputies belonged to the Melliyun party and the balance, with the exception of a few independents, to the Mardum party. However, heated charges of a pre-election agreement between these parties and of discrimination against independent candidates led the Shah to request the deputies to resign. The heads of the parties also resigned their posts, with Dr. Eqbal also resigning as Prime Minister to be succeeded by Jafar Sharif-Emami. On October 31 Queen Farah gave birth to a boy,

Reza Cyrus 'Ali: the nation rejoiced, and the ruler was delighted to have finally produced an heir to the throne.

In January 1961 a second round of elections was held amidst charges of rigged elections and featuring a student demonstration that resulted in the closing of Tehran University. The ruler opened the XXth Majlis on February 21: it included 70 members of the Melliyun party, 60 from the Mardum party, and about 20 independents. The National Front which had boycotted the elections continued to attack the government, and on May 4 backed a massive demonstration in support of striking teachers. Apparently disturbed over a lack of firmness in handling the opposition and the absence of a progressive policy, on May 5 the Shah dismissed Sharif-Emami and named Dr. 'Ali Amini as Prime Minister. On May 9 the ruler dissolved the Majlis. In selecting Dr. Amini, the ruler had picked a man who would not be his "servant," but who would form his own policies and stand or fall by his success or failure in carrying them out. His announced program of reforms placed special emphasis upon the elimination of corruption, the distribution of land to the peasants, and upon efforts toward financial stabilization.

The National Front insisted that the article of the constitution which provides that new elections must follow shortly after a Majlis has been dissolved must be enforced, and made plans to hold a massive demonstration at Tehran on July 21. The previous day many of the leaders of the National Front were arrested, while those who gathered at the site of the meeting were dispersed by the police. In addition, the government announced that no public protest meetings would be permitted, while on August 19 some 200,000 people assembled to hear the Shah outline his program of social reforms.

In January 1962 Tehran was again the scene of a student demonstration which became riotous as both conservative elements and the National Front incited the students, with both these elements demanding early elections. Of great significance for the future of the country was a decree entitled "Agricultural Reforms," prepared by the cabinet and signed by the Shah on January 15. Replacing a law passed by the Parliament in May 1960 which limited the acreage which could be held by an individual, the decree stated that no person could own more than one agricultural village, and provided that excess holdings would be purchased by the state and then resold to the peasants living in the villages. Implementation of the program of land distribution was assigned to the Minister of Agriculture, Dr. Hasan Arsanjani, and in March the Shah distributed deeds to land to peasants in Azerbaijan. Throughout the year this program gained increased momentum.

In April the Shah and Queen Farah made a state visit to the United States: it was reported that he sought increased military aid and a firm commitment for the financial support of Iran's Third Five-Year Plan. On July 18 Prime Minister Amini resigned, blaming tardy American economic aid and the reduction of military assistance for his action. However, at Tehran it was believed that he was exhausted by his efforts in office and discouraged by his inability to reduce drastically the budget of the country which reflected a huge deficit. The Shah named Asadullah Alam to take his place: his choice of a long-time associate indicated that the ruler again intended to play an active role in supervising the day-to-day activities of the government.

Developments in the political, social, and economic fields from 1962 through 1966 are reviewed in the concluding chapter.

V. THE GOVERNMENT OF IRAN

Until the revolutionary movement of 1906 which secured for Iran a constitutional government, the country had been for over twenty centuries under the rule of absolute monarchs. Taking into account this background, and the fact that during the fifty years since then Iran has been so often subjected to foreign pressure, the amount of progress made in democratic government has been considerable.

Constitutional Government

The original Constitution of 1906 has been modified by a supplement of 1907 and amendments of 1925, 1949 and 1957 while sections which were outlined in general terms have been made both more specific and more comprehensive by Parliamentary law. The document is modern and liberal on the pattern of the constitutions of the European democracies, but also contains provisions relating to the state religion of Iran—the Shi'a sect of Islam. It provides for a government composed of three branches: the executive, whose power is vested in the cabinet and in the government officials who act in the name of the Shah; the judicial composed of a hierarchy of courts from district courts up through a Supreme Court; and, the legislative, whose bills do not become law until signed by the Shah.

The Constitution provides for a Senate, which was not brought into legal being until 1949 and first met in 1950, and a *Majlis* or Parliament, which serves for a term of two years. Its members, or deputies, are elected from each district in proportion to the population, and are not required to be residents of those regions from which they are elected, but to represent the interests of the nation as a whole. They must be between thirty and seventy years of age, and may be reelected for additional terms. The Armenian, Hebrew, and Zoroastrian communities elect deputies to represent their collective interests.

Up to and including the nineteenth session of the Majlis some 136 members were elected for terms of two years. However, in 1957 amendments to the constitution established the number of deputies at 200 and provided for four-year terms, including that of the nineteenth session. All male citizens who have reached the age of twenty-one are entitled to vote, with the exception of members of the armed forces and convicted criminals. Elections are not held on the same day throughout the country, but take place over a period of weeks or months, and the total number of votes cast is very small in proportion to the voting population. A number of types of influence may be credited with the victories of local candidates; these include expressed wishes of landowners and tribal leaders, the manipulations of the Ministry of the Interior and of military commanders, and the fancied preferences of the Shah himself. Given the length of the election period a candidate defeated in one area may run in one or more other districts, but, in general, there is a swing toward electing candidates having close ties with their districts.

Parliament receives proposed legislation from the cabinet ministers and usually refers it to one of eight committees, then receives the committees' reports and discusses the bills, which may be passed by a majority vote. Deputies may also initiate bills if the bills are signed by fifteen other deputies. Parliament may ask ministers of the cabinet to appear and answer oral or written questions, and normally one or more cabinet ministers attend each session.

The Constitution gives Parliament the authority to control the policies and acts of the cabinet on matters vital to the interest of the nation. It must approve any disposal of State property or funds, internally or foreign managed concessions and monopolies, government borrowing, and proposed construction of roads and railways.

Sessions of the Majlis are held in the Baharestan, set in a large park in the heart of Tehran, while the Senate meets in its ornate new building. The proceedings of the public meetings are published in an official journal. Private or secret sessions may be held upon the written request of ten deputies or of one of the cabinet ministers. The discussion in recent

Parliaments has been vigorous and at times even violent, but always unsuppressed.

Over the years the composition of the Majlis has been fairly consistent: prior to World War II about two-thirds of its members were landed proprietors, about one-fifth were merchants, less than a fifth were from the professional classes, and the balance from a number of additional categories. Currently the trend is away from the preponderance of landlords toward a larger representation from the professional and intellectual groups.

Half of the sixty-man Senate is elected in two-stage elections in which the group chosen by popular vote makes the final choice from among its members. Fifteen of the thirty elected members come from Tehran. The balance of the Senators are appointed by the Shah. Half of the membership is replaced every two years after a drawing by lot eliminates thirty names. Membership of the Senate is composed of rather elderly, conservative individuals among whom are numerous former Prime Ministers, cabinet ministers, and retired generals. The Senate was brought into being to play the role, if necessary, of a check upon the more exuberant Majlis. It does not have all the powers of the Majlis; for example, financial matters are the exclusive field of the Majlis.

The Role of Political Parties

Persian voters may elect municipal councils and may vote for senators but their most effective way of participating in constitutional government is through the election of deputies to the Majlis.

In the opening years of constitutional government several ephemeral political parties sprang into being. During the reign of Reza Shah political parties were not permitted, although at one period consideration was given to the establishment of a majority party in the Majlis which would attract support to the regime.

Since the end of 1941 political parties have played, and are bound to continue playing, an increasingly important role in government and national life. Up to the present the new parties have ranged all the way from the extreme right to the extreme left. The first parties to be formed in 1942, some of which were sponsored by merchants and landowners and used Tehran newspapers for their party organs, were weak in organization and vague of program. The parties of this first period bore names of such popular appeal as Justice, People, Fatherland, Fellow-Comrades—the last offering a socialistic program, while other rather liberal parties included the National and the Iran.

During the war years the most active and influential parties were the *Eradeyi Melli*, or National Will, and the *Tudeh*, or Masses.

The National Will party was led by Sayyid Zia ad-din Tabatabai, who had been for a short time in 1921 Prime Minister of Iran and had then been exiled from the country for many years. In 1943 he returned to Iran and was elected to Parliament. His party published a detailed program proposing social and economic reforms, but he and his followers were soon attacked as reactionaries by the Tudeh party, while he himself was singled out for the hostile attentions of the Russian press and radio. The party had followers in the Parliament and published newspapers at Tehran; its funds were said to derive from local businessmen and it was believed that its leader had British backing. After his arrest in 1946 the leader and party faded from the political scene.

The Tudeh party was organized in the fall of 1941 by a group of educated men most of whom had been imprisoned under Reza Shah as suspected Communists. It strove for a tight organization, was exceedingly vocal, solicited members from the newly formed trade unions, and elected eight members to the 1944–1946 session of Parliament. In the province of Azerbaijan the militant branch of the party assumed the name of the Democratic Party of Azerbaijan and led a separatist movement which isolated that region from the rest of the country from the end of 1945 until the winter of 1946.

Studies of the Tudeh party have appeared both in Iran and abroad and this is not the place to present a detailed account of its operations. However, it is of importance to note the manner in which its role was the result of promoting principles which reflected popular motivations and interests. Also, it is of value to concentrate on its pattern of activity, since this pattern should offer an instructive comparison with the operations of avowed or concealed communist parties in other parts of the world. In nearly every respect the party was developed to a higher degree in internal organization and variety of activities than corresponding parties in neighboring countries and this concentration reflected Soviet desire to dominate Iran as soon as possible.

In February 1949 the reaction to an unsuccessful attempt to assassinate the Shah was the banning of the party. Some of its leaders were jailed, while others fled abroad to come to the surface in countries behind the Iron Curtain, or even in France, while still others escaped from prison at Tehran in 1950. Reza Radmanesh, Executive Secretary of the party, attended the XIXth Congress of the Communist Party of the Soviet Union, held at Moscow in October 1952. For years before this time the Tudeh party in Iran had spread the fiction that it was a national, liberal party with no external ties, but Radmanesh demolished this fable when he informed the congress that: "The Tudeh party is the sole party of the workers of Iran; inspired by the ideology of Marxism and Leninism it guarantees the liberty and independence of our people. The Tudeh party is based upon democracy and socialism, at the head of which (forces) are to be found the USSR and Joseph Stalin, our great standard bearer." By means of foreign direction, members of the Tudeh party were instructed in multiple efforts to create and foster internal dissension, distrust, and disorder in Iran. Front groups, a favorite Soviet device, appeared in quantity. Among these were the Peace Partisans, the Democratic Women of Iran, the Democratic Youth, the Society for the Protection of Children, the Society against Illiteracy, the National Society against Colonization, the Society to Defend the Rights of Villagers, and the Moslem Socialistic Association. In 1952 and 1953 such groups were publishing as many as 65 newspapers and periodicals, while the Tudeh party papers *Mardum*, *Razm* and *Zafar* streamed from concealed presses in Tehran and its environs. The total amount of Soviet-slanted propaganda and of hatred directed against the government of Iran, Iranian institutions, and the western powers was enormous.

Illegal as it was, the Tudeh party continued to operate along its customary lines, with cell meetings and a program of steady recruitment. Trusted party members headed each and every front group, so that these were arms of the party. Throughout its entire existence the Tudeh party had endeavored to establish a united front with other political elements in Iran, an objective briefly achieved in 1946. In addition, the Tudeh party had several specific goals. From the goal of sabotaging economic and social projects came attacks upon Point IV and upon negotiations for settling the oil issue. From the need to destroy or damage the sources of internal unity came attacks upon the Shah and upon the Moslem religion. Quotations from the front publications of the party from 1953 illustrate the intensity of these attacks. In February the watchwords for the "Day of Anti-Colonizing Youth" included: "Long live the great Soviet Union, the torch of peace and the defender of oppressed peoples," and "Long live the struggle of the Iranian people against American spies." In the spring the paper *Besuye Ayandeh* wrote, "Point IV is one of the most important centers of espionage and sabotage of American imperialism in our country," while another paper stated, "the proletariat is against the intervention of the court in the affairs of the country, is in favor of expelling American spies, and demands interruption of the oil negotiations with the imperialists." In June a front group stated that the aims of the United States in Iran were, "to solve the oil issue on imperialistic terms, to extend American colonization, and to attack the anti-imperialist and democratic movement of the Iranian people." On July 21 a huge Tudeh-inspired demonstration commemorated the rioting of the year before and among the demands of the speakers were the following: "that the court, the center of plots, never again be allowed to interfere in the affairs of the country; that the

Majlis be dissolved by popular referendum; that all centers of espionage and American imperialism be closed; that an attempt be made to sell oil to the Soviet Union and other peace loving countries; and that a single front of the anti-colonizing forces be established."

During the Mossadeq period the Tudeh party increased in strength and boldness. Although in official declarations and in the statements of its front groups it opposed Mossadeq's government, it supported certain of his actions and constantly urged his government toward actions designed to alienate Iran from the western world. Party strength increased within the armed forces, while a ruling of a Tehran court in March 1953 to the effect that its activity was not illegal since the party neither carried on activity against the constitutional monarchy nor propagated the communist doctrine heartened its adherents and indicated the extent of its penetrations among officials of the government.

Several months after the removal of Mossadeq, the Tudeh party issued a pamphlet admitting errors and blaming traitors within the party for its failure to take command of the situation in August 1953. During 1954 membership declined sharply, although Radmanesh brashly informed the VIth Congress of the Bulgarian Communist party that he brought homage from "the Iranian masses, at the head of which is the Tudeh party." In September 1954 military authorities announced the exposure of the military organization of the Tudeh party within the armed forces, with its five sections corresponding to different functions. Hundreds of officers were arrested and detailed confessions made by many of them. It appeared that one of the decisions taken by the party after August 1953 was to concentrate upon recruiting within the armed forces and upon establishing militant cadres. Many officers confessed to espionage in collecting information of all kinds on the army, to propaganda efforts against the constitutional monarchy, and to the training of Tudeh youths for street fighting and for partisan warfare against the government. At a series of trials more than a score of the Iranian officers were condemned to death and then executed. As a result of these disclosures, the Parliament passed a bill providing for prosecution with regard to activities by members of organizations that follow the communist doctrine, that are against Islam and the constitutional monarchy, and that include members of the Tudeh party or other groups which have been declared illegal.

Leaders of the Tudeh party who had fled from Iran established the headquarters of its Executive Committee at Leipzig where it remains, broadcasting its attacks on the government of Iran from Radio Peyk-i-Iran. In 1962 the former commander of the armed forces of the briefly autonomous regime in Azerbaijan, Gholam Yahya Daneshiyan, became head of this Executive Committee. However, within Iran party activity was at its lowest ebb.

Among the parties founded in 1942 only the Iran party continued active throughout the postwar years. In 1944 it entered into temporary alliance with the Tudeh party, an action which has been held against it by recent governments. The Iran party issued pamphlets describing its liberal program but the intention was not to attract a mass following. Instead, the effort was concentrated upon winning over key figures within the government and in private life to become unpublicized but active proponents of its policies.

About 1950 Dr. Mozaffar Baghai founded his Toilers' party, designed to speak for the industrial workers of Iran. His lieutenant Khalil Maleki, previously a Tudeh party leader, broke away to establish the Third Force, a socialistic, anti-communist grouping of intellectuals. Lunatic fringe groups also appeared: the national socialist Sumka party, mystically dedicated to the active life, to courage and discipline, and to the struggle against colonization, communism, capitalism and the parliamentary system; and the Pan-Iranists, ardent nationalists who are resolved to recover territories lost in the last century to the Russian empire and to other neighbors of Iran.

In 1950 the National Front, a loose amalgamation of individuals and groups, attached itself to the personality and prestige of Dr. Muhammad Mossadeq. In time it came to include the Iran party, the Toilers' party, religious leaders, and independent deputies in the Majlis. Members of the Iran party became cabinet ministers and ambassadors. By the middle of 1953 the Sumka party, the Pan-Iranists, and the Toilers' party had deserted Dr. Mossadeq but after his fall his most vehement nationalist followers gathered into the underground National Resistance Movement which put out a clandestine paper, The Path of Mossadeq, in 1956 and 1957.

In July 1960 the National Front was reactivated in order to contest the elections for the XXth Majlis: it was composed of the Iran party, the Pan-Iran party, elements of the Third Force, the National Resistance Movement, and the tiny People of Iran party. Although the elections of August 1960 returned none of its members, in January 1961 its head, Allahyar Saleh, was elected from Kashan.

Since the summer of 1961 the National Front has concentrated its efforts upon demanding that Parliamentary elections be held, and in strengthening its organizational structure. The National Front has a Central Council of up to 50 members and a small Executive Committee, headed by Allahyar Saleh of the Iran party. While its headquarters are at Tehran, it has considerable strength among students and self-exiles in Europe and in 1962 opened a number of provincial branches in Iran. A loose coalition of groups and individuals demanding observance and enforcement of all the provisions of the constitution, its membership is not known.

The Melliyun and the Mardum parties, established in 1957 as detailed elsewhere, concentrated initially upon attracting adherents and then upon competing against each other in the elections for the XXth Majlis. After that body was dissolved in 1961 their activity declined, and it was uncertain whether, under new party heads, they would again play roles on the national scene.

The Governmental Bureaucracy

Available figures on the number of people working for the government of Iran vary widely, that quoted in 1962 being 250,000 or over twice the number employed prior to World

War II. Some 29% of the bureaucracy is illiterate. The government civil service includes nine grades with grade nine as the highest. Promotion is based primarily on length of service, and a college graduate reaches the top grade after eighteen years of service. At that level the employee receives less than $100 a month, much less than the salaries of judges or of university professors, while the lower grades earn from $15 to $30 a month. One quarter of all those employed earn between $27 and $40 a month. Since the minimum living costs at Tehran for a family of this general social level are at least $75 a month, a typical civil servant must do one of three things. He may try to have his schedule so arranged that he can take a second job, he may borrow at ruinous rates of interest, or he may resort to corrupt practices to obtain funds.

Successive cabinets have given consideration to the plight of the bureaucracy. While it is agreed that the number of employees should be reduced, no cabinet has been willing to take such a step. At the same time these cabinets have resisted pressure to raise salaries in view of the fact that 70% of the national budget is allotted to payment of salaries of these employees and of the members of the armed forces.

The Shah

In 1925 a specially formed Constituent Assembly acclaimed Reza Khan as *Shahinshah*, King of Kings, of the Empire of Iran. He selected the ancient Persian term *Pahlavi* as the name of the new dynasty, and upon his coronation in April 1926 took the name and title of Reza Shah Pahlavi.

Under the Constitution the heir presumptive to the throne is the first male child of the reigning Shah to be born to a woman of Iranian origin. If there are no male children, a successor is to be proposed by the Shah and the choice approved by Parliament.

Reza Shah's first son, Shapur Muhammad, was born on October 27, 1919. Educated in Switzerland, he has a very good knowledge of French and English, and was and continues to be active in sports. In 1939 he married Princess Fawzia, eldest sister of King Farouk I of Egypt, and their daughter, named Shahnaz, was born in 1940. After the abdication of Reza Shah, he ascended the throne on September 27, 1941, as Muhammad Reza Shah Pahlavi. In 1948 his marriage to Fawzia ended in divorce and in 1951 he married Soraya Esfandiari whom he divorced in 1958. In 1959 he was married to Farah Diba and on October 13, 1960 a crown prince, Reza Cyrus 'Ali, was born.

The powers of the Shah are exclusively those specified in the Constitution: the naming and dismissal of cabinet ministers; the command of the armed forces; the declaration of war and the conclusion of peace; and the conferring of military rank. He has the power to call special sessions of the Parliament and to dissolve a session.

The Shah's position as head of the armed forces brings him into close touch with military leaders and military affairs. Beyond the scope of his powers he exerts, of course, considerable influence upon the course of government by personal contact with cabinet ministers and officials. He may also patronize special causes or movements, and as Shah he has evinced a deep concern in fundamental social problems and has given very large sums, inherited from Reza Shah, for the construction of hospitals, for the expansion of education, for irrigation projects, and for other worthy causes.

The determination of the Shah to influence the course or social reform is exemplified by his program for the distribution of crown lands. These lands, assembled by Reza Shah, were ceded to the state by the present ruler in September 1941. In 1949 the Majlis reconveyed title to the throne, with the understanding that all income would be handled by the Imperial Organization for Social Services. Under pressure from Mossadeq, in May 1953 the court returned the properties to the government, but following the accession of the Zahedi government title was definitely recovered by the throne. The property in question consists of some 2,000 villages with their surrounding farm land, about 2,000 pasture lands, and 2,400 parcels of land occupied by buildings: the whole yielding an annual income of $500,000. Under the distribution scheme, which was completed in the spring of

1962, the peasant families received title to about 20 acres of land, with the discounted price to be paid in installments over 24 years.

In 1952 the Shah took the initiative in establishing the Bank Omran (Bank of Development and Rural Cooperatives) which was to employ its capital and the installment payments from the farmers to aid the new landowners. Agricultural cooperatives were established and village councils formed, and the Near East Foundation, funded by Point IV, was active in supervising aspects of the general program. Wells were drilled, baths constructed, and select seed grain and farming equipment made available. All these efforts were designed to enable the farmers to become self-supporting and self-reliant as soon as possible, including the assumption of responsibility for the operation of the cooperatives.

Since August 1953 the Shah has played a more direct role in stressing to the deputies and public officials the type of activity which must be undertaken in order to enhance economic and social development. He is said to have favored the constitutional amendments of 1949 and 1957, including the article of 1957 which permits the ruler to withhold assent to legislation enacted by the Parliament.

The Prime Minister and the Council of Ministers

When a Prime Minister is to be chosen, Parliament discusses and votes on a list of candidates, and the person receiving the support of Parliament is then named Prime Minister by the Shah. After he has chosen his cabinet ministers and presented them for royal approval, the cabinet then draws up and presents to Parliament a program of government. If it is approved, the Prime Minister remains in power until he chooses to resign or until Parliament records a majority vote of "no confidence."

Cabinet Ministers must be Persian citizens of the Moslem faith and may not be ranking princes of the royal family. Parliament may submit to the Supreme Court charges of misdemeanors against cabinet ministers.

Continuity within the executive branches of the government is not seriously dislocated by the recurrent changes of Cabinets. Each ministry is headed by an Under-Secretary and the major divisions of the Ministry by Directors-General, high officials who usually retain their posts for a number of years and are thoroughly familiar with the normal activities of their ministries. Then too, the various cabinet posts tend to be held by a limited number of individuals so that an experienced official will be familiar with the operations of several ministries.

Ministers without Portfolio

Each cabinet usually includes one or more Ministers without Portfolio, or Ministers of State. Their function is to advise and assist the Prime Minister and to perform special duties, including important investigations and inspections.

Ministry of Court

The Minister of the Imperial Court has equal rank with the other members of the cabinet but does not attend cabinet meetings and is not responsible to Parliament. This Ministry has charge of the royal finances, represented in part by the sum assigned to the Court in each annual budget and in part by the permanent property of the Court in the form of money or land. The divisions of the Ministry are concerned with ceremony and protocol, with the upkeep of the royal palaces and gardens, with correspondence and records, and with the maintenance of the royal hunting preserves.

There are a number of royal palaces in and near Tehran. Several were built as early as the eighteenth and nineteenth centuries and are noted for their splendid gardens. The *Gulistan* (Rose Garden) Palace at Tehran is an older structure with a large throne room used for official state receptions. In a western quarter of Tehran are large grounds containing the royal palaces, built and furnished in modern style, which house the Shah and members of the royal family. In the mountain resort district some eight miles north of Tehran is a section of about one hundred acres belonging to the Court, where are royal palaces and the summer offices of the Ministry of the Court. The Sa'adabad palace, at the highest point of this wooded land overlooking the city of Tehran, is like a gigantic jewel box. Each of its rooms is decorated in a different scheme by the most highly skilled craftsmen of the country.

Ministry of Foreign Affairs

The Ministry of Foreign Affairs has a number of special departments which deal with routine business, with protocol and ceremony, with accounts, passports and economic information, with the United Nations and with the maintenance of the library and archives. There are also five political departments. The first handles affairs with contiguous Moslem States; the second, Soviet Russia and Eastern Europe; the third, other European countries; the fourth, the United States and the other American countries; the fifth, the Arab States, India, Pakistan and Southeastern Asia.

Iran has consulates, legations, or embassies in over thirty foreign countries; in the United States an Iranian Embassy in Washington, D.C., and Consulates General in New York City and San Francisco.

Iran was an early member of the League of Nations and participated in the organization of the United Nations. Treaties and agreements are in force between Iran and other countries covering commerce, customs duties, navigation, rights of nationals of both countries, etc. Iran's relations with her neighbors are still governed by the Sa'adabad Treaty, signed by Iran, Afghanistan, Iraq, and Turkey at Tehran in 1937, by which the signatories agree to refrain from interference in each other's internal affairs, to respect their mutual frontiers, to refrain from aggression against each other, and to consult together in the event that an international conflict should threaten their common interests. Along with Turkey, Pakistan, and the United Kingdom, Iran is a member of CENTO (Central Treaty Organization).

Ministry of Defense

The Ministry of Defense, comprising the army, navy, and air force, is responsible for national security. The present strength of the army is more than 150,000 men. It is made up of six army corps, totaling twelve divisions and several independent brigades. The first corps at Tehran comprises the 1st infantry division and the 2nd armored division; the second corps of Azerbaijan includes the 3rd and 4th divisions; the 3rd corps includes the 11th division of Kurdistan and the 12th division of Kermanshah; the 5th corps includes the 9th division of Isfahan, the 6th division of Fars, and the 8th division of Kerman; and the 6th corps has the 10th division of Khuzistan and the 5th division of Luristan.

The Shah is commander-in-chief of the army and also is in direct command of the Tehran corps. The royal family is in the care of the Imperial Guard, a body which demonstrated its loyalty to the throne at the time of the political crisis in 1953. Iranian generals commanding corps bear the title of *Sepahbod*, generals of divisions *Sar lashgar*, and generals of brigades *Sartip*.

Under Iran's system of compulsory military service young men are taken into the army when they reach twenty-one and serve for two years, although those who are vitally needed for the support of a family are usually passed over. Some adult education courses are available to the recruits, and graduates of secondary schools and of the University serve for shorter periods and are normally given training as officers. A magnificent Officers' Club in Tehran was provided as a means of creating a sense of unity and pride within the officer corps.

The primary function of the army has been to deal with internal disorder, and although campaigns against the nomadic tribes have been conducted fairly recently, Iranians hope that such troubles are a thing of the past. Under normal conditions the Security Guard is well qualified to maintain order. Cavalry forces no longer play as vital a role as in the Iranian armies of earlier centuries, and the modern army has mechanized equipment. Nearly all the small arms, clothing, and light equipment of the army are produced in government factories and arsenals.

Since 1942 an American military mission has been active with the accounting, supply, and training sections of the Iranian army. In 1950 Iran came under the Mutual Defense Aid Program and by 1961 the United States had contributed over $550,000,000 to the modernization of the armed forces of the country, largely in the form of military equipment and supplies, but also in the construction of bases and budgetary assistance. In Iran the United States Military Mission (ARMISH) and the Military Assistance Advisory Group (MAAG) supervise the programs of military support.

The operations of the Iranian Navy are confined to the Persian Gulf and the Caspian Sea where patrols attempt to prevent smuggling and gun-running. The naval command center is at Khorramshahr. Since 1953 the American military mission has supplied naval vessels and equipment and arranged for the training of personnel. Elements of the growing fleet have taken part in maneuvers in the Persian Gulf with units of the American fleet.

The Iranian air force has a strength of some 5,000 men. Pilots and technical personnel had been trained in the United States to operate the over 100 American jet fighters supplied to the force.

Civilian interest in flying and a source of air force recruits appears in the semi-official National Aero Club of Iran which has its own field, hangars, and club building to the west of Tehran.

Ministry of Finance

The Ministry of Finance employs a large personnel, and its vital operations embrace a great many spheres of activity. An immense modern building of reinforced concrete and brick meets the needs of the ministry for office space.

There are two main divisions. The financial division is concerned with the customs service, direct and indirect taxation, the annual budget, accounts and inspection, buildings, foreign

16. Village life: the threshing floor with wheat from sheaves to grain

17. Urban life: active and passive bureaucrats. The *zur khaneh* in the National Bank of Iran

18. Village life: children are seen but not heard

19. Village life: weaving a Persian rug from a full scale pattern

exchange, the mint, government property, ministerial courts, income from concessions, oil and minerals, and a school of financial training. A few of the many departments of the economic division are those dealing with purchasing, accounts, inspection, warehouses, transport, grain storage, and tobacco.

The annual national budget is prepared from the statements of anticipated receipts and expenditures submitted by all the ministries. Very rarely in the last decade has the Majlis approved a complete budget; instead it votes permission for the government to pay its way from month to month upon the basis of the trial budget. Accurate budget figures are difficult to obtain and official releases may be contradictory.

The figures which follow, given in rials, represent approximations or estimates for some recent Persian calendar years;

	Revenues	*Expenditures*
1966	190,468,000,000	192,112,000,000
1965	175,046,000,000	176,062,000,000
1964	140,953,000,000	144,444,000,000
1963	92,745,000,000	98,999,000,000
1962	86,600,000,000	88,800,000,000
1961	90,431,000,000	93,048,000,000

All of the above figures include special developmental budgets. In several recent years budget deficits were met by direct financial aid from the United States, but such assistance came to an end after 1961. In normal practice budget deficits and all state obligations are met as the Ministry of Finance borrows the required amounts from the National Bank of Iran.

In recent years about 35% of estimated expenditures are earmarked for the armed forces, including the frontier guards, the gendarmerie and the police. The next largest item is 18% for the Ministry of Education, followed by the Ministries of Health and Finance, each spending about 3% of the total.

On the side of income, customs revenues amount to about 30%, followed by receipts from the tobacco and sugar monopolies, by receipts from direct taxes and by taxes on petroleum products consumed internally. Varying percentages of the revenues from the operations of the oil consortium are assigned to the annual budget. As the tax structure now operates some 86% of annual revenue comes from indirect taxes and only 14% from direct taxes. In many other countries these proportions would be reversed.

The income-tax law now in force dates from 1955 and represents a mixture of modern practices and traditional customs. For example, some 40 types of tradesmen and craftsmen are exempt from income taxes: sign painters, peddlers of head and feet of animals, felt makers, horseshoe makers, bird sellers, peddlers of hot beets, menders of samovars and of spectacles, etc.

In 1957 the tax system of Iran was studied by Philip E. Taylor, an American expert, who submitted a detailed report stressing specific measures which might be undertaken by the Ministry of Finance to put the tax structure on a sound footing and to enhance revenues. In the report emphasis was placed upon the desirability of increasing the direct taxes on income and on fixed property. It was indicated that while about 50% of the national income derives from cultivated land, only from 2 to 4% of annual revenues comes from taxes on this production. In 1966 the statistic office of the Central Bank estimated that the average national income in Iran was $200 a year.

Ministry of the Interior

The Ministry of the Interior is responsible for the internal administration of the country. Iran is divided into 14 *ostans*, or provinces, whose boundaries correspond fairly closely to those of very ancient regional divisions such as Azerbaijan, Khorasan, Gilan, Fars, Khuzistan, and Sistan. Each province is in charge of a governor appointed, as are most of the other high provincial officials, by the Ministry of the Interior at Tehran. Taxes collected in the provinces are sent on to Tehran as part of the national revenue.

Many Iranians feel that their government is too centralized. The Constitution provides for the election by the local inhabitants of provincial and district councils to be responsible for the improvement of conditions within the provinces, and in recent years an increasing number of such councils have been elected. In fact, elected councils at the village level are no longer a rarity. Within the Parliament deputies are developing strong interest in their own constituencies and in the projects of the Plan Organization special attention has been given to the needs of the small towns.

Within some 156 larger towns the National Police Administration, totaling over 21,000 men, maintains public order under direct supervision from Tehran. Nation-wide internal security is maintained by the gendarmerie, or Security Guard, a force of 24,000 men operating under the Ministry of the Interior. The country is divided into 16 administrative areas for this purpose, and each area is staffed with from one to three regiments. Since 1942 an American Mission has been advising the gendarmerie on reorganization and modernization and has channeled quantities of modern equipment to this service. In September 1953 the American mission to the gendarmerie merged its administrative organization with that of the American mission to the Iranian armed forces. Point IV has made available substantial sums for the construction of gendarmerie posts and for the education of illiterate security guards.

These security guards are a familar sight to travelers on the roads of Iran. They man check posts on the highways, are stationed on stone towers commanding isolated areas, and patrol from village to village by jeep or horseback.

The interest of the United States Operations Mission to Iran has led to the extension of the operations of this Ministry. A newly established Development Bureau supervises projects under the USOM-sponsored Agrarian Development Program and the Block Development Program. A Department of Extension Services has also been established and a General Department of Public Statistics: time will tell whether these organizations will be firmly integrated within the Ministry.

Ministry of Justice

The Ministry of Justice is concerned with the enforcement of existing laws. Iran's judicial system, modeled after that of France, is a hierarchy of courts from the district courts on the lowest level up to the Supreme Court, which is the court of final appeal but has not the power to determine the constitutionality of current legislation. Judges try all cases except those few for which juries are called, and frequently receive permanent appointments.

Since 1925 there has been a complete revolution in the Iranian concept of law. Before that time the country was subject to a system of religious law based upon the Qoran, augmented by the interpretations of learned theologians, and enforced by the Moslem clerics. This type of law not only was poorly adapted to the conditions of the modern world, but placed too much responsibility and power in the hands of the clergy. It is surprising, however, that a series of new laws could so rapidly efface a heritage of so many centuries.

In 1925 an extensive commercial code was enacted by Parliament, followed in 1926 by a criminal code, and in 1928 by a civil code of some nine hundred articles. These three basic codes established the new legal system, while certain other laws were aimed at the "modernization" of Iran. A law of 1928 abolished the so-called "capitulations," which up to that time had given foreigners resident in Iran some immunity from arrest as well as the right of trial by their own consular representatives. Laws passed in 1931 and 1935 established the legal ages for marriage and enhanced the divorce and property rights of women. Laws of 1928 and 1935 did away with the ancient Persian costume and made western clothing and headgear compulsory, and the use of honorary titles, another holdover from the autocratic past, was abolished in 1935.

The most systematic and extensive legal changes were undertaken after 1933 by Minister of Justice Davar who was given full powers to put laws into effect and then to submit them to the Parliament for approval after they had been tried out in practice. More recent governments have paralleled this experiment for short periods.

A peculiarly Persian tradition which has managed to survive the enactment of modern codes of law is that of *bast*—the act of taking sanctuary within mosques, royal stables, telegraph offices, etc., where fugitives were safe from arrest. Currently political figures have sought bast within the Parliament grounds and at the gate of the royal palace.

In general, the judicial system is not held in high esteem by the Iranians. It is felt that wealth and prestige may influence the decisions of the courts and that the courts do not provide adequate protection for abuses of individual rights. However, the cry for social justice, heard so loudly in some other countries of the region, is not yet loud and persistent in Iran.

In all the towns and large villages there are official registration offices staffed by the Ministry, in which all such documents as marriage certificates, birth certificates, rent contracts, and property and land deeds must be recorded. This service has been of real value in establishing complete and permanent records of land ownership, for in earlier periods the boundaries of land holdings were always very loosely defined and led to many disputes over titles.

Ministry of Education

The Ministry of Education is charged with Public Instruction, Religious Endowments, and Fine Arts.

The term "Religious Endowments" is the translation of an Arabic word *vaqf* meaning "gift for religious education or for charitable purposes." These might be gifts of money but were more often farm land, shops in the bazaars, or orchards, whose annual income was to be devoted to a worthy cause. Some of the older mosques have inscriptions describing in detail the gifts which were to provide for their perpetual upkeep; other gifts met the expenses of public baths, religious schools, and hospitals. The records of all such gifts and of the spending of the funds were formerly kept by the Moslem religious leaders, but a number of years ago the function was turned over to the Ministry of Education.

The Department of Antiquities, whose offices are in the excellent modern museum at Tehran, is responsible for recording, protecting, and maintaining the ancient structures of Iran, and for supervising archeological excavations throughout the country.

The Ministry of Education is assisted in its long-range plans by the Higher Council of Education, composed of ten advisory members and ten voting members, which approves general regulations and text books, strives for constant improvement and development in the educational system and is a stabilizing influence against reactionary or radical trends.

Ministry of Agriculture

The Ministry of Agriculture is divided into technical sections: 1) a general bureau for records, accounts, and inspection, 2) a technical office for the study of sugar beets, sugar cane, flowers, vegetables, and forests; for veterinary and animal husbandry work; for the construction of dams and irrigation projects; and for agricultural machinery, 3) a second technical office for agricultural training, investigation, and research, and 4) the Office of Institutes comprising an agricultural secondary school and college at Karej; a veterinary school at Tehran, a sugar beet institute at Karej, the Razi Institute for serum production at Hessarak, a school of animal husbandry at Haidarabad which has conducted a mass inoculation of animals throughout the country; a land rental administration at Karej; and an insecticide plant at Karej. The agricultural school and college at Karej gives the students a thorough course of study as well as a certain amount of practical application in field, orchard, and garden. But its students are drawn largely from Tehran and other towns, and after graduation few of them are interested in working in the smaller farming communities.

The primary functions of the ministry are the improvement in types and production of crops and livestock, agricultural advice and training for specialists and farmers, and the development of irrigated land areas. Although the department has existed as a separate ministry for only a few years and perhaps too much attention has been given to theoretical activity and statistical studies and too little to direct contact with the farming communities, its published studies of the agricultural resources of each section of the country have been essential to the establishment of a firm groundwork for more practical activity.

In 1943 an important forward step was taken with the establishment of the Office of Irrigation as a separate division of the ministry, with its own independent budget originally intended to total over one million dollars a year. From 1948 until the present more and more effort has been concentrated upon this field with the Plan Organization selecting and financing projects.

In 1945 a survey was conducted in Iran by the Near East Foundation, an American organization which since the first World War has carried out programs for general relief, rural education, and agricultural training in the countries on the eastern periphery of the Mediterranean. The Foundation's Iranian program, begun in 1946 and gradually increased to cover some 300 villages, is carried on with the active interest and support of the Iranian government, and its field staff works with both the Ministry of Agriculture and the Ministry of Education. Its purpose is to raise the level of education, general hygiene, and agricultural methods and production in a selected group of villages as an experimental laboratory, and then apply its findings to the rest of the country.

Both the United States Operations Mission to Iran and the Ford Foundation have supported the program of the Near East Foundation. The USOM has also been responsible for the creation or reorganization of activities of the Ministry of Agriculture, in addition to those named earlier. These include the Livestock Bureau, the Forestry Bureau and the Agricultural Extension Service. The Forestry and Livestock bureaus pool their interests through the High Council of Range Management. The Vocational Agricultural Teachers' Training School at Mamazon, established by the Near East

Foundation, helps to staff nation-wide community development programs.

Ministry of Health

Since 1935 the Ministry of Health, one of the last branches of the government to become a separate Ministry, has made a great deal of progress in attacking the problems of public health. In recent years there has been a shift in emphasis from curative to preventive medicine. Within the Ministry the Department of Public Health spearheads this effort, opening Public Health Centers and sponsoring Public Health Cooperatives with the aid of the United States Operations Mission to Iran. The Ministry has taken over the Palasht Sanitation School, established by the Near East Foundation.

The activities of the Ministry in such fields as the eradication of malaria and the construction of hospitals are covered in the pages devoted to the health and welfare of the people of Iran.

Ministry of National Economy

In June 1947 the Cabinet of Ministers decreed the establishment of a Ministry of National Economy, which took over all the departments and sections of the long established Ministry of Commerce, Industry, and Mines. Its legality was later approved by the Parliament.

The establishment of this Ministry was the outcome of earlier concern with industrial planning. As early as 1937 an Economic Council had been appointed and given responsibility to centralize all economic studies and planning. In 1944 this body was succeeded by the Higher Economic Council and in 1955 a law detailed the duties and powers of this same fifteen-member Higher Economic Council. This Council is supposed to channel and smooth relations between the ministries and departments and the Plan Organization.

The functions of the Ministry may change along with successive governments: it has been charged with the implementation of economic policies of the government; with the supervision of foreign commerce; with the supervision of privately owned industries and mines; and with the management of internal price controls.

The Department of Mines controls the exploitation of those leased to local companies, makes surveys of the mineral resources of the country, and prepares maps of mineral deposits and geological formations.

The activity of the Arts and Crafts Department is of particular interest, since efforts are being made to revive certain of the ancient handicrafts and to improve the quantity and quality of production of the current crafts. The department runs a Higher School of the Arts at Tehran and branch schools at Mashhad, Tabriz, Isfahan, Shiraz, and Shahi. It also maintains a School of the Beautiful Arts at Tehran which was once headed by one of Iran's leading miniature painters, and a Dyeing School and a Women's Handicraft School. Training is given in miniature painting, carpet designing and weaving, the manufacture of pottery and tiles, wood carving, brocade weaving, silver and inlay work, and wood-block printing on cloth. Its purpose is to establish a high level of technical skill and to restore to design the intrinsic good taste of the past, which by the end of the nineteenth century had been almost lost through the influence of inferior machine products from Europe.

In a cabinet which came into office in April 1957 the functions of this ministry appear to have been turned over to a revived Ministry of Commerce, a revived Ministry of Industry and Mines, and a newly established Ministry of Customs and Monopolies. Such changes in the total number and the assigned functions of the various ministries occur fairly frequently.

Ministry of Roads and Communications

This ministry has jurisdiction over the Iranian State Railways, as well as responsibility for developing and maintaining the road system of the country.

During World War II some 2,989,079 long tons of supplies were shipped toward the USSR over the Iranian railways. Iranian supervisory and operational personnel worked closely with British, Russian, and American forces on different sections of the line. At the end of the war the Iranian government purchased locomotives, freight cars, machine tools, and equipment of all kinds from the American army. In more recent years attention has been concentrated upon repairing damage to the roadbeds suffered during the war and to a continuing effort to replace coal-burning locomotives with mountain-type diesels. The problems of railroad maintenance in Iran are many and difficult. For example, all ties must be brought across the high mountains from the Caspian coast, at each watering point water-softeners of large capacity must be kept in good operating order, rails must be imported from abroad, and because the entire line is single-track schedules must be carefully planned and maintained. At the present time the volume of freight and passenger traffic is not large enough to balance revenues against expenses.

The extension of existing lines and the construction of new ones is covered in a later chapter.

The Ministry is responsible for the maintenance and extension of the network of roads and highways. Both railway and road construction is performed through contracts awarded to private companies, but the upkeep of roads is in charge of government officials posted through the entire country. All the main roads and many of the secondary ones are gravel over a base of crushed stone, the materials for which are produced in crushing plants or broken up by hand. Work gangs from villages along the road periodically smooth down the traffic damage and spread a fresh layer of gravel over the surface. When the roads of this type are well maintained they can carry heavy traffic, and passenger cars can make very good time.

Before the war the ministry had had short stretches of highway asphalted and most municipalities had asphalted their main avenues. Hundreds of miles of asphalt were laid by the Allies during the war, and more recently the ministry has arranged for the asphalting of a number of main highways. However, the responsibility for contracting for new work is now shared with the Plan Organization. Operating at an accelerated rate and on an expanded scale, it is certain that the highway network of the country will be completely transformed within a matter of a few years.

Ministry of Posts, Telephone, and Telegraph

The postal, telegraph, and telephone systems of Iran are under the direct management of the Ministry, and the Ministry conducts special training schools which turn out operators and technicians for these services. The first postal system to be modelled after those of the European countries was introduced in 1865, and in 1877 Iran became a member of the International Postal Union. Within the country the mail is generally transported by autobus or truck although there is a local airmail service between Tehran and the major towns. Domestic rates on first class mail are considerably lower than in the United States.

The first telegraph line within Iran was constructed in 1859. At this time the British government was very anxious to establish a system from Europe all the way across the Near East to India, and in 1864 and later the Indo-European Telegraph Company was granted the right of building telegraph lines across Iran, with the provision that they were to serve internal as well as through traffic. These lines entered Iran from the west and divided at a point on the central plateau, with one section joining a submarine cable at Bushire on the Persian Gulf and the other line continuing overland through Baluchistan to India. Much later Iran constructed additional lines of her own and finally in 1932 Great Britain agreed to turn over the lines of the Indo-European Company to the Iranian government. At present about 25,000 miles of telegraph wires are in service within the country.

Radio Tehran and Radio Tabriz are the principal broadcasting stations, although such towns as Shiraz, Isfahan, Ahwaz and Mashhad may send out limited programs on 500 watts of power. All these stations are government owned and the Iranian army has its own network which it uses for educational and training programs. The station at Tehran is housed in an impressive complex of structures a few miles north of the city. It handles commercial traffic with foreign countries by means of directional antennas beamed at Europe and the United States. For some years the maximum power at Tehran was 20,000 watts, but in 1955 a 50,000 watt unit was put into operation.

Radio Tehran sends out general programs on both short wave and standard broadcast waves. The radio day begins about six in the morning with a rather unusual program which combines western setting-up exercises with the drumbeat and chant of verses of epic poetry common to the *zur khaneh*. The station comes back on the air in the afternoon and broadcasts until about ten at night. Typical programs are periods of recorded Western or Persian music and song, programs for children, readings of literature and poetry, news in English, French, Russian, and Arabic as well as in Persian, and talks on current events or subjects of general interest. A sustained effort is now being made to produce programs which will appeal directly to the vast rural audience.

There are some 900,000 radio receivers in Iran. The Persians pay particular attention to local and foreign news broadcasts, while the press reprints much of the broadcast news from abroad.

There are locally owned television stations at Tehran and Abadan and a United States Armed Forces station at Tehran, all of which are on the air in the evenings. Some 85,000 television receivers are in operation.

Iran's telephone system, formerly operated by a privately owned company on a special concession from the government, was nationalized in 1950. There are some 120,000 telephones, of which 85,000 are in Tehran's dial system. Service between towns is quite well maintained and the rates are low.

Ministry of Labor

On May 18, 1946, the Cabinet of Ministers published a comprehensive Labor Law, formulated to meet the urgent requirements of modern conditions. Before the law was put in force Iran had no complete labor code, and there were no adequate provisions for the country's representation in international labor organizations, the more necessary since its labor regulations were out of line with those of other countries. The forty-seven articles of the new law regulated working hours, wages, holidays and paid vacations, and labor by women and children; and provided for contracts between employers and employees, safeguards for the health of workers, an unemployment service, unions, boards of conciliation and arbitration, savings societies, and social security.

On August 10, 1946, a Ministry of Labor was created by cabinet decree and entrusted with the implementation of the Labor Law. This Ministry, the establishment of which had to be confirmed by the XVth Parliament, consists of an administrative division and three technical sections covering Labor, Publications and Publicity, and Reforms and Construction. The important labor section is subdivided into separate offices dealing with the subjects enumerated in the Labor Law, and an Office of International Labor Relations. Iranian representatives have already participated in international labor conferences.

One of the first steps taken by the new Ministry was the issuance of a decree increasing the shares of all farmers who work on land owned by others by a flat fifteen per cent, beginning with the 1946 harvest season. This decree was not seriously enforced and soon became inoperative. In the fall of 1952 the government was ready to promulgate a new law on this subject. Sharecroppers were to receive an additional 10% of the harvest, while the landowners were to contribute an additional 20% of their share of the crop to be devoted to local public works. In 1954 this arrangement was put into force.

Throughout recent years the Ministry of Labor, always very short of funds, has endeavored to carry out a progressive program. Efforts have been made to purge elements of the Tudeh party from the unions. Several independent or semi-independent unions have been established, but their leadership has not been of the type to win the confidence of the members nor to secure benefits for the workmen. Unemployment has continued to be a most serious problem. The Ministry has taken sound steps in opening workers' cooperatives and in instituting a program of workers' insurance. In this program the employers are responsible for 6% of the contributions and 4% is paid in by the workers. In 1962 the name of this Ministry was changed to that of the Ministry of Labor and Social Services.

New Ministries

In 1964 several new ministries were established: Ministry of Water and Power, Ministry of Information, Ministry of Housing and Development, and Ministry of Culture.

VI. THE PEOPLE AND THEIR LIFE

Population and Ethnic Elements

In 1962 a projection of the census of 1956 placed the population of Iran at 21,400,000 people. Of this total some 7,651,000, or 35.7% of the people, lived in towns of 5,000 or more. The rest are either peasant farmers, living in 45,500 villages of fifteen or more houses, or are among the estimated two million members of the migratory or semi-nomadic nomads. Tehran, the capital, has 2,300,000 people; Tabriz 387,000; Isfahan 340,000; Mashhad 312,000; Abadan 302,-000; Shiraz 230,000; and Kermanshah, Ahwaz, Rasht, and Hamadan are all slightly above the 100,000 figure. In these towns the average family appears to have five members.

The average density of population in Iran is thirty-three to square mile, compared to a United States average of forty-five. In the great Iranian deserts and much of the southeastern section of the country the average is less than ten to the square mile, while in the northwest and along the Caspian the figure reaches one hundred. The population of the country as a whole suffered a sharp decline in the eighteenth and early nineteenth centuries, but it is now on the increase. There has been a considerable movement away from the villages to the newly important industrial centers, and the population of Tehran has trebled within the last quarter century. Population increase is estimated at 2.5% annually with some 210,000 marriages and 35,000 divorces taking place each year.

The "Iranian" population derives from the early Aryan mass movements into the region, in the second millennium B.C. Little is known about the pre-Aryan peoples of Iran, who have been referred to as Caspians or Caucasians, but certainly they intermarried with and were absorbed by the Aryans. Some Arab groups entered the country during and after the seventh century A.D., and settled in the northeast and east, and from the tenth to the fourteenth centuries Turkish or Turanian tribes moved in in considerable numbers. The nomadic tribes further complicate the ethnic and linguistic picture. Some of them, judging from the anthropological evidence of their head types, may have been resident in Iran for many centuries, others moved into the country during the Islamic era, and still others have moved or have been transferred from one part of the country to another. Some of these groups speak languages apparently acquired and not consistent with their ethnic origin.

The bulk of the inhabitants of the towns and of the farming communities—from two-thirds to three-fourths of the entire population—speaks Persian. One-fifth of the total population, dwelling in the densely-settled northwest province of Azerbaijan and thence southward in a large triangle reaching almost to Tehran, speaks a Turkish dialect called "Azari," which has a simple grammar and has absorbed many Persian words. A goodly number of these people acquired the language following the Mongol conquest or in more recent times. While it is hard to draw the line between the Turkish elements and the Iranian elements who now speak Azari, it is certain that the Turkish element is composed of "Iranian" Turks who derive originally from central Asia and have little racial affinity with the Ottoman Turks of the present Turkish Republic. The Qashqa'i tribe of the southwest speaks a dialect very similar to Azari, suggesting that this group migrated from the northwestern corner of the country.

The population of Iran therefore reflects the mass movements into the region and the residue from recurrent invasions, but at the same time there is rather more homogeneity of population than in most other countries of comparable size. There is also a basis for national unity and national self-consciousness in the overwhelming adherence of the community to the Shi'a sect of Islam and in the all-pervading influence of Persian literature, culture, manners and customs, and way of life.

Ninety-eight per cent of the inhabitants are Moslems, and 90% of this number are Shi'as. The Sunni sect has many followers among the Kurds, Baluchi, and Turkoman. There are relatively few minority groups within the country, and the Iranians have always been tolerant and shown comparatively little of the discrimination of other lands toward minor racial or religious elements. In the northwest are some 120,000 Armenians, who are also prosperous merchants in the large towns, and some 70,000 Nestorian Christians. Jews are settled in the large towns and in certain ancient farming communities, although many members of this community have gone to Israel in recent years. There are a few thousand Protestants and Roman Catholics. An official government estimate places the Bahais at 50,000 but this figure may well be far too low. At Yazd and Kerman, and in fewer number at Tehran, Isfahan, and Shiraz are colonies of Parsis, Iranians who still hold to the religion of Zoroaster and still worship in fire temples. The Parsis, or Zoroastrians, are famed as gardeners and merchants.

The Persians are brunets, with dark brown or black hair and dark brown eyes, and of medium height and build. Complexions range from quite fair to swarthy, with general coloring similar to that of the Italians or the Greeks.

The Nomadic Tribes

The most important of the tribal groups which are widely distributed over Iran are the Kurds, Lurs, Bakhtiari, Qashqa'i, Mamasani, Khamseh, Shahsevans, Arabs, Baluchi, and Turkoman. The first five named are found primarily in the Zagros Mountain chain. Certain of the tribes, including the Kurds and the Arabs, have veered toward a settled agricultural life, but the true nomads keep to a pastoral economy founded on large flocks of sheep and goats. The Kurds, Lurs, and Bakhtiari speak dialects which may be related to Old Persian or to another ancient Indo-European language; the Arabs north of the head of the Persian Gulf still speak Arabic; the Qashqa'i of the southwest, and part of the Khamseh group, who are neighbors of the Qashqa'i, and the Shahevans speak a Turkish dialect; and the Baluchi of southeastern Iran speak a dialect of Persian. These nomads and many lesser groups are the most picturesque element of the Iranian population, representing the best physical type with a bravery which has always furnished the stiff backbone of Iranian armies, and several ruling dynasties have sprung from tribal warriors. A tribe, called *eel* after the Turkish term, may be very numerous or may number only a few hundred. In the case of the Qashqa'i, who may total some 300,000, the tribe is divided into numerous smaller divisions or parts, with a division either a unit or itself subdivided into ten, twenty, or fifty smaller groups. Such sub-tribes or clan groupings are variously known as *tayifeh*, *tireh*, and *dasteh*. In several regions the tribal leader is known as the *khan* and the heads of the sub-tribes as *kalantars*. Certain tribes claim ownership of large areas, basing their claims on awards of *tiyul*, or fief, made by earlier rulers of Iran, frequently in return for military service.

According to season the tribes move from their *garmsir*, or winter quarters, to the *sardsir*, or summer quarters. These Persian terms are paralleled by the Turkish terms, *qishlaq*, and *yeylaq*. In the fall the tribes of the Zagros range move down to the warm low plains along the Iraq frontier and to the shores of the Persian Gulf to sow their cereal crops. In the spring, leaving behind some members of the tribe to reap the harvest, they migrate again into the highest mountain valleys where their flocks can find good grazing throughout the summer. The seasonal migrations may cover distances of more than two hundred miles and may take weeks. The rate of movement is dictated by the slow progress of the flocks of sheep and goats, which the men and boys drive ahead while the women and children ride perched in precarious fashion atop the baggage lashed to donkeys and camels. Each evening the tents are pitched along the side of the road. Visitors to Iran may expect to see the tribes only at the times of their migrations, for their summer and winter quarters are usually remote from the frequented highways.

The tribes are a law unto themselves, ruled by the strict authority of their elected or hereditary leaders. Many of the khans are men of excellent education; some of the current leaders were educated in Europe, while others attended the former Alborz College at Tehran. They usually own houses in towns or on the tribal lands but spend much of their time in the tents of their tribal groups.

Family life is pursued in the black tents which are made of a tough goat's-hair cloth woven by the women of the tribes. Their vertical side-walls and slightly sloping tops are supported by stout poles, and the tent can be quickly struck and packed in a small space for transportation from one sight to another. The furnishings are extremely simple. The floor coverings are usually rugs woven by the women, or thick felt mats; the blankets are piled against one wall and along the other walls are placed the copper utensils, goat-skin containers for liquids, earthenware jars, bags of grain, and occasionally a wooden chest for clothing.

The flocks themselves sustain the nomadic life. They furnish milk, butter, and cheese, and their wool is used for tribal weaving while both the animals and their wool are sold in the towns. The tribal lands occupied in the summer often contain orchards and groves of nut-bearing trees which are an added source of cash income. Scrub oaks are burned to obtain charcoal, which is sold in the towns. Ready cash is used for the relatively few items not produced by the tribes themselves: sugar, tea, cotton piece goods, arms and ammunition, and jewelry. The fascinating jewelry worn by the women usually include strings of old silver and gold coins, and represents the whole accumulated wealth of the family group. Other valuable property of the tribe is the herds of horses and the guns; the men are fine marksmen and very proud of their weapons.

The men do the hunting and care for the flocks and the herds of horses, and the women gather fuel, carry water, and do the cooking, sewing, and weaving. Polygamy is comparatively rare among the tribes, and the women are not veiled. The social life of the tribe centers around the guest tent of the tribal chief. There the tribal dances are held to the stirring rhythm of flute and drum, ballads are recited, stories told, and news, gossip, and rumor exchanged. Acquaintances and strangers are welcomed to the generous hospitality of the guest tent. Tribal boundaries are fairly well defined, and in recent years intertribal raiding and warfare have been on the decline. The tribes may go in for a certain amount of highway robbery, but more as a form of diversion than as a steady occupation.

Comparatively little is known about the tribes. In the past, attention was concentrated upon determining the exact names of each tribe, sub-tribe and clan, and estimating their numbers. Even these efforts were not very successful, for the figure of two million for the total number of tribesmen in Iran is only a rough estimate. Only scant attention has been devoted to a study of their religious beliefs, their folklore and superstitions, their ballads, and the details of their mode of life—attributes which tend to be modified or to disappear as the old gives way to the new in Iran. However, a few collections of their songs and stories have been made and published at Tehran and Persian authors have published detailed accounts of the composition, life, and customs of a few groups. In the next stage of investigation trained anthropologists must reside among the tribes. Interesting material is on display in the Ethnographical Museum at Tehran which has several rooms devoted to tribal culture, with tents set up and representatively furnished and cases containing life-sized figures of men and women clad in everyday costumes or in the rich and brilliant costumes worn at weddings and on feast days.

The nomadic groups and the stationary population tend to be mutually distrustful. In early periods the central government tried to break the armed strength of the tribes by transferring entire groups to lands remote from their accustomed haunts, and more recently tribal revolts have been severely quelled and attempts made to settle the nomads in newly built villages. The tribal question is of vital importance to modern Iran, for no nation can be truly united if one-ninth of her population remains aloof from the rest of it. On the other hand, the settlement of the tribes in villages does not appear to be an adequate solution. The nomads would be uneasy, unhappy, and unproductive in so alien a way of life, and also the basic reason for nomadism is the acute shortage of good farming land, and until the situation is remedied through irrigation projects there is simply not enough land to go around. In a country where more milk, meat, and wool is needed to raise the general standard of living, effective aid might be given the nomads to improve the quantity and quality of their flocks.

Official awareness of the tribal problem resulted in the establishment, in 1953, of a Higher Tribal Council under the direction of the Ministry of Court. This organization was to improve tribal health and education, develop tribal agriculture and improve the general economic situation, introduce administrative reforms in dealing with the tribes, cultivate intra-tribal unity, and inspire devotion to Shah and nation.

Villages and Village Life

The countless farming communities of Iran exist wherever water for drinking purposes and for irrigation is available, and where the soil is suitable for growing crops. In those regions where adequate sources of water supply are far apart the villages are concentrated near them and therefore tend to be larger, while in sections where mountain streams, springs, and qanat lines are available small hamlets dot the landscape at intervals of only two or three miles. The traveler along the main roads will see many such villages, but by far the largest number are hidden away in remote mountain valleys. He will also see ruined and deserted villages, evidence of the economic decline which has been arrested only in the last decades.

Only along the shores of the Caspian are isolated houses set in the midst of the fields; in all other sections of the country the farmers live in compact and crowded settlements and work in fields which may lie at a considerable distance from the village. Until a few years ago all the villages were protected against marauding bands by high walls of mud brick, pierced by a single bastion-flanked doorway. Today such walls are no longer necessary, and only occasionally are they still standing in good condition. Within each village is a haphazard network of narrow lanes, sometimes paved with cobblestones, and usually one straight main street along which runs the water channel which is the sine qua non of village life. There is usually a village square, an irregular open space made conspicuous by a few towering trees and fronting on it the village mosque or the domed tomb of some local saint. At one edge of the village is always the community threshing floor.

The narrow lanes are bordered by high mud walls, in which double doors lead into the courtyard of each house. The typical courtyard contains a few trees and flowers, and a pool, filled at intervals from the main channel passing through the village, which provides water for all domestic purposes except drinking. The houses are built of mud brick, the type of construction varying with each region. In areas where timber is plentiful crossbeams and overlapping straw mats support a flat roof of earth, which after each rain is packed down with a stone roller kept on the roof for just that purpose. The flat roofs provide a cool place for the family to sleep during the hot summer months. In other sections of the country the houses are roofed with tunnel-vaults or domes in mud brick which are erected by local masons, following an age-old technique, without any supporting scaffold.

The houses usually occupy one short side of the court and contain three or four rooms, but larger dwellings occupy two or three sides. The houses face toward the south so that the warmth of the winter sun can carry directly into the main rooms, and a porch across the front of the house intercepts the rays of the high summer sun so that the rooms are shady all day during the hot months. The better houses have one reception or living room in which the cherished possessions of the family are on display. Rugs, often locally woven, cover the floor, and quilts, mattresses, and pillows are neatly piled in a niche in the wall. An oil lamp stands in another niche. There is always a mirror on the wall, and usually a few bright lithographs of religious subjects or colored pictures from Persian or foreign magazines. There are no chairs or tables or family heirlooms. At mealtime a cloth is spread on the floor and the men of the family gather around food served in dishes on a large brass tray, and at bedtime the mattresses and blankets are spread out and everyone retires early.

The large houses have a vaulted room below the main part of the building which remains pleasantly cool even in the middle of the summer. In the courtyard is a brick oven where the characteristic flat sheets of bread are baked by the women of the house, and where the family cooking is done in copper vessels over a charcoal brazier. At one corner of the courtyard is the simple sanitation arrangement which is much like the outhouse of any country. If the family owns a pair of oxen and a donkey these animals are kept in a separate section of the courtyard, although in some regions the entire ground floor is given over to the farm animals and the living quarters of the family are all on the second floor.

Many villages have a bath. The building, constructed at the expense of the local landowner, has a series of rooms which are mostly underground so that only the upper part of the domes with their glass lighting apertures project above the surface. One man is put in charge of the community bath and it is his duty to keep it clean and see that steaming hot water is available for a given number of hours each week. The villagers can bathe as often as they wish, and everyone helps to support the bath attendant by contributions of wheat, straw, fuel, and fruit.

Usually each village has a mill in which a water-wheel turns one great millstone against another. The miller grinds wheat and barley for the community and receives from each villager a share of the flour ground.

Each village has a headman, or *kadkhuda*, who maintains order and looks after the interests of the owner or owners. There may also be a *mirab* who supervises the network of irrigation channels, diverting the proper amounts at established intervals to houses and fields. Inter-mural and intra-mural violence most frequently flares from disputes over the distribution of water.

Stores and schools are much less common than baths and mills. There may be one very small shop in every seven or eight villages, whose stock in trade is limited to sugar, tea, tobacco, rice, spices, thread, needles, nails, salt, dyes, cotton piece goods, matches, kerosene, lamp chimneys, and similar items. Elementary schools or *maktabs* are to be found in only one out of every twenty-five or thirty villages. Fundamental difficulties in extending the public school system to the villages are, first, that the average village family is small, and the help of the children in cultivating the fields is an economic necessity; and second, that the curriculum common to the urban schools has little relation to the life of the farming communities.

On the outskirts of the large villages a few houses stand among orchard or groves of poplar trees, and then the farming land begins abruptly just beyond the last walls of the village. The villagers keep their own sheep and goats and in the summer make up a village flock which is sent to the mountains in charge of the young men of the village. Most of the sheep are of the fat-tailed variety which look so comical when they are seen for the first time. An early traveler to Iran has a story about them which seems quite worthy of belief: "The Sheep are prodigiously large, trailing Tails after them of the Weight of Thirty Pounds, full of fat, which sometimes prove such Incumbrances that unless small Carts with two Wheels were provided for their Carriage they would trail upon the Ground and wound themselves against every sharp Stone and rough Place of the Ground."

The staple food of the village people is bread (normally the price of bread is about four cents a pound) or rice, according to the section of the country, *mast* (milk which is clabbered by the action of bacteria), cheese, and clarified butter. Eggs, chickens, a very small amount of mutton, onions, cucumbers, radishes, melons, fruit, nuts, and tea round out their simple diet. Mast churned with butter makes a very popular drink called *dugh*. Special events call for the more elaborate foods which are part of the regular diet of the town dwellers.

The farmers may wear a modified version of European dress, but the native costume of cotton shirt, baggy black or blue cotton trousers and a long blue cotton coat is generally worn. The women wear black trousers which are gathered at the ankles, a shirt, and a length of cotton piece goods draped around the body and over the head so that it serves as both head covering and veil, although the village women were never closely veiled as were the women of the towns. There is a natural division of labor; the men till the fields and the women look after the house and weave rugs. Marriages are arranged between heads of families, and the wedding celebrations are among the gayest occasions in village life. The groom displays his possessions in cash and kind, and the bride's family supplies quilts, clothing, and simple housekeeping equipment.

The inherent virtues and qualities of these village people can scarcely be too highly recommended. They have a quick natural intelligence, a ready sense of humor, and a lively interest in the world about them. They are extremely hospitable and friendly, and will place all their meager resources at the disposal of their honored guests. Village life is very orderly, with most disputes between individuals confined to heated discussions while more serious matters are settled by the headman of the village. There is little robbery within the villages and none of the vices of urban life. Probably the only destructive feature has been the practice of opium smoking. Opium was a means of escape from the monotony of daily toil, but it was more important as a method of alleviating the pain of diseases and sickness for which no medical treatment was available.

The villagers have only limited contact with the outside world, when the men travel to the larger towns with donkey loads of straw, fuel, fruit, and vegetables or when at less frequent intervals the families go to town to shop in the bazaars. Small detachments of the government Security Guard are stationed in certain villages and patrol the trails, maintain order, and assure the collection of taxes, but the average villager feels that he receives little benefit from the government at Tehran.

In village life there is no distinction between the hours of toil and those of amusement and recreation. There is no organization of leisure hour activity as in the West, and indeed there is little leisure except in the winter months. Conversation is the chief form of diversion and relaxation, when groups of men gather to drink tea, to discuss the weather, and to exchange news and opinions. These meetings also help to perpetuate the stories, song, and ballads of the region and to keep alive the love of poetry which is so characteristic of the Persian people.

Now, however, after centuries of somnolence the tempo of village activity is increasing. Visits to the towns and the stories of the young men who have left the villages for industrial employment have tended to create desires for material progress. Then too, outside agencies are having a direct impact upon village life. Programs of various ministries, of the Plan Organization, of ICA, and of the Near East Foundation show concrete results in such fields as prevention of disease, expansion of education facilities, improved sanitation, more productive methods of farming, cooperative marketing ventures, greater facilities for obtaining low-interest loans, and the establishment of village councils empowered to spend funds on local facilities.

Towns and Urban Life

Many of the towns of Iran fit into a pattern, populated by between 40,000 and 100,000 persons and situated about eighty miles apart along the main highways. Most of their sites were chosen because they were originally points of intersection of important trade routes, and some of them serve as collection and distribution points for farming regions. Mashhad and Qum owe much of their importance to the fact that they contain holy shrines visited by a great many pilgrims. Quite a number of the towns were developed as the capital of the country especially during the Islamic centuries when the capital was shifted from one to another of these: Isfahan, Maragha, Tabriz, Sultaniya, Qazvin, Mashhad, Shiraz, and Tehran. Such towns as Kerman, Yazd and Damghan were the seats of important local rulers.

Every town bears testimony to the program of modernization begun in the reign of Reza Shah. Beginning about 1930, wide avenues were cut through crowded residential quarters, and helped relieve congestion in the towns and to provide space for the new buildings. In only a few cases have the new avenues destroyed some of a town's former charm; at Shiraz the fine vaulted bazaar was cut through and one of the old palaces was destroyed. All the towns have newly constructed primary and secondary schools, which are quite adequate to meet local needs, and several have handsome buildings which house branches of the National Bank of Iran. Other new structures include hospitals and other government buildings. Stores line the new avenues and tend to attract shopping activity away from the older bazaars. On the outskirts are to be found the recently constructed grain silos, the electric light plants, the oil storage areas, and the factories. The principal avenues and streets of all important towns have been asphalted in the last few years and in a score of towns systems of piped water are in operation or under construction.

The larger towns boast large, modern hotels, while the smaller ones provide more simple accommodations with clean rooms and good food. There is also at least one garage equipped to do fairly complicated repair jobs on cars and trucks. It also serves as a passenger station, and in some towns there are available for travelers buildings that are a combination of the old caravanserai and the new garage.

In spite of the fact that shops line the avenues a good deal of the retail and nearly all of the wholesale business takes place in the bazaar. Essentially the bazaar is a single long street, from fifteen to twenty-five feet wide, which is covered for its entire length by vaults of fired brick so that merchants and shoppers have complete protection from the summer sun and winter rains. It is lined with small shops, usually about fifteen feet wide and twenty feet deep. At intervals wide portals lead into structures resembling caravanserais, each with a large central court surrounded on all sides by offices or store rooms and, in the finer bazaars, roofed with vaults of fired brick. These buildings are the headquarters of the wholesale merchants, and the courts are usually crammed with piles of rugs, skins, and hides; bales of cotton and cloth; boxes of spices, and other merchandise. The bazaar entrance is on the main square of the town, and the bazaar itself may run for as much as a mile until it dies out in a residential quarter. Often it pursues a winding course, and the larger bazaars have secondary branches parallel with and at right angles to the main street. The shops are stocked with both local and imported merchandise, and sales are made by bargaining rather than by fixed prices. However, both the merchant and the shopper are familiar with the current price of any article, and the give and take of the bargaining process is enjoyed to the utmost by both parties.

The public baths of the towns are considerably more elegant than those of the villages. Some are recently constructed, but many are more than a hundred years old. The older baths are as much as thirty feet below the street level so that clear, fresh water from underground channels or wells can flow directly into their tanks. The floors are paved with glazed tiles, the lower walls lined with marble or alabaster, and the upper walls and vaulted ceilings are plastered and decorated with painted designs. Among the series of rooms for the various stages of the cleansing process is usually one spacious hall which serves as a general lounging and gossip center. A few sentences from an account of a bath written in the eighteenth century give a still valid description: "Immediately within the Porch is the greatest Cell, or rather a large Room, where they doff their Cloaths, and being undressed leave their Garments; in the midst of this Place is a cistern of cold Water coming into it by several pipes. All the other Cells are so conveniently planned, that every one may breathe a different Air as to degrees of Heat; for some want a Hot Bath, others Tepid, and others a cold Bath. The Pavements are all Marble, on which, the more Hot Water is thrown, the more it increases the Heat, although at the same time the Subterranean Fire be as Hot as it can be. On these Marble Floors they at last extend themselves, when they think they have tarried in long enough, that the Barbers, whose business it is, should wind and turn every Limb and Joint of the Body, before, behind, and on every side, with that Dexterity and Slight, that it is admirable to behold them perform it; whereby they leave no Muscle, Nerve, or Superficial Joint either unmoved or not rubbed."

In the more crowded residential quarters the houses are very similar in plan and construction to those of the villages.

Those of wealthy people may be considerably larger and built of fired brick, but the open court and the reception room, opening to the south and sheltered by a porch, remain the principal elements of the plan. The best of the houses are usually on the outskirts of the town in the midst of spacious gardens. To the north of Tehran thousands of apartment buildings have sprung up in the last decade and this same trend is reflected in the other large towns. Amazing to the visitor is the rapidity with which the gardens of these new buildings, established on barren ground, become luxuriant within three or four years.

The dress of the townspeople is the result of the steps taken to modernize the country. A law passed in 1929 provided for the replacement of an ancient Persian dress with a European type of costume, and after 1935 European hats were the required headgear. The western style of suits, overcoats, and felt hats are made in countless small shops. The women of the towns, before the reign of Reza Shah, wore a length of black cloth, called the *chadar*, which covered the entire figure and was drapped over the head and held like a veil to cover all the face except the eyes. The women of the upper classes also wore a black visor which projected over the eyes. After 1936 the veil was discarded, and the head was left uncovered or crowned by a western style hat. Since 1942 there has been a trend toward a length of figured cotton cloth wound around the body and carried over the head, and this may be used as a veil. There are many dressmakers and shops handling women's clothing in the towns, and copies of *Vogue* and similar magazines are in great demand.

Persian women now enjoy a degree of freedom and equality still denied to their sisters in some other Moslem countries. A law passed in 1931 placed marriage on a civil rather than a religious basis, another law of 1935 fixed the lowest marriageable age for women at fifteen and for men at eighteen, and still other laws gave women control over their personal property. Polygamy, provided for in the Qoran, is still in force, but recently it has been discouraged by such restrictions as, for example, that a man may not take a second wife without the full knowledge and consent of both wives. In actual practice polygamy is on the wane, due partly to economic reasons but also to the changing attitude of the people.

Children are the objects of most tender parental affection. Boys are especially favored, but not so heavily as in the earlier days when the birth of a girl was an occasion for condolences rather than for congratulations. This attitude was caused by the inferior status of women; socially, even though the Moslem religion had given her a higher standing than before, and economically, in that the boy was more essential to the family and would eventually take over its support. Mothers still protect their babies and young children against the evil eye, and against sickness and disease, with superstitious rites and charms. The boys become independent and self-reliant at a very early age, and are quite capable of running a shop in the bazaar, working at a trade, or tending a flock of sheep in the high mountains.

Earlier in this century the cost of living in Iran was very low but the impact of World War II on the local economy set off an inflationary spiral which is still rising. The original cost of living index which began with the base value of 100 for 1936 was adjusted in 1959 with that year as the new base value of 100. The inflationary trend is reflected in the following table:

1936	6.6
1940	10.7
1945	58.1
1950	51.6
1955	77.1
1960	108.0
1965	115.5

Not all the items represented in the general index have risen at the same rate. Rents have risen almost three times as much as other items, with speculation in land and building in the larger towns accelerating this trend.

In general, the budgetary expenditures of a family of

average means have been distributed in approximately corresponding amounts during recent years. A table representing these expenditures in 1959 follows:

food	58 %
lodging	12 %
fuel and light	8 %
clothing	16 %
miscellaneous	6 %

The 58% item for food was spent in the following manner:

bread	16.5%
sugar	8 %
tea	2.5%
butter and cooking oils	5.5%
mutton	7.5%
chicken	0.4%
rice	4 %
vegetables	1 %
fruits	2.5%
tobacco	2.5%
cheese	1 %
flour	0.5%
other items	7.1%

The diet of the townspeople is considerably more elaborate than that of the villagers. Rice is the main course of many meals and as cooked in Iran is never moist and sticky, but fluffy and dry and altogether delicious.

When rice is prepared with meat, vegetables, or spices it is called *pelow*. Other foods may be mixed with the cooked rice, or sauces poured over it. One such rice sauce, usually served with fried chicken, contains almonds, pistachios, orange peel, and dates. Another rice dish contains pieces of fried smoked fish and a mixture of chopped parsley, leeks, dill, and coriander, and a delicious sweet-sour sauce is made of large pieces of duck, pomegranate juice and ground walnut meats.

Kababs or pieces of lamb roasted on a spit are also a favorite article of diet. A popular thick soup, called *awsh*, contains spin-

ach, beet greens, peas, beans, or lentils, and often contains *mast*.
Fine omelets are made with greens and herbs.

There is less emphasis on desserts than in our country but
during the proper season a great deal of fruit is eaten. The
Iranian melons, of which there are at least twenty distinctive
varieties including the familiar watermelons, have been famous
for centuries. As soon as the season arrives everyone begins
eating melons and, according to one old account: "They will
eat at that time a matter of ten or twelve Pound of Melon a
day, for a Fortnight or three weeks together; and this is as
much for Health's sake as it is to please the Palates, for they
look upon it as a great refresher and colorer of their blood.
After the first Melons, there come up different sorts every
Day, and the later these Fruits are, the better. The latest of
them all are White, and you would swear that they were
nothing but one entire Lump of pure Sugar." Isfahan in particular is noted for its melons, and in one small area north of
the city grows a much relished variety which is so fragile and
delicate that if a horseman gallops by the fruits will split open
on the vine. During the seventeenth century, melons were
sent all the way from Iran to the court at Agra in India. They
were carried by men who suspended two baskets, with a melon
in each, hung on a pole over their shoulders, and walked for
eighty days to reach their destination. The hardier melons are
stored in caves below the ground and keep very well throughout the winter.

Sherbets are still very popular, although apparently less so
than they used to be. The word itself is a Persian one which
has passed directly into the English language. Sherbets were
either drinks cooled with ice or snow or the same ingredients
frozen into flavored ices: "Sherbets are made of almost all
Tart pleasing Fruits as the Juice of the Pomegranates, Lemons, Citrons (limes), and Oranges which are brought to the
Markets." One popular drink was made of violets, vinegar
and pomegranate juice and another consisted of water, sugar,
lime juice and a touch of garlic juice. A currently common
warm weather drink is made of water, vinegar, sugar, and
sliced cucumbers. In the earlier days such drinks were served

20. Aerial view of the Iranian petroleum installations at Abadan

21. The Baharestan, housing the sessions of the Parliament at Tehran

22. The Ministry of Foreign Affairs at Tehran

23. The Nemazee Hospital, a unit in the new Shiraz Medical Center

in huge porcelain bowls and sipped from the large spoons with beautifully carved handles which were the specialty of the wood-carvers in the town of Abadeh, where such carving is still done. However, carbonated soft drinks are now enormously popular: there is a Pepsi-Cola bottling plant on the outskirts of Tehran and a plant to produce ginger ale under construction. The country turns out considerable quantities of local white and red wines, beer, vodka, and other alcoholic beverages.

The large towns have mechanical ice plants but throughout most of the country there are only the local ice houses, whose most important feature is a mud wall at least ten yards high and running in an east-west direction. On the north side of the wall several square pits are dug, and when freezing weather arrives water is put into the pits. Usually the cold will be sufficient to freeze only an inch or two of water during the night, and each day the accumulated ice is broken up and more water added while the high wall prevents the sun's rays from melting the ice during the daytime. After a week or so when each piece of ice is five or six feet thick, it is removed to a special storage chamber under a roof thickly insulated with brush or reeds. Snow is also commonly used during the summer, collected and stored by dwellers in the highest mountain villages, and when hot weather comes, carried on donkey back to the nearest town.

The townspeople normally have a better education and higher social position than the villagers, and are the products of long centuries of cultural continuity. Social graces have been developed to a very high degree. As far back as the seventeenth century a visitor to the country wrote: "The Persians are the most Civilized People of the East, and the greatest Complimenters in the World." Another traveler remarked: "Friendly and Courteous Salutation is no where so much promoted as among the Persians, for the very Plebians, in other parts surly and unconversable, are here Affable and Kind, not Rude and Unmannerly." Indeed, the Persian tradition of politeness and hospitality dates back to a most remote period. In the Old Testament we read of the tolerance shown by the Persians to other races and religions, while history has recorded incidents of their kindly behavior toward defeated enemies at a time when barbaric cruelty was common to the ancient world.

The many forms of polite address have grown into a formal ritual of almost endless variety. Such ingrained habits of speech are not easily cast aside, and today the people, including even those who endorse a complete break with the past, begin speaking with such phrases as "I make the humble remark," or, "This slave believes that . . . ," while the phrase "you and I" will be rendered in Persian as, "This slave and your honor." The phraseology is, however, less ornate than in former years. To say a man was dead the speaker used to say, "He has made a gift of the share of life which he had, otherwise he might have lived still many years; but out of the love he has for you he has joined them to those you still have to run."

A characteristic form of Persian politeness was the use of honorary titles. When these were conferred by the Shah on his generals and nobles, they often took the place of personal names. Common titles meant: "Upholder of the Realm," "Intelligence of the Empire," and "Splendor of the Country." Titles other than those conferred by the Shah were also in common use, and during the seventeenth century a book was compiled which listed the proper title for every class of man from Shah down to shoemaker. A few years ago a law was passed which forbade their granting and use, but cabinet ministers and members of the older generation are still known by their titles.

Social and community activities reach their greatest development at Tehran. Fifteen or more larger towns have motion picture houses; Tehran has about twenty, as well as several legitimate theaters. Many of the plays are based upon the *Shahnama* of Firdawsi, while others are original modern compositions or translations and adaptations of western works. Musical programs also are popular at Tehran, and the city has an excellent orchestra which plays not only the standard classics of the western composers but Iranian works as well, based upon the folk music of the country. There are concerts given by the orchestra of the School of Music and by some of the school choirs.

Certain forms of entertainment more common in former days still linger on both in the older residential quarters of Tehran and in the towns. The magician makes his rounds, and the fortuneteller attracts his clients. The snake-charmers put on a show which includes, strangely enough, an educational lecture on the life and behavior of various species of snake. Dervishes in their picturesque costumes were much in evidence until about fifteen years ago, when the authorities decided that they were out of place in the modern picture and forbade them to enter the towns. Now they have begun to appear once more. The word dervish is itself a Persian one, meaning "humble," "poor," or "one who lives by alms." The dervishes really correspond to our Christian monks, and are divided into a number of religious orders each with its own tenets and regulations. In Iran the dervishes lead a more wandering life than in the other Moslem countries. A minority are deeply religious men who have taken vows of poverty and chastity, but the majority have lived by their wits and on the credulity of the common people. Their usual costume is a long varicolored patchwork cloak belted with a rope girdle from which hangs a string of wooden beads. Over their shoulders is draped a dressed panther or wolfskin, and on their heads is a skullcap embroidered with verses from the Qoran. Their matted hair hangs to shoulder length and their feet are often bare. Slung over one shoulder is a horn and they carry a weapon for protection against wild beasts, usually a steel battle-axe or a wooden club studded with sharp spikes, and a begging bowl made from a hollowed gourd and decorated with fine carving.

On entering a village or town the dervishes blow loud blasts on their horns and cry out, "Ya Hak, Ya Hak" or "O Truth." They then bring into play whatever specialty they have developed for obtaining gifts of food and money. Some claim to have medical skill and sell "Pills of Gladness," composed of herbs mixed with earth from the sites of holy shrines. They also sell amulets or talismans: scraps of paper bearing religious verses which will serve to ward off the evil eye and to prevent disease or injury. They tell fortunes using several different devices, the most usual one being four brass dice loosely fastened together on a metal shaft which give four-number combinations each of which has its own special interpretation. To the crowds which gather around them they also tell stories; Persian poetry is their specialty, and they may know hundreds of verses from the *Shahnama* as well as many selections from Hafiz and Sa'di.

The *zur khaneh* or "house of strength" is an old Iranian institution which continues to flourish both in Tehran and in the provinces. Its organization is like that of a physical culture society, and its members are drawn from every occupation and social level. It is believed that the zur khaneh originated in a remote period when Iran was occupied by foreigners and the youth of the country trained in secret against the day when they would be able to expel the invaders. Each zur khaneh has one large room containing a pit about twenty feet square and three feet deep, a raised platform for the drummer, and a space for spectators. About twelve men, clad only in gaily embroidered knee-length trousers, enter the pit and perform to an accompaniment of stirring drum beats and the chanting of verses from the *Shahnama*; they do push-ups in unison, juggle large and very heavy Indian clubs, and jump high in the air and spin about. The military origin of the zur khaneh seems to be attested to by exercises with large wooden shields and iron bows which have links of iron chain in place of a bow string. Wrestling matches, in both Persian and European style, are the climax and finale of each session.

Tea houses and cafés are the popular public gathering places of the small towns where men drop in for tea, for friendly conversation, for a game of backgammon, and to smoke the water-pipe. Tea is the Persian's favorite drink: it is served in glasses with plenty of sugar, although often the drinker holds a lump of sugar between his teeth and sips the tea through it. The custom of tea drinking seems to have come from Russia fairly recently, for during the seventeenth and eighteenth centuries the Persians drank a great deal of coffee, which was quite unknown in the West until European travelers discovered it in Turkey and Iran. In 1652 a Mr. D. Edwards, who was a merchant trading with Turkey, began to call himself a "coffeeman" and to import the berries to England, where coffee drinking soon became a fashionable fad. An Englishman who visited the coffee houses of Isfahan in 1627 wrote: "The coffee, or coho, is a drink black as soot, or rather a broth, seeing that they sip it as hot as their mouth can well suffer out of small China cups. 'Tis strongly scented and somewhat bitter, distrained from berries beat into a powder and boiled with water: if supped hot comforts the brain, helps raw stomachs, aids digestion, expels melancholy and sleep. However unsavory it seems at first, it becomes pleasing and delicious enough by custom."

At Tehran cafés replace the tea houses of the towns. Many of them are in pleasant gardens and in the late afternoon they are crowded with family groups who linger for coffee, tea, a cold drink, ice cream, and pastry. Restaurants are, of course, to be found in every town but Persian families nearly always eat in their own homes.

One of the most common family diversions is a holiday trip into the country. The weekly holiday of the Moslems is Friday, and on this day the families pack a picnic lunch and set out by train or bus or on foot for some shady garden beyond the edge of town. There are fifteen official public holidays in the year and all are of a religious nature except those which mark the New Year, the birthday of the Shah, and the anniversary of the Constitution.

No Ruz, the New Year, is March 21, the first day of spring and the sun's vernal equinox. The Iranians have celebrated the arrival of spring for many centuries as evidenced by the long rows of sculptured reliefs at Persepolis showing groups of people from every part of the mighty Achaemenid empire bringing their tribute to the ruler of Iran on this occasion.

Preparations for No Ruz begin well in advance. Fifteen days before the festival, each household plants in a shallow bowl seeds of wheat or lentils which by the proper time have sent up a thicket of fresh green shoots several inches high as a token of spring. Several days before No Ruz the small villages are treated to an amusing spectacle. The "man who burns fire" parades through the streets, accompanied by a masked troupe of performers wearing high hats and cloaks of many colors to which are fastened small bells. The troupe may include a tightrope walker, wrestlers, a trained monkey and a dancing bear. One of them strikes two boards together and repeats:

> The fire-maker has come.
> He comes once each year.
> I am the fire-maker and an orphan.
> I am poor one day each year.
> Intestines and guts have come.
> Whoever wasn't here has come.

The last Wednesday of the old year is a special festival called *Chahr Shambeh Suri*. On the eve of this day each family used to prepare bundles of dry wood or desert thorn and make a bonfire. Everyone in the house then jumped over the flame while they addressed to the fire these verses:

> You take the yellowness from me,
> I take your redness.
> You take the coldness from me,
> I take your warmth.

The fire must not be breathed upon, and the dead ashes are to be scattered at a crossroads. Certainly this custom is a survival of rites performed in very ancient times.

For No Ruz household servants and minor government employees receive an extra month's wages, the house receives its spring cleaning, and everyone dresses in new clothes. On New Year's Eve a light must burn in every room in the house and a special table is prepared. The centerpiece consists of a mirror and candlesticks, and grouped around it are a copy of the Qoran, a large sheet of bread, a bowl of water in which floats a green leaf, a glass of rosewater, nuts, fruit, candy, colored eggs, chicken, and fish. A large plate or tray contains the *haft sin*—seven articles whose names begin with the Per-

sian letter S. *Sepand, sib, sir, serkeh, samanu, sabzi,* and *sumaq*
are the English wild rue, apples, garlic, vinegar, a paste of
malt grain, greens, and sumac.

As the time of the vernal equinox approaches all the household is grouped around the table to await the exact moment of
the New Year, said to be marked by the moving of the leaf on
the surface of the water or by the rotation of an egg placed on
the mirror. In large towns a cannon is fired to announce the
New Year. Not all the customs and ceremonies associated with
No Ruz are now performed in the towns, but those described
below are observed by every family.

The New Year begins a period of five days of official holidays devoted to social calls. During the first two or three days
the eldest members of the family remain at home to receive
calls from friends and relatives, and large sums are spent on
the entertainment of the guests. Return calls are paid, and the
atmosphere of these days is one of contentment and rejoicing.

On the thirteenth day of the New Year, considered an un-
lucky day, the bowls of green shoots grown in the houses are
thrown out into the streets, if possible into running water, and
everyone troops out into the open country for a promenade in
the fresh green fields. Each family takes along as elaborate a
supply of food as its means permit, and spends the entire day
in the open. The people believe that in this way they do not
only welcome the spring but carry the bad luck associated
with the thirteenth day away from their homes and abandon
it in the country where it can do no harm. On this day the
young girls recite the good luck verses:

> The thirteenth outside for good cheer,
> And before another year
> It will bring a husband dear,
> And a child in my arms.

Tehran

Writing early in the twelfth century a geographer mentioned Tehran as a village in the district of Ray. For centuries
it remained small and obscure, with a limited reputation for

its fine fruit and shady groves. The Safavid rulers camped at the site and in A.D. 1785 Karim Khan Zand had a royal palace erected there. In 1788 the Qajar ruler Aqa Muhammad chose Tehran as the capital of the country: at that time it had fewer than 15,000 people. This ruler began the Gulistan palace and his successor Fath 'Ali Shah built the once vast palace and garden called the Qasr-i-Qajar north of the town in the early nineteenth century and also the Masjid-i-Shah, or Imperial Mosque, still standing in the bazaar area.

Nasr ad-din Shah, 1848-1896, who made several trips to Europe, tried to emulate European towns and provided Tehran with a horse-drawn tramway, factories, administrative structures, a hospital, a power station, post-office, etc. The covered bazaar and the impressive Sepahselar mosque were erected near the end of his reign as were royal palaces in the Shemiran area. The population reached 170,000.

Slowly growing Tehran took a fresh lease of life during the fifteen-year reign of Reza Shah. An entire new town sprang up on the northern outskirts of the older one. Wide, asphalted avenues, marble-clad buildings for the ministries, a monumental officers' club, and a central police headquarters and a national bank building both modeled after the architectural style of Achaemenid times. Since 1946 this growth has been even more rapid; a few years ago Shah Reza avenue was at the northern limits of the city but now the built-up region stretches far beyond.

Two wide avenues climb some six miles to the Shemiran area, several hundred feet higher than Tehran and much cooler in summer, and a third highway is under contruction. Hundreds of new houses and apartment houses are gradually filling up the entire distance between the city and its resort suburbs. It is indeed fortunate that Aqa Muhammad selected Tehran as the capital, for no other town in Iran could have provided such a suitable, well watered and wooded topography for such vast expansion.

Travel about the city of one and a half million people is by taxi, station wagon, and bus—all relatively inexpensive. Parking in town is a problem and in the late afternoon many of

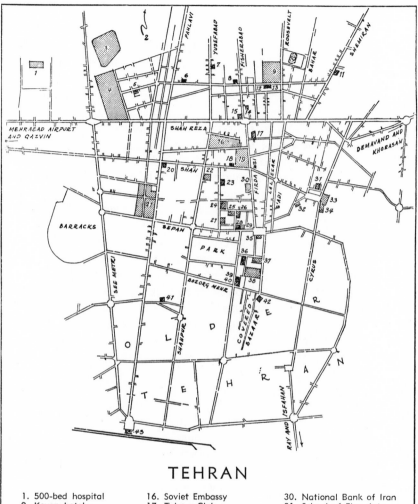

TEHRAN

the main avenues are jammed with traffic; most of the country's automobiles are concentrated at Tehran. There are at least ten adequate or better hotels most of them quite new and situated near the business and shopping area. There is also a handful of interesting restaurants, some located in gardens during the summer months. Houses and apartments are available for high rents; houses in Shemiran usually have a spacious garden and a pool for swimming.

Most of the shopping takes place between Shah Reza avenue and Istanbul avenue to the south. Visitors are attracted by the colorful carpet shops and the many stores, concentrated along Firdawsi avenue, crammed with Persian antiquities and modern handicrafts. Lalezar avenue has its own row of fascinating jewelry shops where pieces may be made to order.

The visitor has a considerable choice of things to see and do. In the city are the Archaeological museum; the Ethnographical museum; Sepahselar mosque; the old bazaar and the Masjid-i-Shah; the extensive Gulistan palace featuring a royal museum with two jewel-encrusted thrones and the imperial collection of illuminated manuscripts and miniatures; and the National Bank complex with its display of the fabulous crown jewels and the athletic displays of its zur khaneh.

The Shemiran area comprises some 60 villages nestled in the foothills of the Elborz range. The Qajar palace Sahib Qaraniyeh is at Niavaran and just above Tajrish are the extensive grounds and the summer palaces of the present royal family. Throughout the area footpaths along mountain streams wind steadily upward passing falls, pools, orchards and meadows and many charming picnic sites.

With a car the visitor can cover a wider area. Historical remains are to be found at Ray, five miles south of Tehran and once one of the mightiest cities of the mediaeval world. Shah Abdul Azim, just adjacent to the ancient site, has its saintly shrine, crowned by a golden dome, and nearby is the stately mausoleum of Reza Shah. Varamin, twenty-five miles south of Tehran, has monuments of Moslem architecture of the thirteenth and fourteenth centuries—a mosque, tomb tower, and shrine. Demavand village, some 35 miles east and north of Tehran at a height of nearly 7,000 feet, is located in a picturesque mountain setting, dotted with structures of the Seljuq and Mongol periods. In the summer many people pass through Demavand village on their way to climb Mount Demavand; the climb itself is not difficult but sulphur fumes make the experience somewhat trying. In winter skiing is featured at Ab 'Ali, some 30 miles east of Tehran.

Tehran offers three different faces to the foreign visitors or resident: the crowded area of the old town which has little to attract him; the cosmopolitan, bustling new city, teaming with traffic and with new construction springing up everywhere; and the surrounding countryside with its countless pleasant retreats from the turmoil of the town.

Isfahan

Above all other towns in Iran, Isfahan rewards the tourist in search of the monuments and atmosphere of the country's glorious culture. An hour by plane from Tehran or a short day's run by bus or car, Isfahan is particularly delightful in the spring when flowering orchards are everywhere and the Zayandeh Rud fills its banks as a noble river should.

The foundation of Isfahan dates from the pre-Islamic centuries and it was a renowned center of trade and culture under local Moslem princes and then the capital of the vast kingdom of the Seljuqs. Spared devastation by the Mongols, it reached its greatest fame under the Safavid rulers and fell into slow decline after siege and capture by an Afghan army early in the eighteenth century.

At the end of the long covered bazaar is the great Masjid-i-Jami', or Congregational Mosque, whose great open court is flanked by dome chambers, ivans, and prayer halls that were erected at intervals over the long centuries. Two dome chambers are of the Seljuq period and feature decoration and inscriptions in brick patterns, while additions of later periods display surfaces of bright faience mosaic.

But the principal spectacle at Isfahan is the remains of the imperial city built by Shah 'Abbas between the old town and the river. Celebrating the New Year festival at Isfahan in 1598 the Safavid ruler decided to move the capital of Iran to this spot. The focal point of the grandiose plan was the Maidan-i-Shah, or Imperial Square, a rectangle 570 yards long and 175 yards wide. A uniform facade in two stories still enclose the square: its shops housed sellers of jewelry, cloth, and drugs. On weekly market days the square was thronged with booths and buyers and on special occasions the Shah and his courtiers played at polo; the stone goal posts stand at either end.

In 1613 work was begun on the Masjid-i-Shah, or Imperial Mosque, situated at the southern end of the maidan and although the ruler pressed for speed the entire complex was not completed until after twenty years of unremitting effort. The mosque is one of the supreme monuments of Persian architecture. From a lofty entrance portal the way leads into an open court flanked by great ivans and arcades; all the bulk of the mosque is turned at an angle to the square itself in order to be oriented directly toward Mecca. Inside and out, the surfaces of walls, pillars, vaults, minarets and dome are clad in multicolored tiles in which light and dark blues predominate.

A monumental entrance to the old covered bazaar was erected at the northern end of the maidan in 1617. Traces of a huge painting which depicted the victory of Shah 'Abbas over the Uzbeks is still visible on the rear wall. Crowning the portal was a musician's gallery where drums and oboes played long and loud every night just at sundown.

Near the center of the long east side of the maidan is the well preserved mosque of Shaykh Lutfullah. This was one of the first structures to be started, although the decorative details were not completed until 1619. From its brilliantly colored portal a corridor leads around and into the single chamber of the mosque; at a higher level the square chamber is transformed into a lovely dome, pierced by sixteen grilled windows. Every square inch of the interior is decorated with mosaic faience and the light streaming through the grilles pours changing patterns of color upon the sparkling walls.

The effect is so elegant, so rich, so dazzling, so unique that the visitor loses touch with time and reality.

On the western side of the maidan stands the Ali Qapu, or Lofty Gateway, the noble entrance to the palace grounds and gardens. In addition to that function it was the administrative center for the royal court, dealing with countless personnel and equipment, supplies and treasures. Rising some six stories, the structure had as many as ten rooms on some levels; a lofty open porch overlooked the entire maidan and eighteen huge tree trunks sheathed with flat strips still uphold the roof decorated in blue and gold. Royal audiences were held at the Ali Qapu and accounts of the arrival of foreign ambassadors with their precious presents make fascinating reading. Inside the structure all the ceilings were decorated with floral patterns in red, blue, and gold, while the walls had scenes of courtly pleasures in country and garden; much of this decoration remains.

Of the many pavilions and palaces scattered through the gardens to the west of the Ali Qapu only the palace called the Chehel Sutun, or Forty Columns, remains. Restored and housing a museum of objects from the Safavid and earlier periods, it is a highlight of a visit to Isfahan. The great open porch with its towering wooden columns overlooks a long reflecting pool and from a recess back of the porch three doors lead into a banquet hall which extends the full width of the structure. Six enormous oil paintings adorn the upper walls and help to visualize the turbulent and lusty life of the seventeenth century: they show battles and royal parties in which dancing and drinking hold the stage.

To the west of the palace area proper was the Chahar Bagh, or Four Gardens, not intended to serve as a busy street as at the present day but as a place of promenade. From a corner of the palace grounds it ran down grade for nearly a mile to the river, crossed by the Allah Verdi Khan bridge, and then up rising ground to a now vanished royal estate called the Hazar Jerib, or Thousand Acres. Eight rows of plane trees and poplars, among which grew a profusion of roses and jasmine, were spaced across the sixty-yard width of the promenade. Five watercourses ran down the avenue and at each change in level was a marble pool with its fountains. Not until near the end of the nineteenth century were many of the fine old trees cut down, while in recent years wide strips at each side have been paved with asphalt. Just enough of the original aspect remains to realize that a seventeenth century traveler was deadly serious when he described it as the most beautiful avenue that he had ever seen or heard talked about.

Both sides of the Chahar Bagh were lined with garden pavilions belonging to nobles and set in spacious grounds: one remains in ruins, the Hasht Behesht, or Gate of Paradise. However, the site of one such pavilion is occupied by a charming later structure, the Madrasa Mader-i-Shah, or Religious School of the Mother of the Shah, completed in the year 1714. An entrance façade of multicolor tile and polished marble leads into a rectangular court. Two-story arcades provide separate living rooms for religious teachers and students and the reflection of the whitewashed arcades shimmer in dark pools. A great dome rises high above the sanctuary chamber.

Crossing the Zayandeh Rud on the bridge mentioned above one reaches Julfa, the settlement of Armenian weavers and craftsmen brought by Shah 'Abbas from Julfa in Azerbaijan. These settlers enjoyed royal protection and built a splendid cathedral in the years between 1606 and 1654 and two additional churches. Today the cathedral is open and deserves a visit, both as an architectural monument and because of the unique manner in which the Persian tilework was used in the interior. In the grounds of the cathedral is a museum of Armenian antiquities and treasures.

As the visitor tours the monuments of the time of Shah 'Abbas and of other periods he has no way of knowing that years of painstaking effort have gone into the restoration and preservation of these structures. National monuments throughout the country are in charge of the Antiquities Service, and at Isfahan skilled tile cutters, masons, plasterers, and engineers have been at work for a quarter of a century. As one example, more than a decade ago the exterior surface of the great domes were in pitiful condition; then they were surrounded by towering scaffolds, and after several years of planning, cutting, and fitting minute pieces of tile these surfaces were restored to their original condition.

Isfahan has its own attractive environs, featuring pleasant villages upstream and along the banks of the Zayandeh Rud. The one requisite to enjoyment is time, for many villages are remote and not near any highway.

Shiraz

This southern town is renowned for its poets, its gardens, and its wine; all three having centuries of tradition. Just over three hours by air from Tehran, it is a long day's journey by car from Isfahan. The trip to the Achaemenid capital of Persepolis only 35 miles to the north is an easy one; hotel accommodations are available at the site.

Shiraz has the long and eventful history common to many Persian towns. For centuries it has been the capital of Fars, or Pars, the area which gave its name to Persia. The town was subdued in turn by Timur, by a great flood, and by the same Afghan army that took Isfahan, but in the middle of the eighteenth century it came back to life and splendor under the benevolent attention of a regent-ruler of Iran, Karim Khan Zand. He embellished the town with a citadel at its center, a magnificent covered bazaar with very high vaults of wide span, the Masjid-i-Vakil, or Mosque of the Regent, his own private garden palace in the town—today housing a museum —and spacious gardens on the northeastern slopes above the town.

The best approach is from the northeast and through the pass of Allaho Akbar, "God is Great," so called from the usual expression of wonder at the sight of blooming, fertile Shiraz. The wide avenue leading down into the town was once lined on either side by gardens and pavilions; a surviving structure houses a hotel which offers a splendid view across groves of orange trees and ranks of stately cypresses. Indeed the soaring cypress trees are the hallmark of Shiraz.

Within the town the visitor may see the Masjid-i-Vakil;

the Masjid-i-No, or New Mosque—built in the twelfth century—and the very famous Masjid-i-Atiq, or Ancient Mosque.
Parts of this monument date back to the ninth century but in
recent years garish reconstruction and repairs have hidden
the work of earlier periods. The soaring, bulbous domes of
revered shrines dominate this old section of the town. Most
of Karim Khan's fine bazaar was demolished in favor of a
broad, paved avenue—a brutal action in the name of progress.

Outside the town there is much to see. To the northeast are
the tombs of Hafiz and Sa'di, places of pilgrimage for all
Iranians. Hafiz lies under an open kiosk, surrounded by other
graves, and in a fragrant garden. Persian visitors take a *fal*,
or augury, at the tomb; his poems opened at random give
the answer to questions in the minds of his devotees. Some
distance to the east is the tomb of Sa'di. A few years ago the
old structure sheltering the grave was replaced by a new building, combining elements of Moslem style and of modern construction. On these slopes above the towns and on its other
outskirts are to be found some of the fine old gardens, or
baghs, of Shiraz, such as the Bagh-i-Eram, Bagh-i-Delgosha,
Bagh-i-Golshan, and the ruined hillside Garden of the Throne,
or Bagh-i-Takht. Gradually these gardens and others will disappear as the town expands.

Not all the interest of Shiraz is in its past for the town has
a lively, busy air not to be rivaled in Iran. The Shirazis are
local boosters as well as poets and there are many signs of this
public interest. The portal at the Allaho Akbar pass is a gift
to the town by a local merchant, and others have contributed
land or buildings related to modern requirements. To the
northwest of the town is situated the wonderfully modern and
well-staffed Shiraz Medical Center, with its Nemazee Hospital
and Nursing School. Adjacent is the Khalili Eye Hospital,
now under construction. The Shiraz Medical School is in this
same vicinity and the new Pahlavi University is also situated
in this same general area.

Tabriz

Tabriz, capital of the province of Azerbaijan in north-western Iran, is two hours by plane from Tehran. Long one of the leading commercial centers of the country, located on the great highway across Asia, it was also the capital of the region during the Mongol period and again in Safavid times. Until this century the crown prince had the post of governor-general of Azerbaijan. Rainfall is more abundant in this region than over most of the plateau and dry farming is customary; the area is an abundant granary.

Tabriz itself has few monuments of great interest. The remains of the huge vaulted Mosque of ʿAli Shah, built early in the fourteenth century and later incorporated into the citadel are visible, and the badly battered Blue Mosque displays the finest mosaic faience and carved alabaster. Tabriz is a center for excursions to towns and sites such as Maragha, Marand, and Rezaieh. Roads lead to Turkey and to Iraq. Tabriz has long been the terminus of a wide gauge railway which entered Iran from Russia at Julfa. Now the new Iranian line coming from Tehran to Tabriz is being extended to the Turkish frontier.

Mashhad

Rivaling Tabriz in commercial importance but far more noted for its holy shrine, Mashhad is some three hours plane flight from Tehran and at the end of a branch line of the Iranian railway which traverses the northeastern part of the country. Long the capital of the province of Khorasan, Mashhad —the very name means "burial place of a martyr"—owes its chief fame to being the site of the burial shrine of ʿAli Reza, eighth Imam of the Shiʿa line. The Imam Reza was poisoned in the ninth century.

The town is bisected by a north-south avenue and at its heart a circular avenue encompasses the shrine on all sides. Conditions vary from year to year: sometimes the entire shrine area is open to non-Moslems and at others they are allowed only in the outer courtyard. Great open courts are on other side of the complex containing the actual tomb chamber. That to the west is the oldest and is represented by the Mosque of Gawhar Shad, built between 1405 and 1417. That to the east is largely of the Safavid period and various Safavid and Qajar rulers supplied the funds for gilding the great dome, its flanking minarets and the arched portal nearest the tomb chamber. The chamber itself has lower walls encased in tiles and upper walls and ceiling entirely covered with mirror work. The great sarcophagus, set in one corner, is sheltered within silver grillwork. Throughout the years streams of pilgrims come to the shrine from all corners of Iran, and from Pakistan, Afghanistan, and Iraq.

The finest treasures of the shrine—carpets, hangings, bronzes, manuscripts, miniature paintings and illuminated Qorans—are housed in a modern museum building which is open to all visitors. Among modern products the fine carpets of the province and the turquoises, from mines in the vicinity which have been worked for centuries, are outstanding.

Religion

Islam is the official religion of Iran. *Islam*, as used in the Qoran dictated to the Prophet Muhammad, means "submission to the will of God." Its five obligations are: the confession of Faith expressed in the formula "There is no God but Allah and Muhammad is His Prophet"; the five daily ritual prayers; the fast from sunrise to sunset during the month of Ramadan; required and voluntary alms; and the pilgrimage to Mecca.

The history of the rise of Islam and the position of the religion in Iran has been given in another section. Attention must now be centered upon the origin, growth, and beliefs of the Shi'a sect of Islam, for ninety per cent of the people of Iran belong to this group, which also has adherents in Syria, Iraq, Afghanistan, and India.

The sons of Muhammad died in childhood. His daughter Fatima, who married 'Ali, was the only one of his daughters to give him male heirs. The two sons of 'Ali and Fatima were named Hasan and Husein.

Upon the death of Muhammad the question of a successor and spiritual head of the new faith arose at once, and the choice fell upon Abu Bekr, who held the post but two years, from 632 until 634. Then came 'Umar, who was assassinated in 642, and after him the aged 'Uthman, another son-in-law of Muhammad. Dissatisfaction against 'Uthman arose on many sides, and a respected companion of Muhammad and other influential people began to preach in favor of 'Ali and of the rights of his family to the Caliphate, or headship of the religion. In 656 'Uthman was killed and 'Ali was chosen as Caliph. Moawiya, governor of Syria and cousin of 'Uthman, refused allegiance and fighting broke out, and in 661, 'Ali was assassinated by a member of still another hostile group.

After his death the Shi'ites, or the "partisans" of the family of 'Ali, chose his son Hasan as his successor. However, the power was held by Moawiya, who moved the capital from Medina in Arabia to Damascus, and whose line was known as the Omayyads. Before his death Moawiya named his son Yazid as his successor but Husein, the younger brother of Hasan, was urged to press his rightful claim to the Caliphate. He and his small band of faithful followers were surrounded on the plain of Kerbala in Iraq, and after a period of ten days they were all put to death.

In 749 the Omayyads gave way to the 'Abbasids whose line was descended from the uncle of Muhammad. The 'Abbasid Caliphs settled at Baghdad and held temporal and spiritual power as heads of the Sunni sect of Islam until the line was wiped out by the Mongols in 1258.

Shi'ism continued strong in Iran whenever such successive local dynasties as the Saffarids, the Samanids, and the Buvayhids flirted with the sect, partly from conviction and also because it served to differentiate Iran from the Arab world, although Shi'a dynasties also sprang up in Egypt and North Africa. One reason for the appeal of Shi'ism to the masses was a popular myth according to which Husein had married a daughter of the last ruler of the Sasanian line.

According to the Shi'ites, the true successors to the spiritual leadership of Islam continued through the line of 'Ali in the series of the twelve Imams. Each Imam of the line was considered to have divine infallibility, each could work miracles, each named his own successor, and each met with death by violence. The Twelfth Imam, known as the Hidden Imam, disappeared into a cave while still a young man, and it is believed that he will eventually return as the Mahdi when the world approaches its end. Divisions arose within the Shi'a sect over the question of the line of the Imams. The Zaid Shi'ites of Arabia place their faith only in the first five, while the Karmathians and Isma'ilians recognize only the first seven. The Isma'ilians within Iran, a powerful group first led by Hasan as-Sabbah and known to the western world as the Assassins, were finally overthrown by the Mongol invaders.

The Shi'ites of Iran believe in the entire line of the Imams, and follow the teachings of J'afar, the sixth Imam, who was greatly respected as an authority on law and tradition. Shi'ism came into its own in Iran with the Safavid rulers whose ancestor, Shaykh Safi ad-din, claimed descent from the seventh Imam, and has been the official religion of Iran since about 1500. The Constitution designates the Jafarite sect as the religion of the country, and provides that the article in which the faith is proclaimed is to remain in effect until the appearance of the Mahdi, the Imam of the Time.

Shi'ism and Sunnism have split less on questions of belief than politically, as opposing factions or states made use of the division to promote their temporal power. The Shi'as are, of course, ardent believers in the authority of the family of Muhammad and do not, as do the Sunnis, admit that of the companions of Muhammad. They believe that Muhammad recognized 'Ali as his successor, and bless the names of 'Ali, Hasan and Husein. The Shi'a doctors of religious laws are held to be inspired by the Hidden Imam, and their statements are granted much greater authority than those of the Sunni theologians. The Imams are worshipped as martyrs, and the Shi'ites make pilgrimages not only to Mecca but also to the shrines of 'Ali at Nejef and of Husein at Kerbala, both in Iraq; of 'Ali Reza, the eighth Imam, at Mashhad; and of Fatima, the sister of Imam Reza, at Qum. There are also many lesser shrines of local saints, the so-called Imamzadehs, or sons of the Imams, scattered throughout Iran.

The public religious holidays observed in Iran are the anniversary of the Birth of 'Ali; the Mission of the Prophet Muhammad; the Birth of the Twelfth Imam; the Wounding of 'Ali; the Death of 'Ali; the *Fetr*, or festival marking the end of the fasting month of Ramadan; the *Ghorban*, or day of sacrifice; the *Ghadir*, or investiture of 'Ali as the successor of Muhammad; the *Tassoua* and *Ashura*, or days of the Martyrdom of Husein; the Martyrdom of Hasan; and the Birth of Muhammad.

The Shi'as of Iran mark the tragedy of Kerbala with sermons, processions of flagellants, and the type of drama called *ta'ziyeh*. These tragic plays are grouped into three cycles—the state of affairs before the battle at Kerbala, the battle itself, and the aftermath of Kerbala. During the reign of Reza Shah the processions were forbidden and the plays discouraged; recently both manifestations of mourning and grief have been revived.

A number of special aspects of Islam continue to be practised in Iran. The *sufis*, or devotees of mysticism, are to be found at all social levels and many draw inspiration from the shrines of the renowned mystics of earlier centuries. Sects other than the Shi'as are active, such as the Isma'ilis, headed by their new Aqa Khan, and the Shaykhi, centered at Kerman. Indeed, Islam is a self-reforming religion and at any moment many movements of reform are ardently or quietly active.

While Islam has no organized hierarchy, certain titles or designations are used to distinguish special members of the Moslem community in Iran. A descendant of the prophet Muhammad uses the title Sayyid as a part of his name. Religious pilgrims are less distinguished for this fact than formerly, but a man who has been to Mecca may be known as Hajji; one who has been to the tomb of Husein as Kerbeli; and one who has visited the shrine of Imam Reza at Mashhad as Mashhadi or Mashdi.

A Moslem cleric of limited training in theology is a *mullah*, while one who has studied at such a higher institution as the Sepahsalar Theological College at Tehran may become a *mujtahid*. A few of the most important Iranian religious leaders, resident either in Iran or at the Shi'a shrines in Iraq, bear the honorary title of Ayatollah. At Tehran the learned mujtahids and Ayatollahs may come together in a Body of Ulemas to render decisions relative to religious doctrine, while the Shar'ia court at Tehran may try purely religious controversies. The Imam Jom'eh of Tehran, currently a doctor in law from a French university and a member of the noted Imam Jom'eh Tehrani family, has the responsibility of reciting the Friday prayers in the mosque on behalf of the ruler.

Lacking a governing hierarchy, there is no operative means by which an Iranian Moslem may be excommunicated or brought to account for irreligious actions. It is true that the religious leaders resident at the Shi'a shrines in Iraq or the highly respected leader at the shrine at Qum may issue decrees which have the force of law to the faithful, but these leaders generally refrain from activity in that field where politics and religion mingle. Thus it is that in the last few years some of the more worldly clerics have been free to agitate for retrogressive social customs, to support fanaticism, and to engage in political activity—including assassination. Several such groups or societies were active during 1951 and 1952 and there was even friction between various religious elements, such as between the followers of Ayatollah Sayyid Abol Qasem Kashani and those of Navab Safavi, fanatical head of the Devotees of Islam. In addition, Soviet-inspired front organizations succeeded in capturing a small handful of secondary clerics who acted as propagandists for these front groups. As a result, the spiritual direction of Moslem life in Iran appeared confused and unproductive.

As many as fifteen religious papers, most of them weekly, were published at Tehran in 1957. The international Islamic Propaganda Center has offices at Tehran and publishes a weekly periodical and an annual almanac.

Education

Iran's history of education goes back to a very remote period. In Achaemenid times the young men were taught not only to ride and to shoot the bow, but to know the value of truth and to distinguish between good and evil. After the Arab invasion and the adoption of the Moslem religion, education was based upon the Qoran just as in Europe it was based upon the Bible. For many centuries Moslem priests taught, in return for a very small sum of money from each parent, in schools called *maktab*, where the children memorized the Qoran by chanting its verses in unison and learned to read and write Persian and do simple arithmetic. There were also many religious colleges, something like the western theological seminaries, where advanced students, gathered around men renowned for their learning, worked at such subjects as the interpretation of the Qoran, religious law, and religious philosophy. There were no formal examinations. No place for girls was provided in this system of education. Although the religious schools and colleges have largely given way to secular education, they still function, especially in the smaller towns and villages for the training of *mullahs*, or clerics. In 1962 there were 233 higher religious schools in which 13,000 students were under 522 teachers.

Fairly close contact with some of the European countries was established in the early seventeenth century, and from this time on interest grew in foreign ideas, languages, and way of life, culminating in the establishment in the nineteenth century of schools modeled on western ones. One of these was the *Dar al-Fonun*, or House of Learning college, founded at Tehran in 1852, which at first specialized in military subjects, but soon broadened into the field of the liberal arts and performed a vital service in educating the young men of the leading families. The first Ministry of Education was founded in 1855, but the essential form of the present educational system dates from the organization of an Education Council in 1897, when the decision was taken to use the French system of education as a model. This system, with its emphasis on the accumulation of a great mass of fact, is still in force, although the schools run by the American Presbyterian Mission aroused a good deal of interest in American methods of teaching.

Iranian schooling requires about the same total number of years as our grammar and high schools and colleges, but the division before the college level is somewhat different. The elementary schools—in 1963 there were 11,566 schools attended by 1,720,000 pupils—are free and attendance is compulsory; children enter them at seven years of age and attend for six years. In the lower grades boys and girls may be in the same classes, but later on they are either in separate classes or in separate schools. At first most of the school periods are devoted to the Persian language, manners and morals, and games and arithmetic; later the number of courses is increased to thirteen and the subjects are much the same as those taught in American schools. The lower grades make extensive use of Persian readers. The second reader now in use contains short articles about being careful in the streets, when filling the oil lamp and when playing near the edge of the courtyard pool; animal fables; lessons about geography, animals and plants; lessons on keeping clean and helping around the house; and simple stories based on ancient Persian history and poetry. This reader and those for the higher grades contain a much greater amount of poetry than would be found in an American school reader.

The secondary schools, which are neither compulsory nor free, require six years and students usually enter when they are thirteen. At the end of the third year there is a general examination, and near the end of the course the students can prepare for more advanced studies by specializing in literature, mathematics, commercial subjects, or the natural sciences. Seventeen subjects are studied with from one to four hours a week devoted to each one. Of the foreign languages, Arabic is stressed since it is the language of the Qoran, and French, which was once the most popular foreign language, has been supplanted by English within a period of about fifteen years. In 1963 there were 1,207 secondary schools with 326,856 students.

In 1957 there were thirteen higher level schools, including universities, religious colleges and teachers' training colleges, with 954 teachers and 14,000 students. Outstanding in this field is the University of Tehran, founded in 1935, which has autonomous status and is run by a faculty council. In 1963 this university had 13,700 students and over 1,000 faculty members in twelve co-educational schools and colleges. Over 2,000 of the students are women. Such faculties included Moslem Law and Theology; Medicine, Dentistry, and Pharmacy; Veterinary Medicine; Law, Political Science, and Economics; Literature; Agriculture; Secondary Teacher Education; Natural Science and Mathematics; and Engineering. A School of Fine Arts is associated with the university.

Tabriz University which was founded in 1947 has 1,535 students and five faculties. Mashhad University opened in 1956 and now has three faculties and nearly 1,000 students, and the Pahlavi University at Shiraz has four faculties and well over 1,000 students.

In addition, thousands of Persians go abroad for their college years. After 1926 the Iranian government selected about one hundred students a year to study in Europe and the United States at government expense. After World War II this trickle of official students was swelled by a flood of those going on private means. Year after year the Iranian government has had difficulty in arranging to supply the foreign currency required by these students. In 1966 there were about 20,000 students in foreign countries. Of the 4,500 in the United States, a great many were in California. It must be said that many of these students become disoriented with respect to their own country and seek to remain abroad. Aware of this difficulty, the students themselves have formed organizations designed to promote their mutual interests and to prepare for their return to Iran. In the United States there is a very active Iranian Students' Association which publishes a monthly in English called the Danneshjoo.

Persians display a special gift for acquiring languages, as shown by the fact that the Iranian students abroad become fluent in the language of their studies within a few months.

The Ministry of Education is responsible for the School of Nursing and for the very promising School of Music. There are also technical and trade schools on the secondary level; one of these is the School of Dyeing which trains students for the rug weaving industry.

The training of teachers is a very important part of the Ministry's work. Prospective teachers complete the first three years in a Secondary School and then enter one of the Elementary Normal Schools, and after two years of study receive certificates permitting them to teach in elementary schools. If they wish to teach in secondary schools they must attend the Teachers Normal College and obtain a second diploma from that institution.

For the last twenty years one of the basic policies of the Ministry of Education has been the encouragement of group activities. Persians are strong individualists, and there were no organizations in which boys or girls could get together for pleasure or for more serious pursuits until the government sponsored the Boy Scout movement and brought from the United States a trained leader who soon became tremendously popular with the boys. Uniforms were the same as those worn by American scouts, and a great deal of emphasis was placed upon cleanliness, hiking, and sports. By World War II the movement had lost much of its early vigor, but is now being revitalized. Sports also are encouraged and facilitated by the schools, which hold at Tehran an annual sports festival attended by the best athletes from every section of the country. The present ruler of Iran, who before he came to the throne was an enthusiastic supporter of the Boy Scout movement, is the chief patron of sports and is himself an unusually strong tennis player. The most popular and most widely played game is soccer. In the schools field and track events and mass gymnastics are held; wrestling is popular, and boxing somewhat less familiar. Neither American football nor baseball is played, but there are some good basketball teams. Other sports not directly associated with the schools are skiing, tennis, and ping-pong.

It is fairly easy to see that Iran's present educational system is better adapted to the cities and towns than to the small village communities; the material in the school readers, for instance, has little value for the village children. Responsible leaders in Iranian education are convinced that the village schools must be more closely related to the life of the people;

that the teachers should come from the community in which they teach, and that the curriculum should be tied in with the improvement of farming methods and of sanitary conditions. At the present time even in the more heavily populated areas there is only one school for every eight or ten villages, so that only a small percentage of the farm children receive the benefits of education.

Progressive Iranians are convinced that the solution to the problems of rural education, widespread illiteracy, and lack of national unity lies in an all-inclusive system of education. In 1943 Parliament passed a law which provides for free, compulsory education for a given period for every Iranian child. This will require a tremendous effort and the construction of thousands of new school buildings, and although up to now the funds for putting the law in effect have not been allocated, the major problem will be one not of funds, but of training the necessary teachers.

The American schools conducted by the Presbyterian Board of Foreign Missions have brought to thousands of Persians sound training in cooperation, unselfish service, and good character. After the first school opened at Rezaieh (then called Urmiya) in 1836, others, attended largely by Assyrians and Armenians, were organized in the vicinity. Schools of higher grade for both boys and girls were gradually established by the Americans in other cities, and were attended by an increasingly larger proportion of Persians. A school for boys was established in Hamadan in 1870 and one for girls twelve years later. In Tehran an elementary school for boys was opened in 1873 and one for girls the following year. At about the same time schools were opened in Tabriz, and a school at Rasht developed into separate schools for boys and girls in 1907. The last American school was opened in Mashhad in 1926.

From small beginnings with a few elementary classes the schools developed into a complete program for both boys and girls from kindergarten to college level. In 1933, 1708 boys and 1346 girls, or a total of over three thousand, were being educated in American schools. Alborz College at Tehran, the outgrowth of the American High School for boys, in 1928 received a temporary charter from the Board of Regents of the University of the State of New York and in 1932 this charter was made permanent. The development of this institution was the life work of the late Samuel Jordan, principal of the school from 1899 and president from the time it became a college until his retirement in 1940. The appreciation of the people of Persia is a well-deserved tribute to his devotion. Arthur C. Boyce, who was long associated with Dr. Jordan in this enterprise, also devoted many years to the youth of Iran.

At the same time the Sage College for Women was being developed as a continuation of the Nurbakhsh School for Girls, operated in relationship to Alborz College. In addition to these American schools there were British, German, French, and Russian schools in operation in various parts of the country. In 1940 all foreign-run schools which were educating Persian students were taken over by the Iranian government; a private explanation of this action was that it was taken to halt the spread of Soviet propaganda through the media of the Russian schools.

In a recently published history of education in Iran Dr. Issa Sadiq, former minister of education, outlined the major current developments in this field. These include a steady rise in the total number of pupils; the continuing campaign of school construction; the emphasis upon village schools so that two thirds of all elementary schools are now in small villages; the great progress made in teacher training; the stress on manual and technical training, especially in the village schools; and the ever increasing shift toward the American methods of teaching.

Public Health

Throughout the entire country widespread disease and illness are related to undernourishment and to low levels of housing and living, and the struggle against disease must be strengthened by such social and economic reforms as will help to raise the general standard of living.

Infant mortality is very high in both towns and villages.

The average household numbers five people, and nearly every family loses at least one child at an early age. Most authorities have stated that the general state of health of the farming population is poor, but some observers believe that such statements are exaggerated.

Cholera is rarely found in Iran. Outbreaks of typhus have occurred in recent years, but on each occasion strict quarantine measures have controlled them. A virulent type of smallpox is endemic in the country and was once a real menace, but the vaccination of school children and adults is proving very effective against it. Venereal diseases are all too common, although the disease types seem to be less destructive than those in western countries.

Trachoma is widespread, as is the *salak*, a festering boil apparently caused by the bite of a sandfly, which often leaves a considerable scar.

Water- and food-borne diseases, such as typhoid fever and amoebic dysentery, are prevalent but are less damaging than might be expected, since the people seem to have developed a partial immunity against recurrent attacks.

Tuberculosis strikes both farmers and townspeople. Only recently has malaria been recognized as the cause of the fevers which sapped the strength of a large percentage of the population. Though malaria was known to be rampant along the damp coastline of the Caspian Sea it had not been realized that the malaria mosquitoes also infested the high altitudes and dry climate of the Iranian plateau. The Ministry of Health, encouraged and supported by ICA, arranged for crews with motor-driven spraying equipment to penetrate into all malarial areas and spray the houses and mosquito breeding areas with DDT. The program has been so successful that malaria has been all but eliminated in many parts of the country.

Water-borne diseases and those transmitted through human waste are prevalent in Iran, although the hot, dry climate does act as a neutralizing agent to cut down on these types of infection. No towns in Iran have sewage systems and it seems most unlikely that any such systems will be installed. Towns and larger villages employ a primitive septic tank arrangement with the disposal shafts frequently located under the streets and lanes. In the smaller villages both private and communal privies are found and it is common practice to collect the human excreta to fertilize the field crops.

Within recent years striking progress has been made upon the installation of systems of pure, piped water. Shiraz led the way when a private benefactor, Mohammed Nemazee, supplied funds for the entire system, including a purification plant. Work began on the system for Tehran about 1950 and in 1955 the first connections were made to houses in the city. Here, as at Shiraz, there are numbers of free outlets located throughout the urban areas. Now piped water systems are completed or under construction in scores of towns.

The Pasteur Institute at Tehran, founded in 1921, is headed by a most competent staff and performs a valuable public service in the study of local diseases and in the preparation of vaccines and serums against smallpox, typhoid fever and, more recently, against typhus.

Since 1930 many hospitals have been constructed by the government. Tehran has several very large hospitals, of which the largest is known as the "thousand bed hospital." There is also a special women's hospital in Tehran. Most of the large towns have government hospitals, and that at Mashhad is especially well equipped and well managed. The government maintains free clinics in the towns and has endeavored to bring these clinics to the farming villages, but a shortage of nurses, the unwillingness of capable doctors to live in the villages, and the shortage of funds has hampered this program. The village clinics' whitewashed walls, and neat and spotless interiors offer an object lesson in the protection against disease implicit in personal and home cleanliness. The villagers have no inherent prejudices against modern medical treatment and flock to the clinics. The government has also established a tuberculosis sanitarium high above Tehran, in the grounds and buildings of a nineteenth century royal palace.

Conspicuous at Shiraz is the Shiraz Medical Center, comprising the Nemazee Hospital and a School of Nursing both offering facilities equal to those to be found anywhere.

Supervised by The Iran Foundation of New York City, this institution stems from the concept and funds of the donor of the Shiraz water works and it is of interest to note that profits from the water works are assigned to the running expenses of the hospital.

A sizable medical school is affiliated with Tehran University and additional schools, newly established, are in operation at Shiraz, Mashhad, and Tabriz. In 1961 there were said to be some 5,990 doctors in Iran. Of this number 3,000 were products of the local schools and 300 were women. According to these figures there is one doctor for every 3,500 people in the country. No current figures are available as to the number of hospital beds in Iran, but a rough estimate may be 34,000 beds. Private physicians often maintain their own private hospitals and clinics, among which are a number of maternity hospitals and hospitals for children.

Foreign-owned and -operated hospitals have rendered a tremendous service to the people of Iran. Over a long period of years the Presbyterian Board of Foreign Missions has built and run hospitals in the north of the country and in them trained both doctors and nurses, thereby helping to eradicate the popular belief that nursing was not a very respectable occupation. The American hospitals were then asked by the government to establish the first state-sponsored and state-supported schools for nurses. At the present time the American hospitals at Kermanshah, Hamadan, Mashhad, and Tabriz are open, but the large hospital at Tehran remains closed due to lack of personnel. The Church of England conducts a hospital at Isfahan and carries on medical work at Shiraz and Kerman. Soviet Russia now operates a small hospital at Tabriz and a larger one at Tehran which is very competently staffed; the rates are considerably higher than those of the government or mission hospitals.

Child labor is regulated by law but in actual practice is widespread, particularly in the rug-weaving industry where the small hands of young children are so useful in the tying of knots. The economic pressure of village life forces the children to take their part at a very early age in the raising of crops and the tending of flocks, and mindful that this kind of work is detrimental to the physique of the growing children the Ministry of Labor plans to supplement and rigidly enforce appropriate legislation.

For a good many years the practice of opium smoking helped to undermine the constitutions of many Iranians. While it offered a facile escape from deadly drudgery, its continued use sapped the energy and the will to act, and its cost absorbed so much of the addict's limited cash that from the economic point of view the practice has been disastrous. No doubt it will be very difficult to stamp out, but the Iranian government has now displayed an earnest determination to halt the production and use of opium.

Intellectual Activity

The educated Persians of today are very well informed on both local and international affairs and display far-reaching intellectual interests. Several bookstores at Tehran and many kiosks stock a considerable number of foreign newspapers, magazines and books, and the continental editions of American newspapers and of the popular weekly periodicals are sold in quantity. The Iranian government operates Pars, a telegraphic press agency which subscribes to the major foreign agencies and translates and distributes this material to the Persian press as well as dispatching Persian news abroad.

Persian is, of course, the principal medium for local publication and within recent decades the language itself has undergone "Persianization." In 1937 the Iranian Academy made a study of the language of the country, and found that throughout the centuries so many Arabic words had been taken into Persian that it actually contained more Arabic than Persian words. Writers had found that they could command a larger audience if they wrote in Arabic, and there was also that fact that a knowledge of Arabic was excuse for a display of erudition. Persian histories and other works of the tenth and eleventh centuries had contained only about five per cent Arabic words, but by the fourteenth century the more erudite authors were using as much as ninety per cent Arabic. It was also pointed out that the language was weak in technical terms and that many European words related to such subjects as mechanics, aviation, engineering, chemistry, botany, hygiene, and medicine were being taken into the language unchanged. The Academy stressed the fact that good Persian words existed for nearly all the Arabic ones in general use, and decided to meet both these problems by publishing periodically pamphlets containing lists of purely Persian words to replace the Arabic, and of new technical terms based upon appropriate Persian roots. Lists of technical terms continue to be issued at intervals. The program was never so stressed that all foreign words were "purged" from the language and the results have been salutory. In general the ornate style and elaborate imageries of earlier times have given way to directness and clarity of expression.

Newspapers and magazines are regulated by law, that in effect having been enacted by Parliament in 1963. According to this law only an Iranian citizen of good character and education and possessing funds to operate for a stated period may apply for a license to the press commission. The violation of a number of prohibitions, such as attacks on the royal family, printing false news, revealing military secrets, publishing material injurious to Islam, or printing obscene material, may result in suspension of publication, fines, and imprisonment.

At any given time there may be outstanding two or three hundred permits for the publication of newspapers. Until September 1953 Soviet-front papers were very active in Iran, and each such paper would appear under different names as one permit after the other would be suspended. Usually there are about a score of daily papers being published at Tehran, and half this number come out at rather irregular intervals. The larger provincial towns publish their own papers; a town such as Shiraz may have one daily and three or four weekly papers.

Certain Tehran papers have established positions. *Ettela'at*, owned and directed by 'Abbas Massoudi, began publication in 1927. It appears daily in either eight or twelve pages, normally supports the government in office, and circulates about

80,000 copies. *Keyhan,* its leading rival, has almost as great a circulation. *Ettela'at* appears in an airmail edition. Both papers appear in English language editions: one with the *Tehran Journal* and the other Keyhan *International.* In the second rank may be mentioned *Post-Tehran, Bamshad, Mehr-i-Iran,* and *Paigham-i-Imruz*: most are four pages and circulations range between 2,000 and 7,000 copies. The lesser papers may print as few as 500 copies and are organs for the personal political or social views of their owners or editors. Launching a new paper is an uncertain and expensive venture in view of the crowded field, the high cost of imported newsprint, the limited amount of advertising available, and the difficulty of attracting readers. To meet some of these problems sensationalism may find considerable expression in the more ephemeral sheets. The Persian press does give very full coverage to international events and adequate treatment to the local political scene. Crime news is played down, human-interest stories are not featured, comic strips are rare, and daily columnists are missing from this scene.

The press also caters to special needs. An official daily, *Akbar-i-Iran,* carries announcements and items released by the government as well as the texts of the meetings of Parliament. Tehran has a daily published in French, one or two English-language dailies, and two press reviews, issued in mimeographed form, which summarize news stories, editorials, and special articles.

In the realm of the periodicals the *Ettela'at* publishing house, which has its own excellent printing facilities, puts out a weekly called *Ettela'at Haftegi,* and a monthly, *Ettela'at Maianeh.* An illustrated weekly of some 40 pages called *Tehran-Mossavar* has maintained a circulation of some 30,000 since its inception in 1949: the successful mixture includes anti-Soviet and anti-communist material, continued stories, articles on the unusual and bizarre within Iran and abroad, and material in support of the throne and the regime. A weekly, *Khandaniha,* founded in 1940 after the pattern of the *Reader's Digest,* has attained a circulation of about 30,000. Reprinting provocative material from foreign and local papers and magazines and including material critical of local conditions and events, it plays an important role on the local scene. Rather more characteristic of the nationalistic, socialistic press read by the intellectuals is *Roushan Fekr*, founded in 1954 and with a circulation of between 30,000 and 35,000 copies; its thoughtful articles may influence official thinking.

Literary journals include *Yaghma* and *Sokhan*. The latter, founded in 1949, appears monthly and features the work of national-minded poets, novelists, and scholars; it has a circulation of about 2,000 copies. In addition, periodicals are published by several ministries of the government, and by the Plan Organization. There are also popular women's magazines, magazines for children, a scientific journal, an architectural magazine, and cinema magazines.

In the field of book publishing there are concrete signs of an amazing expansion of the number of readers and book purchasers. It is estimated that about 650 books were published in Iran in 1959. Although the majority appear with paper covers, they are quite expensive in relation to the income of their readers. A few years ago much of the current publication was in the fields of translations of European novelists, religious works, and editions of established and modern poets. Now a score of publishers and several large organizations are active. The Institute for Translation and Publication specializes in translating world-renowned works from German, French, English, and Greek into Persian and has put out some 30 titles in editions of from 2,000 to 5,000 copies. Franklin Publications, Inc., a non-profit organization with its main office in New York City, has been most active at Tehran. In 1962 this organization had published a total of three hundred fifty-three titles in Persian, with editions ranging from 1,000 to 45,000 copies. Few of the titles were novels; the demand was for works on the history of science and on intellectual and cultural development. The University of Tehran sponsored its own series of scholarly publications and by 1960 had put out more than 400 titles in the fields of scholarly research and editions of manuscripts. There is an Iranian Publishers Association and a monthly bibliographical publication called *Rahnamayi Ketab*, or Book Guide.

Scores of prose writers and poets have been active on the local scene. Sa'id Nafisi is most highly regarded as a scholarly editor, novelist, and short story writer. The novels of Muhammad 'Ali Jamalzadeh displayed society in ferment and satirized contrasts between older and contemporary ways of life. Sadiq Hedayat, who died tragically in 1951, enjoyed unrivaled popularity for his short stories which combined psychological insight with broad caricature. Other established novelists include 'Ali Dashti and Muhammad Hejazi. A dozen others specialize in historical romances laid in ancient Iran or in its neighbors.

In view of the number of practicing poets and the high esteem each has of his own works it would be rash to single out any of the current crop for special praise. Mention will be limited to three: Parviz Khanlari, Golchin Gilani (Dr. Majd ad-din Mir-Fakhrai), and Feridun Tavalloli. Producing works of very different character, they have in common a simplicity of imagery and a sparse, controlled use of words which are contemporary qualities.

Creators of special literary niches are Fazlullah Subhi, the teller of fairy tales over Radio Tehran, and Husein Kuhi Kermani, collector and publisher of folk poetry and folk tales. Scores of local writers produce regional histories and guidebooks to the larger towns. All over the country there is great interest in the languages of Iran. This interest ranges from valuable studies of the ancient languages of the country to current investigations of a score of the modern Persian dialects, of such Turki dialects of Azerbaijan as Tati, Harzani, and Keringan, and of variations in the Gilaki tongue spoken in Gilan. Dictionaries of high merit appear, including a dictionary of colloquial Persian.

The extent and depth of the current fascination with reading is reflected in the revision of the texts, illustration, and printing fonts of the readers used in the Persian schools. In summary, in comparison with some of its neighbors Iran appears to be in the midst of a literary and intellectual renaissance.

The cinema is very popular in Iran, so popular that the prosperous theater owners have increased the number of large, modern movie houses as well as embellishing the gardens in which films are shown during the summer months. Several films have been produced locally but the sophisticated audiences laughed at some of the features of acting, settings, and direction; the home industry has not as yet recovered from this type of reception. Foreign films must be screened by a local board of censors. The majority of films are from the United States, with fewer imported from England, France, Italy, Russia, Egypt, and India. Westerns are popular, probably because their rental costs are lower than first-run productions. Until quite recently translations of the language spoken in the picture were projected on the edge of the screen but now Persian is dubbed in in a highly proficient manner.

Recent years have seen a notable increase in musicology and the performance of music. Students of the history of Persian music now emphasize that its origins are to be found in the Sasanian period and have tried to destroy the theory that it was merely an offshoot of the music of the Arabs. Composers, trained in Western musical theory, have sought to combine traditional songs and themes into melodic sequences and at Tehran more orchestras and many more performers are available to give concerts of Persian and Western music.

It may be said that interest in all the arts and culture of Iran is on the increase. The Persians have become "tourists" in their own land, visiting important historical sites throughout the country and—like Americans—taking countless pictures. Instead of collecting Russian porcelain, Bohemian glass, and French paintings of the romantic school, the wealthier Persians have turned to interests in the ceramics of Ray, Sultanabad, Kashan, and Gorgan, in miniatures of the Qajar and Safavid periods, in ancient bronzes, and in the highly decorative contemporary arts and crafts.

Clubs and societies show a steady growth. Merchants form their chambers of commerce and professional men have societies of engineers, of doctors, and of lawyers. Just recently a branch of the Rotary Club was organized in Iran and tomorrow may see the appearance of pressure groups, designed to promote the interests of segments of society.

The modern Persians are very sports-minded. In the Olympic games held in 1956 the Iranian team finished seventeenth but gave a most impressive account of itself in the fields of weight-lifting and free-style wrestling.

Charitable organizations are very active. Outstanding is the Red Lion and Sun Society, the Persian equivalent of the Red Cross, while the Society to Combat the use of Opium did a most effective job in marshaling high-level public opinion behind this goal.

VII. THE DEVELOPMENT OF
NATURAL RESOURCES
Minerals

Surveys indicate that Iran possesses extensive and widely varied mineral resources. Until about fifteen years ago all mining had been done by laborious hand methods, but with the erection of modern plants for processing ores more efficient systems of extraction have been introduced.

The sub-surface riches of the country are the subject of a special Mining Law, last revised in May 1957, which divides all such resources into three categories. If materials of the first category—limestone, building stone, marble, and gypsum—are found on privately owned land the proprietors may exploit the deposits and pay the government 5 per cent of the value of the materials. If the materials are in the second category—metallic minerals, solid fuels, salts, precious minerals and precious stones—the owner must obtain a license for exploration and exploitation and the state receives 4 per cent of their value. The third category includes petroleum deposits and all radioactive materials, and the rights of exploitation belong exclusively to the government regardless of the ownership of the land. The government may lease such deposits to local companies or may conduct its own mining operations. Foreign companies are granted concessions for the location and exploitation of petroleum or mineral deposits only through special action by Parliament.

In 1962 the first and second categories included 820 explored mines of which about 270 had been exploited to some degree. The following list is not intended to include all recorded deposits, but is indicative merely of the types and locations of certain minerals. The bituminous coal fields situated on both the northern and southern slopes of the Elborz Range from Zenjan to Mashhad are mined at Zirab, Shimshak and adjacent sites to meet the industrial requirements of Tehran. Cokable coal appears near Kashan and in recent years reserves of good quality coal to an estimated 180 million tons have been located north and west of Kerman; ambitious plans have been made to ship this coal to Pakistan. Copper ore is currently mined at Zenjan and near Sabzevar in the north with other deposits known to exist at Anarak and near Kerman. The region to the north of Tabriz contains many ancient mines. Copper is refined in a modern plant at Ghaniabad, just to the southwest of Tehran. Iron ore deposits are scattered along the line of the Elborz Mountains and at Shamsabad, near Arak, some 20 million tons of hematite have been located. During the reign of Reza Shah an iron foundry was partially constructed at Karaj and then abandoned, so that Iran continues to import all its finished iron and steel. In 1956 representatives of Demag and Krupp were in Iran planning to construct a foundry at Shamsabad. Chromite is found at Abbasabad and Sabzevar in the north and in important quantities in the south, north of the port of Bandar Abbas; a refinery is planned for the southern area. Deposits of associated lead and zinc ores are quite numerous, and sulphur is found along the Persian Gulf and at several inland sites. The ores of nickel, cobalt, manganese oxide, arsenic, antimony, and tin have been located.

The mines at Anarak, well within the limits of the Dasht-i-Kavir, show signs of having been worked for long centuries, originally for the extraction of silver, but now also for nickel and lead. The known gold deposits would seem to require placer mining to put the extraction of this precious metal on a profitable basis.

Chemical salts such as the borates and sulphates of various minerals are found in rich layers, while table salt is obtained either by mining rock salt from the many salt domes or by allowing the flow of salt springs to crystallize in settling basins.

Building materials including stone, gypsum, and lime are available throughout the country, and there are quarries of marble and alabaster near Maragha, Yazd, and Shiraz. The proper earths for pottery, baked bricks, and special firebrick are common. Such precious and semi-precious stone are found as the topaz, emerald, sapphire, carnelian, and turquoise; near Nishapur are countless shafts and galleries from which the matrix embedded with fine turquoises has been extracted for many years.

Even in the present stage of development, the export of minerals is an important source of revenue to Iran. In 1962 exports amounted to 140,505 metric tons, including the following ores: manganese 1,270 tons, chromite 67,670 tons, lead 21,275 tons, zinc 21,559 tons, and iron ores, including red oxide, 28,732 tons.

Petroleum

Petroleum springs were seeping up through the rock of Iran when the earliest man appeared on the plateau. Oil flows or the escaping gas from the oil-bearing beds were ignited, probably by lightning, and became the object of wonder and worship. Much later, when the cult of Zoroaster became the official religion of the Achaemenids and truth and light were venerated, some of the temples housing an eternal flame were erected over or close to springs of oil or gas. The ruins of one such monument, the Masjid-i-Sulayman, may still be seen in the heart of the producing oil fields. Still later, more practical use was made of the natural petroleum. A European who visited Iran nearly two hundred years ago wrote: "On that side they call Mazanderan, they found the Petroleum of Naptha. It is used in varnishing and painting, and in Physick too, for the curing of raw cold Humors. Also the meanest sort of People burn the Oyl that is made of it."

In modern times the search for oil deposits began near the end of the nineteenth century. In 1901 a British subject, William D'Arcy, heard of the possibilities, and the Iranian government granted him exclusive rights for exploration and exploitation of all of the country except the northern provinces. The concession, which included the exclusive right to building pipelines to the Persian Gulf, was to run for sixty years. D'Arcy's first companies were personally financed. In May 1908 the first free-flowing well was sunk in an area about 125 miles north of the head of the Persian Gulf. The following year the Anglo-Persian Oil Company was formed in London and took over the operation of the concession. In 1912 the British government made its first contribution to the financing of this company, and later bought control of 52 per cent of the voting power of the outstanding stock.

In 1932 the Iranian government, dissatisfied with certain terms of the contract between the company and the Iranian state, suddenly canceled the concession, and in 1933 negotiated a new contract. Briefly, that contract had provided for: 1) a concession until 1993; 2) limitation of the concession to an area of 100,000 square miles; 3) loss of the exclusive right to build pipelines to the Persian Gulf; 4) payment to the Iranian government of four shillings on every ton of oil either sold for consumption within Iran or exported, and 5) an annual payment equal to 20 per cent of all annual dividends of the company above the amount of 671,250 pounds sterling. All these payments must total at least 750,000 pounds each year.

In recent years the Anglo-Iranian Oil Company had six fields in production in the hilly country north and northeast of the head of the Persian Gulf. The crude oil from these fields was pumped through several pipelines to Abadan, on the Gulf, where is situated the largest and one of the most modern refineries in the world—its pipelines, refinery, and port facilities at Abadan can handle over 700,000 barrels of oil a day. At the fields the gas which escapes with the flowing oil is drawn off and burned, wasting every day some 100,000,000 cubic feet of gas. Since the pressure of the gas in the oil-bearing strata is just sufficient to force the oil to the surface, the company has developed a special process by which the heavier oils remaining after the refining process are pumped back from Abadan to the fields and injected into the strata to build up the underground pressure.

The Anglo-Iranian Oil Company employed some 65,000 Iranians and a large British and foreign staff. In 1949 the production of the Anglo-Iranian Oil Company totaled 27,200,-000 tons, and in 1950 it reached 32,259,000 tons. In 1949 royalty payments by the company to the Iranian government were listed as equal to $37,779,958. The oil company also expended an amount in pounds sterling about twice that of the royalty payments for the purchase of the Iranian currency essential to its operations in Iran.

In western Iran a subsidiary of the Anglo-Iranian Oil Company, the Khanaqin Oil Company, exploited the Naft-i-Shah fields near Qasr-i-Shirin, immediately adjacent to the frontier between Iran and Iraq. The oil is pumped over the high mountains guarding the plateau to a modern refinery in the town of Kermanshah, and from there gasoline and kerosene are distributed throughout northern Iran.

In 1937 the Iranian government granted a concession covering the oil deposits of the northeastern section of the country to the Amiranian Oil Company, a subsidiary of the Seaboard Oil Company of Delaware. Survey work was undertaken at once, but in 1938 the American company relinquished its concession. In 1944 American and British oil companies displayed an active interest in obtaining concessions in the southeastern part of the country, while the USSR pressed for the creation of a joint Irano-Soviet company to exploit the possible oil reserves of the northern provinces of Iran. During World War II Soviet occupation forces operated drilling rigs at Semnan, east of Tehran, and along the Caspian coast, and Russian geologists must have definite opinions regarding the potential fields of northern Iran. In fact, Soviet soldiers were stationed at a drilling site near Semnan for several years after the end of the war in order to assert Soviet claims to a nineteenth century inoperative concession covering this Kavir Kurian area.

Following the nationalization of the Anglo-Iranian Oil Company in 1951—a subject discussed at some length in earlier pages—the export of oil from Iran dwindled to a few thousand tons a year. On February 1, 1954 the Anglo-Iranian Oil Company announced that it was meeting with seven other large oil companies with interests in the Middle East to discuss ways of resolving the difficulties which prevented Iranian oil from returning to the world markets, and about this same time the American government stated that should five American oil firms join a consortium they would not be liable for anti-trust prosecution. Technical experts representing the eight companies flew out to survey the condition of the fields and the refineries in Iran.

Protracted negotiations followed and in August 1954 the Iranian government representatives and the international consortium members announced full agreement in principle. The companies making up the consortium were the Anglo-Iranian Oil Company (which name was changed in December 1954 to The British Petroleum Company), Gulf Oil Corporation, Socony-Vacuum Oil Company (now Socony-Mobil Oil Company), Standard Oil Company of California, Standard Oil Company of New Jersey, The Texas Company, The French Petrol Company, and Royal Dutch-Shell Company; and it was their belief that in the first three full years of operation under this agreement Iran would net some $460,-000,000. The agreement was to run for twenty-five years, with provisions for three extensions of five years, and the extremely technical text ran to nearly 50 pages. Ratified by Iran in October, tankers began loading at Abadan at once.

The consortium set up a British holding company called Iranian Oil Participants Limited which holds all the shares of two companies established to operate in Iran. These are registered in Holland and their names—in translation—are the Iranian Oil Exploration and Producing Company, and the Iranian Oil Refining Company. In addition, the consortium established the Iranian Oil Services Limited. In 1955 one-eighth of the interest of the five American members of the consortium was transferred to and divided among nine other American oil companies. All these participating companies buy crude oil at the wellheads from the National Iranian Oil Company and arrange to ship this crude from the oil port or to have it processed at the Abadan refinery prior to shipment.

The law providing for nationalization brought into being two Iranian companies, the National Iranian Oil Company, which operates the fields and refineries and owns all the fixed assess of the former Anglo-Iranian Oil Company, and the Iranian Oil Company, which has prospecting and drilling rights throughout Iran except for the area covered by the consortium agreement.

The income of the National Oil Company of Iran derives from 50% of the net profit of the Iranian Oil Participants Limited, from income taxes paid by the two operating companies named above, from sales within Iran, and from sales of Iran's share of the production. To detail the last two points: (1) petroleum products for internal consumption are purchased from the operating companies substantially at cost, and (2) the National Iranian Oil Company has the option of taking payment in kind up to 12½% of the total crude oil produced and may sell this oil on the world market at its own chosen prices. By law varying percentages of the total oil revenues of the government are turned over to the Plan Organization to finance development projects.

In 1965 the production of the Iranian Oil Operating Companies was 88,500,000 long tons of crude, of which 18,269,000 tons were processed at the Abadan refinery. In that year production was at a daily average of 1,808,000 barrels, a gain of 9.2% compared with 1964. In 1965 payments to the government of Iran were the equivalent of $514,520,000, as compared with $480,200,000 in 1964. The companies employ 18,800 people, while ancillary services operated by the National Oil Company of Iran employ 22,930 workers.

Internal consumption of petroleum products is about 4,000,000 tons a year, largely at Tehran, so that rail facilities from the south to the capital are taxed by oil shipments. In 1954 the National Iranian Oil Company concluded contracts with one British and one French company covering the construction of a 10 inch pipeline from Ahwaz to Tehran, a distance of 820 kilometers. This line was to be completed in June 1957 and to carry gasoline, kerosene and natural gas. However, events had a significant impact upon the plans for this pipeline. In 1952 the Iranian Oil Company began drilling near Qum and in August 1956 the drillers brought in a gusher which spewed out two million tons of oil before it was capped —oil was sold from this lake to buyers who brought their own containers. As drilling continued at Qum, at Sarajeh, some

80 miles southeast of Tehran, and on the Caspian it appeared that the problem was not to get oil to Tehran but to ship it out of the area. In 1957 consideration was being given to plans to pipe oil through the new line between Ahwaz and Abadan at the rate of 1,000,000 tons a year, to laying a pipeline to Rasht on the Caspian for the Soviet market, and to running a line through northern Iran and on to a Turkish port.

In view of the interest of foreign countries in participating in the development of the petroleum resources of Iran it was necessary to do something about the "Mossadeq bill" of 1944 which prohibited members of the Iranian government from discussing the subject of oil concessions with foreign concerns, and in May 1957 the government sponsored a bill to authorize the National Oil Company of Iran to accelerate the location and extraction of oil with, if necessary, the participation of foreign capital.

In August 1957 the Parliament ratified an agreement, comprising some 47 articles and seven annexes, between the National Oil Company of Iran and the Agip Mineraria Company of Milan. The two parties to the agreement are to establish an Irano-Italian Oil Company, with equal participation, which is to prospect for oil and gas, within three defined regions, and exploit and sell these products. Half the profits of the Irano-Italian Oil Company will go to the National Oil Company of Iran and half of the profits which Agip Mineraria will derive from the Irano-Italian Oil Company will go to the government of Iran in lieu of local taxes on income. By 1962 both companies had brought in important producing wells in their areas.

To provide for the expanding future of the industry in Iran, the Abadan Institute of Technology, founded by the Anglo-Iranian Oil Company, was placed upon a more active and expanded schedule. Surveys made by teams from Lafayette College resulted in its conversion to a standard college of engineering, initially under the presidency of Walter A. Groves, formerly of Alborz College at Tehran.

Cultivation and Soils

A full two-thirds of the land area of Iran is taken up by the highest mountain ranges and the great deserts and is therefore completely unsuitable for cultivation. At the present time only about one-fifth of the remaining area is farmed. Allowing for land left fallow, the average cultivated area is 15,000,000 acres, of which about one-third are irrigated, or *abi* land. The productive unirrigated, or *daymi*, land is situated largely in both the northwest and northeast parts of the country. Historical accounts and the direct evidence from flights over southwestern Iran demonstrate that vast irrigation networks once covered large areas. Since 1700 many of the artificial irrigation systems have fallen into ruin, but in the same time the population of the country has decreased by at least 50%, so that, although the area of productive land is now sufficient to meet the needs of the settled population and to supply limited amounts for export, it would not be adequate for an increased population.

Iran has little of the soil familiar to Europe and the United States, a loam containing living organisms resulting from the decomposition of natural vegetation. Instead, Iran's substratum soil, a mixture of gravel, sand, clay and lime, has been exposed after centuries of deforestation and erosion. It is, however, quite fertile except when it is impregnated with alkalis.

Agricultural and Natural Products

Agricultural productivity and the growth of wild vegetation is regulated by the scanty and concentrated rainfall of the country. The cereals, including wheat, barley, and rice, are the staple crops of the country, under cultivation on some 9,300,000 acres. Wheat is grown in every section of the country except along the Caspian coast where its place is taken by extensive fields of rice which is also grown on the plateau in the few places where an abundant supply of water is at hand. The normal wheat harvest totals 3,000,000 tons and the rice crop about 800,000 tons. Some 800,000 tons of barley also are harvested. Wheat is the basic crop of the country and it should be available in surplus. However, in recent years Iran has imported wheat, as producers have declined to sell at prices fixed by the government—about $80 a ton—and as important amounts have been smuggled across frontiers. Other field crops include maize, corn, potatoes, millet, large peas, beans, and lentils. Alfalfa, native to the region, is a crop worthy of more extensive planting since its long roots can penetrate to the sub-soil moisture. Cabbages, turnips, onions, eggplant, cucumbers, and melons are commonly grown, and also sugar beets, cotton, tobacco, and opium poppies.

Iran produces very fine fruits with the annual production about 875,000 tons. Most of them are not equal in size to our own highly developed species, but they have a more delicate flavor. Fruits grown include peaches, apricots, plums, cherries, pears, pomegranates, and apples. The peach and probably several other fruits originated in Iran and spread from there to other countries. Apricots are the quantity crop and are dried for home consumption and export. The apples are rather small in size, probably because the winter cold is not sufficiently prolonged to maintain the period of dormant life required by apple trees.

Citrus fruits, including oranges, tangerines, lemons, and limes, are grown along the warm and humid Caspian littoral and also in such southern regions as the town of Shiraz. The current annual citrus yield is 150,000 tons.

The date palm is cultivated in oasis villages inland along the entire length of the Persian Gulf and in large groves at the head of the Gulf. There are in Iran some 9,000,000 date palms whose present annual production is about 100,000 tons. In the south of the country the date tends to replace bread as the staple article of diet.

It has been estimated that some 400,000 olive trees are grown in a limited area on the northern slopes of the Elborz Mountains. Their crop of fruit and the oil it yields is one of real value, and attempts will be made to raise these trees in other parts of the country.

More than thirty varieties of grapes are grown on the plateau, the methods of cultivating them varying according to local habits. In one interesting method a circular pit is dug to a depth of several yards until moist earth is reached. The vine root is then planted at the bottom of the pit, and as it gradually grows toward the surface the pit is filled in with earth until the established vines are all above ground level. Grapes are a staple of diet during the summer months, are dried as raisins for export in amounts up to 60,000 tons a year, and are used in the making of wine. European types of wine are now produced at several towns, but the distinctive wine of Shiraz, resembling a Malaga in taste, is the most renowned.

Since the cereals are largely consumed in the areas where they are grown, a number of other crops form the principal source of farming cash income. These products, of which the first five are processed in new government-owned plants, are cotton, sugar beets, tobacco, tea, silkworm cocoons, and— until recently—opium poppies.

Under the supervision of a government company which supplies seed and encourages production, the yield of cotton has increased steadily until some 115,000 tons are grown; exports have reached 85,000 tons.

Within recent years the consumption of sugar in Iran has increased at an almost fantastic rate until some 350,000 tons are consumed annually. Twelve state-owned refineries process sugar beets to produce 160,000 tons of lump and granulated sugar and privately-owned refineries turn out 50,000 tons of sugar. Several other refineries are on order but there appears to be no possibility of local production catching up with demand, so that for years to come sizable amounts of foreign exchange must be used for these purchases. Selling the sugar to individual consumers at about ten cents a pound, the Iranian government makes an important profit from its dealings in the vital commodity. Sugar cane is grown along the Caspian and production is being revived in the southwestern province of Khuzistan, formerly noted for the growth of sugar cane.

Tobacco is grown on at least 55,000 acres, principally in the areas of Gilan, Gorgan, Mazanderan, and Azerbaijan with seed tobacco produced in Mazanderan: annual production is about 15,000 tons. The purchase and processing of the crop is in the hands of a monopoly of the government which contracts with growers. The cigarette tobacco is of the Turkish type, and of the categories known to the trade as Trebizon, Tiklac, Basma, and Samsoun. The factory at Tehran turns out some 9,050,000,000 cigarettes annually, and efforts are being made to push the export of tobacco and cigarettes, notably to the Soviet Union. Pipe tobacco production is at 3,600 tons and declining. Tobacco for use in water-pipes is grown in the Khonsar region and amounts are exported to Egypt and Syria.

Tea is the most popular beverage in Iran and 14,000 tons are consumed each year. A score of years ago tea plantations were developed in Gilan, and in more recent years Chinese experts were brought in to improve the quality of the product. The local production never exceeds 10,000 tons, primarily because the Persians prefer the taste of imported teas and will pay higher prices for them. Efforts to increase consumption of local tea, such as licensing local tea growers to import foreign tea in proportion to their own sales, have not proved successful.

In summer the white fields of opium poppies have long been a familiar sight in Iran; the cultivation demanded relatively little attention and the cash return was high. It was less than a hundred years ago that the cultivation of the poppy was fostered in Iran in order to meet the demands of the European market, but the Persians themselves became victims of their own crops and, according to a 1955 estimate, there were 2,800,000 addicts in Iran. The preparation and sale of opium was a monopoly of the government and a very profitable one: in years when production ranged between 700 and 1,200 tons, an average amount of 80 tons was exported. In 1946 a cabinet decree was issued forbidding the culture of the poppy and the sale of opium, but in the years which followed the government continued to process and sell the crops. Strong sentiment against production crystallized in the person of Dr. Jehan Shah Saleh, Minister of Health, and in 1956 a bill was passed which prohibited the cultivation, production, and sale of opium, and provided stiff penalties for violations of the law. Health officials entered on a serious campaign to close down places where opium was smoked, including an estimated 1,200 at Tehran, and to cure addicts. This program met with conspicuous success, and the long established cancer of society is being eliminated.

Mulberry trees grow all over Iran and for centuries many villages raised the silkworms which fed on the mulberry leaves and spun and wove the silk on hand looms, but it was not until 1885 that cocoons of higher quality were introduced from abroad. In 1937 the production of silk became a monopoly of the government, and centers for preparation of cocoons and for weaving were established along the coast of the Caspian Sea. Annual production ranges between 500 and 1,000 tons, and the industry does not reflect a stable situation capable of attracting additional producers.

Not much more than ten per cent of the country is covered with timber, possibly 48,000,000 acres. The dense forests which make up a full one-third of the wooded areas are found along the northern slopes of the Elborz Range, beginning a short distance back from the Caspian shoreline and extending upward to a maximum altitude of 7,000 feet above sea level. Much of this area is virgin forest, of oak, ash, elm, beech, ironwood, box, cypress, maple, and honey locust, and since it represents important potential national wealth all wood cutting is controlled by governmental regulations. Wood in the form of telegraph poles, timbers, and firewood is transported to the plateau by train and truck. A government factory near Babol on the Caspian coast cuts and creosotes ties for the Iranian railway system.

On the plateau proper the wooded areas are usually confined to the higher mountains and consist of sparse growths of scrub oak, whose bark is used in the tanning of hides, and of wild fruit and nut trees. The extreme deficiency of timber on the plateau is met in part by the cultivation of watered groves of poplar trees whose trunks are used in house construction. Willows and enormous plane trees grow in the villages and line the irrigation channels. Groves of fine black walnut trees are found throughout the country, and both almond and pistachio trees are much cultivated, the nuts from these trees constituting a good cash crop for both the nomad and the farmer. In fact, the income received from the harvest of a single giant walnut tree will support an entire family throughout the year. Some 20,000 tons of almonds and 5,000 tons of pistachios are harvested each year.

Deforestation of the plateau has been going on for centuries and still continues. The nomads cut the scrub oaks and burn the wood for charcoal, flocks of sheep and goats devour the new shoots, and everywhere the villagers carry on a constant search for fuel. The reforestation of certain areas of the country is quite possible, but each planted section would have to be protected for a number of years against the ravages just mentioned. Forest products are valued at $50,000,000 annually and the government is alert to the value of increasing production, while halting useless destruction of forests. The organic law controlling the forests dates from 1943, a Forest Service was started in 1949, and a Forest Range School was to open in 1957. Through the efforts of the Forest Service the heavy inroads of the charcoal industry have been slowed down, while nursery trees suitable for dry areas are now available at several centers for village planting.

Certain wild plants and shrubs and their saps or resins are carefully collected and form an important item of export. Some of them are gum tragacanth, gum arabic, gum asafetida, and galbanum, colocynth, and licorice. Some 2,500 tons of the medicinal gums are exported annually. Other plants of value include mastic, rue, absinthe, cumin, and sumac, and a score of herbs are widely grown to flavor rice and sauces served with rice. Coloring matters used in rug weaving come from indigo, saffron, and gall nuts. Henna for coloring hands and feet, hair and beard—used much less now than formerly—comes from the tree of that name. Jute is indigenous to the Caspian littoral where a maximum annual production of 6,000 tons of fiber was once reached. Oils are extracted by pressure from seed-bearing plants such as cotton, linseed, sesame, castor, and poppy.

Flowers are so highly prized by the Iranians that even the

smallest courtyard is bright with flower beds and potted plants, and in early spring both valley floors and mountain slopes are carpeted with wild flowers. Some of those common to Iran are the tulip, grape-hyacinth, gladiola, gentian, bell-flower, poppy, buttercup, crocus, pink, iris, geranium, and dwarf hollyhock, and many wild flowers which are less familiar to other countries. Of them all, first place in popular affection is held by the rose, praised in charming verses by poets of nearly a thousand years ago. In fact, the common word for rose, *gol*, is also the generic term for flower. Many varieties are cultivated or grow wild along trails and water-courses. Noteworthy is the double pink, *rosa centifolia*, and the double yellow, *rosa hemispherica*, believed to have originated in Iran. Rosewater, *golab*, has been prepared in the country for centuries and at Kashan extensive fields of the double roses are still grown for that purpose. It is also of some interest to note that nearly 300 tons of dried roses are exported each year to countries such as Oman, Kuwait, Pakistan, and Iraq.

Water Supply and Irrigation

The fact that Iran's rainfall is very limited and that the fullest possible use must be made of the existing water supply has already been stressed, and it has been mentioned that although a good deal of dry farming is carried on in the north-west and northeast of the country, her agricultural productivity is dependent upon various methods of irrigation.

A system very effective for hillside farming is that in which dug channels angling off from rivers and streams carry water directly to the cultivated fields, the wider channels subdividing into narrow ditches. Parallel ditches at different levels along the slopes are connected vertically by miniature water-falls which can be left open or blocked by stones and brush. However, in this method a very large percentage of the original water supply is lost through seepage and evaporation in the channels and, of course, so much water is taken off near the source of the stream that little is left for areas further downstream.

A logical and more effective version of this method of free-flowing irrigation is to lead off the main channels behind dams or barrages thrown across the rivers. The construction of such dams and barrages may date from Achaemenid times, although no surviving ruins can definitely be assigned to this historical period. It is known, however, that dams and their associated irrigation channels were in operation in southwestern Iran by the first century A.D. Remains of many dams and barrages built during the Sasanian period, between the third and the seventh centuries A.D., have been found over a large area of south and western Iran, a few still largely intact and serving for current irrigation schemes. A most impressive series of dams was erected along the Karun and the Ab-i-Diz rivers, and today the air traveler flying over Khuzistan can easily trace the lines of the broad channels which led off from the reservoirs. After the Moslem occupation of Iran and down to the thirteenth century these dams were well maintained and the systems expanded, with the result that many thousands of acres were then under intensive cultivation which are now completely barren. Coming down to more recent historical times, a few large dams were constructed in the seventeenth century and two of these, one near Sava and one near Kashan, remain in fairly good condition.

Since 1945 the leaders of Iran have become convinced that no one subject is more vital to the future of the country than the expansion of irrigation facilities. The Office of Irrigation has undertaken studies of many sites, and more recently the Plan Organization has taken over the responsibility of financing selected projects. Dams or barrages are planned for, or are under construction, at sites all over the country, such as Ravansar, Bampur, Golpaygan, Mian Khanegui, Zahak, Bar, and Kashf Rud, and are too numerous for description. However, since these projects are to bring well over a million acres under cultivation, it is proper to characterize a few of the larger projects.

In 1954 a project for increasing and stabilizing the flow of the Zayandeh River, which flows past Isfahan, was completed. About seventy-five miles west of Isfahan in the Kuhrang

Mountains is a narrow ridge which divides two main drainage basins; west of the ridge are the abundant headwaters of the Karun River, which flows into the Persian Gulf, and east of the ridge is the upper course of the Zayandeh Rud, which ends in the interior desert. Joining the Karun to the Zayandeh Rud was first thought of by Safavid rulers in the sixteenth century, and thousands of workmen labored to cut a V-shaped trough through the ridge but abandoned the work when it was only about a third completed. In the modern undertaking a tunnel was driven through the ridge and a storage dam erected on the east side to impound the flood waters of both streams and provide electrical power for Isfahan.

In 1961 construction was completed on the Karaj River dam, some 25 miles west of Tehran, at a cost of over $55,000,-000. It provides drinking water and some 75,000 kilowatts of power for Tehran, and irrigates about 25,000 acres. The 103 meter high Sefid Rud dam, completed in 1962 on the north slope of the Elborz Range, irrigates 450,000 acres in fertile Gilan. Also, there were plans to exploit the Lar River which flows into the Caspian by constructing a very high storage dam and leading tunnels from this reservoir through the mountains into the Jaji Rud which flows down the south slope of the Elborz Range. Another related dam would hold water to irrigate vast stretches of the Varamin plain to the south of Tehran.

On the Marv Dasht plain south of Persepolis the remains of six ancient barrages testify to the extensive irrigation of this fertile area in ancient times. Plans for a new barrage at Dorud Zand visualize bringing water to 150,000 acres. In Khuzistan a barrage across the Kharkeh River feeds canals which irrigate 200,000 acres. Khuzistan is also the locale of a bold plan to apply the principles of the TVA to a region of 58,000 square miles: in 1955 the Development and Resources Corporation of New York contracted with the Plan Organization to plan and execute a unified program for the agricultural and industrial development of the area, including a system of dams to irrigate 2,500,000 acres. The major unit in this plan, the great 203 meter high Dez River dam, was completed in 1963.

It may be pointed out that practical irrigation schemes of great value to the country are not necessarily on the scale of those described. Careful field surveys will locate many sites where small dams could be thrown across narrow valleys at points above and adjacent to farming communities. These dams would be filled in spring and the water gradually released during the dry months. Such dams could be built with local labor and from the stone directly at hand, so that only cement and a limited amount of earth-moving machinery would have to be brought to each site. However, preliminary studies for choosing a site would have to cover more considerations than that of mere convenience. In certain types of soil the precipitation from the water would rapidly silt up the reservoir, and care would have to be taken not to bring brackish water to sweet land or to waste good water on ground already heavily impregnated with salts.

The second and most important method of irrigation in Iran is by means of underground channels which in Persian are called *qanat* or *kariz*, a method used throughout the country, especially in areas where there are few flowing streams. The system seems to be almost uniquely Iranian, for it is seldom found outside of the country. Some authorities believe that the first qanats were dug in prehistoric periods. The tunnel of an ancient qanat, the only one known in Egypt, has been found in the oasis of Kharga, over a hundred miles west of the valley of the Nile. Since it is near a temple erected after the conquest of Egypt by the armies of Iran in the fifth century B.C., it seems highly probable that the invaders constructed there a system which was then common to Iran.

A qanat line is constructed to supply water for the needs of a farming village and for the irrigation of its cultivated fields. At the base of mountains, and at the point nearest in a straight line from the village, a master well or shaft is sunk deep into the ground until its bottom is below the summer water table. The water table is a layer of porous rock which retains the water which seeps down through the ground after the warmth of spring has melted the snow on the high peaks. The master shaft is at least two hundred feet deep—near the village of Gunabad in eastern Iran are master shafts nearly 1,000 feet deep which are known to have been dug at least five hundred years ago. Often a series of horizontal galleries fan out from the base of the shaft so that water from a larger area of the water table can be drawn into the completed system. After the master shaft is finished, a trench is started on the slight slope above the village and aimed directly at the distant shaft, and when it reaches a certain depth it becomes a tunnel. As the tunnel is driven through the ground it is pierced by vertical shafts dug at intervals of fifty or more yards, which serve to bring air to the workers in the tunnel while excavated material is placed in baskets and drawn up the shafts by a rope and windlass. Finally, the tunnel reaches the master shaft, and water rushes through it to the village.

The excavation of qanat lines is in the hands of a limited number of specialists from families which have done this work for generations, the town of Yazd being the home of the most skilled qanat diggers. With simple equipment these men lay out the course of the tunnel and plan its slope so that it is just sufficient to keep the water in motion. Occasionally the tunnel is dug from the base of the master shaft toward the village. A qanat line may vary in length from a few hundred yards to a distance of fifteen or twenty miles, and it may take years to finish the digging of a single line. One line at Yazd is over forty miles long. The underground tunnel is about two and a half feet wide and four feet high, just room enough for one digger. In soft or sandy ground a collapse of the tunnel roof is guarded against by lining it with cylindrical lengths of baked tile. Once a qanat line is completed the work is not at an end, for it must be kept clear of silt and debris which has blown down the many vertical shafts. Sooner or later serious cave-ins take place. At first new sections of tunnel may be dug around such points but eventually the entire line becomes blocked and must be abandoned. Thus, when a village is seen from the air the paths of four or five qanat lines may be followed by the heaps of earth around the vertical shafts, but of this number probably not more than one is in active service.

A qanat line which taps a generous water table will furnish a flow of about four cubic feet a second, or an amount adequate for the periodic irrigation of about 200 acres. Water rents vary throughout the country but an abundant qanat represents an annual income of several thousand dollars. The qanat line emerges on the surface on the slight slope above the village, and at first is usually a single channel which supplies the power to turn the grindstones of the local mill. Beyond the mill the channel subdivides, and its branches flow first through the orchards and the grounds of those houses which stand in their own gardens, and then along the village lanes. Beyond the last houses they spread out to cover a fan-shaped area of cultivated fields.

The channels or runnels through the fields pass at right angles to rectangular plots of ground, each enclosed by a dyke of earth a foot in height. Each plot is irrigated by turning the water from the runnel into the plot until it is covered with an inch or two of water. During cold weather the fields of winter wheat receive three or four irrigations; in summer each plot is irrigated at intervals ranging from eight days to two weeks. Normally the problem of water rights is very complicated, for the output of a qanat may be the property of a single person or may be jointly owned by several people, each of whom possesses a different percentage of the total. One or more men are charged with the distribution and diversion of the water supply. The unit of time for measuring the flow to each plot is based upon the time required for a small concave brass bowl, pierced at the base with a tiny hole, to sink in a larger bowl of water.

The third means of irrigation is through water drawn from wells. Comparatively restricted use is now made of this means except in the southwestern corner of the country, where animals are employed to turn water wheels or to draw up leather buckets of water, both methods common to the countries of the Near East and North Africa. However, it is certain that wells will play an increasingly important role in irrigation, for on much of the plateau water lies not too far beneath the surface of the ground. The possibilities of power drilling of wells and of power pumping have attracted considerable attention, and well drilling rigs are at work in towns, villages, and farms throughout the country. The capital expense of a well is far less than that of a qanat, and in places where parts and service for pumps are available the cost of pumping water compares favorably to the purchase of a like amount from a qanat. Artesian, or free-flowing wells may also augment the water supply. Specialists have located a few areas whose general topography and underlying structure hints at the possibility of artesian wells, but it is not probable that suitable formations exist on much of the plateau.

Fisheries

The waters of the Caspian Sea have long been a source of food and of income to Iran. In 1927 a joint Irano-Soviet fisheries company was given a monopoly on the foreign sales of fish and caviar from the waters off the Persian coasts of the Caspan. Although the company was owned in equal shares, the Soviets managed to dominate the management of the fisheries. The sturgeon, spawning in the clear cold waters of the streams which flow from the Elborz Range into the Caspian were the source of the fine caviar, distributed as Russian on the world markets. In January 1952 the concession expired and Iran failed to respond affirmatively to a Soviet request that it be extended. Internal sales and exports are now in the hands of an Iranian company, *Mahi Iran*. Quantities of fresh and smoked fish are still sold to the USSR as well as within Iran. Some 190 tons of caviar are exported annually, largely to the USSR, USA, France, and Switzerland.

Countless mountain streams in Iran offer fine trout fishing. The local people employ a proven method: stones are piled up under water to form a passage leading into a domical area, the fish swim downstream into this trap and are taken out at intervals by removing the capping stone.

The exploitation of the resources of the Persian Gulf has been neglected until recent years. Now a company, backed by the Plan Organization, is establishing a fishing fleet and facilities for preserving and packing the catch. The port of Bandar Abbas is scheduled to become the center of this expanding activity.

Farming Methods

Over most of Iran the farming of the land—the plowing, sowing, and reaping—is done in the same manner as in other countries of the Near and Middle East and by methods in use for thousands of years. The area of land which can be cultivated by a pair of oxen is called a *juft* or "pair," and requires about 2,000 pounds of wheat or barley seed.

The ground is broken by a team of oxen pulling a plow fashioned from a forked tree limb, with the plowshare encased in iron. Donkeys, or even camels, may take the place of the oxen, and the lightweight, modern steel plough is used with increasing frequency. Sowing and weeding are done by hand. The ripened wheat and barley is cut with sickles and tied into sheaves and—just as is recorded in the Bible—the poorer people have the privilege of gleaning the fallen stalks.

The sheaves are carried to the threshing floor, a hard-packed surface of clay located on the edge of each village. There the grain is heaped in piles and threshed by driving oxen, pulling a heavy frame lined with projecting teeth, in a slow circle over and over each pile. Winnowing is accomplished by pitchforking the grain into a strong wind. As the final step the grain is passed through a coarse sieve and the rounded piles of grain impressed with an owner's mark, a decorative motive cut into a block of wood. Flour for local consumption is ground in the village mill while the rest of the grain is sacked and transported by donkey or camel to the largest towns. The government also uses a fleet of trucks to collect and haul the grain to the large silos situated adjacent to the largest towns.

Prepared fertilizers are little used in Iran although quite recently there has been a limited local production of chemical fertilizers. In some areas the farmers dig at the mounds of ancient city sites and scatter the material over their fields. Manure is also used, especially for garden vegetables. On the

Isfahan plain a feature of the landscape is the high circular towers with interiors divided into hundreds of compartments for housing pigeons whose droppings are collected and used on the fields. However, the principal method of restoring fertility to the soil is allowing it to lie fallow. Most villages have far more land than can be irrigated with the existing water supply, and so a field which is cultivated one season is permitted to lie fallow for the next year or two. Crop rotation is also practiced.

Productive farming land is owned by the state, *khaliseh* land; by the ruler, *amlak* land; by the trustees of a religious endowment, *vaqf* (plural *auqaf*); by a landlord, or by the farmer who, assisted by his family, tills the soil. Peasant holdings are neither numerous nor large, such plots running from a quarter of an acre to one acre, or to ten or more. A landlord may own five villages with the surrounding fields and one or more qanat lines, may own twenty or more, or, in exceptional cases, may own over 100 villages. However, many villages are each owned by a number of people in sixths of the total. The stable landed aristocracy is limited in number and found in only a few areas, as inheritance laws and conditions of insecurity tended to break up holdings. In recent years established landowners and tribal chiefs have tended to dispose of parts of their holdings to newly rich merchants and contractors in search of the prestige and income to be obtained from owning land. State lands are administered through the Ministry of Finance, while the Ministry of Education supervises endowed lands. Royal lands are managed for the benefit of the Imperial Organization for Social Services.

Farmers working for landlords are nearly always sharecroppers and the general system, which is many centuries old, is based upon the five items essential to the growth and harvest of the crops: land, water supply for irrigation, seeds, draft animals and primitive equipment, and human labor. Normally the landowner furnishes the first two items and receives two-fifths of the harvested crop. In poorer areas he may furnish everything except the labor, in which case the share of the farmer is small. However, systems of dividing the crop vary from region to region. In the Khamseh province the farmer with his own oxen and seeds receives four-fifths of the harvest, and in the Isfahan area the man who contributes only his labor is entitled to one-third of the crop. The produce of the orchards is also divided, but trees planted by the sharecropper become his personal property. The farmer grows his own vegetables and has others sources of cash income.

Cultivated land is now taxed 10% of the annual income derived from it by the owner, except that small farmers with an income of less than $400 are exempt. Separate taxes are levied on grazing land, water rights, and water mills.

Agricultural machinery such as tractors, mechanical reapers and threshers has been introduced into Iran. A first effort to farm with machinery on a large scale was made near Bushire after World War I, but ended in failure. In recent years a company was formed for the purpose of farming the level plains of Khuzistan with modern machinery, but it had very little success. The fact is that local conditions work against the use of tractors and other power-driven units. Most of the villages are so remote that it would be difficult to maintain either supplies of gasoline or the trained men to operate and repair the machinery. Further, the basic system of field division into small units for irrigation by flooding hinders the use of tractors which require large, unobstructed areas in order to make their operation economically feasible. Experience indicates that mechanization yields the best results when one or more tractors work out of a point where a skilled mechanic and competent drivers are available. In order to encourage more rapid mechanization the government permitted agricultural machinery, well-drilling machinery, and irrigation pumps to be imported free of duty from 1947 through 1957; near the end of this period there were over 3,000 tractors being used for farming.

Animals and Birds

In a country of many small and scattered villages the difficulty of taking an accurate census of the human population is great, and that of estimating the number of domestic animals is enormous. Official estimates of 1963 follow:

Sheep	31,800,000	Horses	550,000
Goats	12,500,000	Water buffalo	247,000
Cattle	6,000,000	Camels	283,000
Donkeys	2,000,000	Pigs	44,000

The breeding of fine Turkoman, Arab, and Persian horses, which are not used as draft animals, has been carried on largely by the tribes for many centuries. When Alexander the Great came to Iran he made a special trip to the mountains south of Kermanshah to see the famous Nisaean herds. Oxen draw the farm implements, and neither oxen nor cattle are systematically fattened for beef. Meat is not a principal article of diet for most of the population and when eaten it is usually mutton. Pigs are raised at Tehran and Hamadan for consumption by non-Moslems.

In every farming village the donkey is the universal beast of burden.

In general, the cattle are small and poorly nourished and the types of sheep would yield more and better wool if crossbred with foreign types. Progress toward improving the character of the livestock is being made, while many vaccines and serums required to protect the animals from diseases and epidemics are now produced within Iran. The annual production of wool runs to at least 20,000 tons and about 10,000 tons are exported: the USSR takes more than half of the exported wool. Lambskins, hides and animal hair are also important items of export income. Camel hair, in an annual production of 300 tons, is especially valuable.

The wild animal population of Iran defies all census-takers, and it is possible only to enumerate the species found there. The lion, the national animal of Iran, may be extinct. Tigers of great size are common along the Caspian. Brown bears live in the Elborz Mountains and smaller cinnamon bears in the Zagros Range. Panthers, jackals, wolves, and foxes are common. Porcupines, squirrels, hares (but no rabbits), rats, and mice abound. Hunters may find a variety of game: wild sheep and goats in the mountains, gazelle on the plains, wild asses in the salt deserts, and wild pigs in every swampy spot. Of the reptiles, turtles and lizards are numerous, but snakes are less common and only the horned viper of southeastern Iran is poisonous.

Many of the birds of Iran are common to the United States. An incomplete list includes the crow, raven, magpie, jay, oriole, finch, sparrow, lark, wag-tail, warbler, thrush, robin, woodpecker, kingfisher, and owl. Also the green-coated bee eater, turtledove, pigeon, partridge, quail, and pheasant.

Storks build their nests on the tips of the village shrines, and these welcome guests are known as *Haji Lak Lak* or "the pilgrim who cries lak lak." Ducks and geese breed in Sistan. Hens, small of size, scrabble for a living in the dirt and debris of the village: one of their small eggs now sells for more than the price of 100 eggs less than a score of years ago.

Falcons are found inland from the Persian Gulf and are still bred and trained for hunting, principally by the nomads. The sport of falconry has long been popular in Iran and was a favorite of the ancient rulers; the birds were highly prized, some of them being valued at the equivalent of several thousand dollars.

Hunting in Iran features local techniques of proven effectiveness. Gazelle abound over the plateau and are a real challenge to the hunter on horseback. Sighting the horsemen, the gazelle takes off in one direction and will not swerve from that line, so that the riders follow an angle which may intercept the animal's course. Hunting by jeep, introduced by Allied troops during the war, has been the decay of the sport. Such "hunters" have timed the speed of gazelles as high as 50 miles an hour. The pursuit of mountain sheep has its own procedure. Along the lofty game trails holes are scooped out and the hunters lie concealed behind ramparts of earth and stones, while beaters attempt to drive the sheep into position.

Villagers and farmers employ primitive but efficient means of catching quail. A man will hide beneath a brightly colored patchwork quilt and, as the curious birds alight to examine the lure, thrusts out his hand through a hole and grabs the birds.

In certain wide valleys the quail have customary stopping places in their flight across the valley. The villagers spring up from behind blinds and bring down the birds by swinging long bamboo canes; the Tehran game market is supplied by these hunters.

Persian cats deserve separate mention but the fanciers of this type may be surprised to hear that the Persians do not claim it as their own but assign it to Angora (in Turkey). Called the *gorbeh boraq*, or cat with bristling hair, it is not common in Iran except in the town of Yazd. There, it is said, quarters of the town breed their own lines, isolating each from contact with the others. Hairs from the tails of these cats form the delicate brushes used in miniature painting.

VIII. THE DEVELOPMENT OF
FACILITIES

Industry

When Reza Shah opened the first session of the VIIIth Parliament in December 1930, he said: "We wish this Parliament to be known in the history of the country as the 'economic parliament.'" From that time on every effort was made to make Iran as self-sufficient as possible, and the government began the task by assuming the role of the "supreme economic organizer." Industry within the country was to be developed on a large scale but certain measures had to be taken before the factories could be erected and put in operation. The world-wide depression had been acutely felt in Iran, and it was necessary for the government to take over strict control of foreign exchange transactions and to supervise the import trade so that only prime essentials would be purchased with the scanty stock of foreign exchange. The theory and operation of stock companies had to be explained to the merchants, to the new industrialists, and to possible participants. Further, stock companies formed to deal in articles of export and import had also to be prepared to distribute the products of the factories then under construction.

A Ministry of National Economy was set up to regulate the fields of agriculture, commerce, and industry. In 1931 a law was passed requiring the registration of all stock companies, and the compliance by these companies with certain regulations. In 1932 a new commercial code was put into force. The government took the lead in the formation of new companies, some of which were owned outright by the government, in others the government had a controlling percentage, and in still others ownership was divided between the stockholders of the new company, the government, and one or more of the companies already in existence. The operations and ramifications of some of these companies seem worthy of mention.

The Imperial Company was founded in 1931 with a capital of 5,000,000 rials represented by 5,000 shares of stock of which 2,000 shares belonged to Reza Shah, 2,000 to the National Bank, and the remaining 1,000 shares to two German firms manufacturing machine tools and electrical equipment.

The Central Company, capitalized by the Ministry of Finance and the Agricultural Bank, was established to carry on commercial transactions abroad. It also had a controlling interest in the Company for Cotton, Wool, and Hides, which was to process and export these items.

The Cotton Goods Company, which had a paper capital of 20,000,000 rials, of which 52% was held by the National Bank and the rest by the Ministry of Finance and the company directors, was to have a monopoly on the import of cotton piece goods and their sale to private merchants. The merchants were to pay to the company 20% over and above the cost of the goods, and of this profit 15% was to go to the government as payment for the monopoly rights and 5% to the company as commission.

In August 1936 control over nascent industry was strengthened by the passage of a bill which stated that an individual or company which wished to establish a factory or industrial enterprise should make application to the Administration of Industry and Mines. Three categories of enterprises were specifically encouraged: those planned to supply vital local needs, such as sugar, woven goods, and matches; those planned to prepare and package important export items, such as cotton, rice, and fruit; and those associated with the trend toward urbanism, such as cement, glass, and railway ties. Remembering the earlier intervention in internal affairs resulting from loans obtained from Great Britain and Russia, foreign participation was not invited.

In 1936, firms in which the government owned blocks of shares or a controlling interest had a monopoly on the export or import of the following items: silkworm eggs, sugar and matches, opium, silk, cotton piece goods, jute, rice, playing cards, goat and sheep skins, saffron, asafetida, rugs, silk stockings, wool, alcoholic drinks, canned food, dressed skins, handbags, shoes, automobiles and trucks, tires and spare parts, and dried fruits. This meant that the government had direct control of 33% of all imports and 44% of all exports. Profits to the companies were large: one company offered shares for sale with a guarantee of annual dividends of 12%; another spinning and weaving company made profits ranging from 40 to 50%. Favored government officials, merchants, and members of influential families profited materially from these companies but as time went by management was not willing to replace wornout machinery and to promote such efficiency that the local products could compete in quality and price with a growing flood of imports. Typical of the result was the announcement, in 1956, that the important Risbaf textile factory, founded at Isfahan in 1933, had gone into bankruptcy. The profits accruing to the government itself were used in part for the erection of factories and industrial plants. There was, of course, a temptation to set the prices of monopolized imports fairly high, and as a result the people of Iran paid for the industrial development of the country by a form of indirect taxation.

The system of monopolies and controls entered a new phase about 1937 with the conclusion of barter agreements between Iran and Germany, and between Iran and Soviet Russia. Russia sent piece goods, sugar, and other items in exchange for wool and rice.

With the advent of World War II the monopoly system played an even more vital role in the economic life of the country. Limited sources of supply and scarce shipping space made it necessary for the Iranian government to import, often through the medium of Allied agencies, none but the most essential items, and the institution of war-time rationing was also a factor which kept the government in business. Since 1942 a number of the monopolies have been brought to an end, although tea, sugar, and tobacco remain in that category.

Naturally enough Iran had lagged far behind the Western world in the development of the new machine age. At the end of World War I there was little industry within the country except for a few electric light and power plants and some match factories. Before Reza Shah's detailed program of industrialization was interrupted by World War II it had resulted in the erection of some thirty moderately large factories owned and operated by the government, and nearly two hundred other industrial plants. The major emphasis was placed upon textile weaving, with food materials and vegetable products in second place.

The general industrial scheme was a sound one and was executed by foreign specialists and by Iranian engineers who had been trained abroad. Plants were well located in reference to the new railway lines, to mineral deposits, and to areas suitable for the growing of the agricultural products to be processed. Many of the factories were designed by leading European engineering firms, and fine modern machinery was purchased from England, Germany, Sweden, and other countries. According to an announcement by the Plan Organization a number of these state-owned factories which have lost money for some years will be rehabilitated and then offered for sale to private business interests in Iran.

Since the end of World War II industry has developed at an accelerated pace, aided in good part by the steady flow of funds from the International Cooperation Administration. Hundreds of projects approved for financing by the Plan Organization will swell the number of industrial enterprises; the changing aspect of the towns of Iran will become increasingly conspicuous.

Any attempt to present a survey of industry in Iran is complicated by the existence of conflicting figures and statistics, all released by branches or agencies of the government. The concept of editing such statistics is still to be adopted.

There may be about 10,000 large and small manufacturing and processing plants and industries in the country and more than a third of them are situated at Tehran. Seventy-eight are comparatively large state-owned factories. Certain plants produce traditional items, such as the over 900 brick factories and nearly 100 plants turning out decorative faience mosaic. However the new era is reflected by the existence of nearly 150 printing presses, by some nine plastic factories, and by scores of machine repair and metal working establishments.

The number of industrial workers in Iran probably exceeds 200,000. Among the largest categories of employment are oil production, 50,000; railways, 24,000; carpet weaving, 30,000; textile plants, 28,000; sugar factories, 5,000; and match factories, 4,000.

Twelve state-owned sugar factories scattered about the country where extensive tracts of land suitable for the cultivation of sugar beets are available produce some 110,000 tons of sugar a year—about one-third of the present annual consumption.

Cotton is cleaned and ginned in at least 70 small plants and there are 19 cotton spinning plants and 14 plants turning out cotton cloth in the amount of about 236,000,000 meters a year. Production of cotton cloth is augmented by hundreds of hand looms, but the total output fails to increase substantially and comes to less than half the annual requirements of the country. Many small concerns at Tehran make hosiery and knitted cotton goods.

Twelve large wool spinning and weaving plants produce some 4,700,000 meters of cloth annually. Much of this cloth is turned out as blankets and, as in the cotton weaving industry, production is not mounting and amounts to less than one half the annual needs. In an effort to improve the situation the Plan Organization has placed some of the plants under a special company and has provided it with a subsidiary sales company, called Baft, more effectively to dispose of the output. The Plan Organization also intends to bring in new machinery and expand this industry. The state-owned silk weaving factory at Chalus on the Caspian Sea has a current annual production of 400,000 meters—again production has dropped in recent years.

Six vegetable and fruit canneries are located along the Caspian Sea and in Khorasan province and a sardine-packing plant at Bandar ʿAbbas on the Persian Gulf. Vegetable seeds are pressed for oil in some 18 plants for a total of 100,000 tons and 19 soap plants take a large amount of this oil to make

31,000 tons of soap annually. Some 313,000,000 boxes of matches are made in 48 plants and meet annual requirements.

At Tehran the tobacco monopoly company operates a tobacco products factory which employs 1,700 people and produces concentrated nicotine, cigars, pipe tobacco, water-pipe tobacco, and some 9,050,000,000 cigarettes. In 1965 twenty cigarettes retailed for the equivalent of seventeen cents: the price of cigarettes is occasionally increased as the government acts to swell the handsome profits derived from this important monopoly.

Tehran is also the center for the production of construction materials. A group of brick kilns situated on the southern edge of the city, each marked by a brick chimney, taller than any of the minarets which they so resemble, produce more than 4,000,000 bricks a week. It is of interest to note that within less than a score of years the type of brick used in this part of the world for many centuries—square in plan and less than two inches thick—has been replaced by the European type. At Ray, just south of Tehran, is the site of Iran's first cement plant, constructed in 1932 and added to in 1937. A second plant was recently completed at this place and the two plants have a total daily production of 600 tons. A plant, equipped with American machinery, was opened at Shiraz about 1955 and has a daily production capacity of 200 tons. There is also a plant near Mashhad with a daily production rate of 70 tons. By 1962 local production totaled 410,000 tons, and imports of cement had fallen off to nearly one-tenth of that amount. While self-sufficiency was in sight the difficulties of internal transport by road of the weighty product have retarded construction of additional plants.

The construction of plants for the smelting and working of mineral ores has not kept pace with industrial development in other fields. South of Tehran, at Ghaniabad, is a state-owned mill which turns out copper ingots and copper wire. At the outbreak of World War II a large steel mill, which was to include blast furnaces and a rolling mill, was more than half completed at Karaj. As noted earlier, this site will probably be abandoned in favor of a mill at Shamsabad, close to excellent resources or iron ore and coking coal.

The leather industry, producing for local consumption and export, is an important one as is the manufacture of window glass and articles of glass. Many other private or state-owned plants are currently producing sodium carbonate, caustic soda, hydrochloric acid, sulphuric acid, potassium bichromate for tanning, borax, industrial alcohol, beer, wines, soft drinks, furniture, rubbers and galoshes, paints, pressure lamps, bus and truck bodies, and a score of other items which had to be imported until recent years. Typical signs of the times include the fact that there are now 85 ice plants in operation and some 180 electric power plants. A decade ago electric lights were found only in the largest towns; now plants have been installed or are on order for smaller towns throughout the country. In recent years as the population of Tehran grew at an amazing rate and as industrial enterprises multiplied, the city was plagued by a shortage of electricity. Some 35 generating plants came into operation, producing 96,000 kilowatts of power. With the completion of dams in the area of the capital, additional generating power became available at these sites and present total output is on the order of 230,000 kilowatts. Carefully prepared plans for the extension and expansion of these facilities will take care of all future requirements in the capital.

Handicrafts

Long traditional to this entire region of the world has been the production and sale of goods in bazaars. Different covered lanes or sections of such lanes in the bazaar were devoted to the manufacture of basic items, such as tinned copper ware for cooking, quilts, rope, saddles, bridles, farming tools, clothing, chests, and jewelry. At each shop an *ustad*, or master workman, negotiated with purchasers and supervised the work of assistants and of apprentices, or *shagirds*. Guild associations were numerous and influential and families exercised the same craft for generation after generation. This system served to stabilize the social order of the towns through the continued existence of a body of citizens having permanent concern for local affairs.

Less than a half century ago sizable amounts of items of common utility began to flow in from abroad, and as this stream built up the craftsmen in the bazaar found that the market for their goods steadily declined. Today the visitor to the covered bazaars of Tehran, Isfahan, or Shiraz sees that foreign articles predominate in the bazaars, and it will also be apparent that shops handling those locally made articles in most demand have moved into the newer areas of the towns. However, in one broad field the crafts are staging a most effective comeback. This is the field of artistic craftsmanship based upon traditionally fine workmanship. Typical items include hand-blocked cottons, *kalamkar*; inlaid mosaic work of tiny pieces of wood, bone, and metal, *khatemkari*; silverwork in the Isfahan style incised with birds and swirling foliage; silverwork in the Tabriz style decorated with incised geometric patterns; a great variety of silver and turquoise jewelry; caps of gay embroidery; hand knit cotton slippers, *giveh*; copper trays; and Persian miniatures executed on paper or bone. Not only are visitors to Iran entranced with these attractive items but the local people are proud to have these articles in their own home, when a few years ago only decorative objects from Europe were acceptable as an indication of modern taste. At Tehran a School of Fine Arts sponsors the design and execution of articles of exquisite craftsmanship, but the export market for these items may not increase rapidly until controls over packaging, consistency in meeting specifications, and reliability in filling orders have been established.

Carpet Weaving

During the sixteenth century the art of carpet weaving in Iran reached a height never equaled in any other country. Although the weaving of pile rugs and carpets was a national industry for centuries, the earliest preserved fragments date from the end of the fifteenth century. Similar rugs are pictured in Persian miniatures of the fourteenth and fifteenth centuries and in European oil paintings of this same period.

The hand looming of fine rugs continues in Iran on a large scale, and the preparation of the materials, the techniques of weaving, and the choice of patterns and colors follow the earlier traditions. The people of the country cherish these rugs as their most prized possessions. In addition, Persian rugs represent a most important item of export, and up to the present have been able to compete successfully with the machine-woven rugs of western countries. Fairly exact copies of fine Persian rugs are woven in the United States by power-driven looms, but they always seem to lack the vitality and luminousness of the original models, perhaps because the very irregularities of their pattern outlines and colors are the source of their beauty and brilliance.

Most of the rug weaving is done in so-called "factories." A factory may be only a large house in which two or more looms have been installed, for there are comparatively few structures which have been specially built to house looms. The number of weavers regularly employed is about 30,000 and it is probable that the total number of people engaged in part-time weaving may reach 100,000.

Usually the rugs are woven on a base of cotton threads and the pile is made up of strands of wool or silk yarn which are knotted around the base threads and then cut off. Cotton is used in preference to wool for the foundation threads because the knots can be tied closer together on the thin cotton strands. Fairly coarse rugs may have some sixty knots to each square inch, while those of fine quality have over two hundred. The fabulous rugs surviving from the sixteenth century have nearly four hundred knots to the square inch, and even today this figure is sometimes excelled in the very costly silk rugs. The number of knots to the square inch has no relation to wearing qualities, but the finer workmanship gives an extra precision to the outlines of the pattern elements.

The quality of rugs intended for export is controlled, and weavers encouraged to use only permanent dyes. Alizarin dyes are used to a certain extent but at most of the weaving centers the prepared yarn is boiled in vats containing such time-tested local coloring materials as madder, indigo, cochineal, and dyer's weed, and the skins or shells of the almond, walnut, pistachio, and pomegranate.

In the factories a preliminary drawing is made for each rug as well as careful full-scale pictures in color of sections of the pattern. In weaving a large rug three or four adults or children sit in front of the loom while a foreman, following the prepared drawings, calls off the number and color of the knots to be tied by each weaver as the work goes forward.

The rugs are usually finished while still on the looms. As a section about two feet long is completed the foreman carefully clips the pile down to a uniform surface. Work progresses slowly: a rug of moderate size takes about a month to weave, and huge rugs, as large as 15 feet by 35 feet, which are sometimes woven, may take over two years to complete.

The rugs are usually known to the trade by the names of the towns or districts where they are woven, and many towns have their own patterns and combinations of colors by which their rugs may easily be distinguished. Trade names in common use include Tabriz; Heriz (near Tabriz); Qashqa'i and Afshar from the vicinity of Shiraz; Senneh, Bijar and Sanandaj from the region of Kurdistan; Saraband from Hamadan; Mahal and Sarouk from the region of Arak; and the well known Kerman, Kashan, Qum, Isfahan, Mashhad and Turkoman varieties. The center at Arak weaves rugs for firms doing business in the United States and has worked out patterns to appeal to American taste.

A great many rugs are also woven by the women of the nomadic tribes or of the farming communities, and these are not usually exported. No preliminary drawing is made and the bold geometric designs develop as the weaving progresses.

The continued production of large numbers of fine carpets is seriously menaced. With the cost of living rising at a more rapid rate than returns from weaving, numbers of weavers look for more permanent and rewarding occupations. For example, the demand for labor in the new oil field at Qum may mean the disappearance of this long-renowned type. Given the economic pinch, too many weavers contract for carpets, receive the proper amount of wool in advance, and then skimp on the tying of knots in order to finish the job with wool left over which they may sell or may weave into additional rugs. Plans to cope with the economic crisis in this vital industry include the sale to local weavers of washed and pre-dyed yarn. The Iranian Carpet Society was founded in 1936 as a governmental monopoly to supervise production and export sales. Currently its responsibilities are more restricted, although it buys extensively from weavers under contracts and maintains about 1,000 looms at such towns at Kerman, Arak, Kashan, Malayer, Hamadan, Mashhad, and Tabriz. This society attempts to preserve traditional patterns and to maintain traditional quality.

The Lebanon, Switzerland, and Koweit import very large quantities of Persian carpets but all of these countries are re-exporters: the most important purchasers for local sale are the United States, West Germany and England. In 1960 some 6,950 tons of carpets were exported from Iran: this weight would be roughly equivalent to 95,000 carpets, 3 meters by 4 meters, each of which weighed about 160 pounds.

In 1957 local prices for new carpets ranged from a high of about $65 a square meter for the finest of the carpets woven at Kerman, to about $25 a square meter for fair to good carpets from Kashan, Arak, Mashhad, and Qum, down to as low as $15 a square meter for "commercial" quality from Mashhad and Tabriz.

Foreign Investments in Industry and Business

In 1965 there were almost three hundred foreign firms registered to do business in Iran, the majority of them connected with commerce, industry, or transport. About forty of them were industrial firms. In 1965 the United States led in the amount of foreign capital invested in Iran, and Great Britain was second, followed by France, Italy, Holland, and Switzerland.

After World War II, as part of a general reaction against foreign influences, regulations were put into force which appeared to penalize the operation of foreign firms in certain fields. New regulations concerning foreign banks appeared so restrictive that all such institutions except the Soviet-owned Russian Bank in Iran withdrew from the country. A cabinet decree of December 1952 listed rather stringent conditions under which foreign insurance companies could operate, including the withdrawal from the country of no more than 10% of annual revenues, and these concerns began to wind up their affairs.

Quite recently there has been a swing in the other direction as the need for foreign capital in certain fields has become apparent. Near the end of 1955 the Parliament passed a bill of seven articles entitled For Attracting and Protecting Foreign Capital. The bill provides for the withdrawal of the capital in the same currency in which it was brought into Iran, for taking out annual net profits in that currency, and for equitable compensation in case of nationalization. However, the maximum allowable net profit is to be determined by regulations, and in the case of nationalization the amount of indemnity is to be determined by a local commission. In 1957 Iran and the United States exchanged a note which provided for the latter country to guarantee private American capital investments in Iran; in cases of claims against Iran there would be direct negotiations between the two countries.

Industrial Labor

The labor movement had its beginnings in Iran about 1921 and came into being at the hands of devotees trained by the communist party of the USSR. A number of guild unions and unions of government workers were set up at Tehran where the movement was headed by Sayyid Muhammad Dehqan who reported on his efforts at the fourth meeting of the Third International held in 1924. Several of his close associates were to reappear in the Tudeh party or in the autonomous movement in Azerbaijan in 1945. Thus, Ja'far Pishavari supported the unions through the paper *Haqiqat* published at Tehran, Ovanessian played an active role, and Reza Rusta came to Tehran from the Caspian area in 1927 to become one of the moving spirits. May Day celebrations were held at Tehran from 1925 through 1927 but in 1929 the government of Reza

Shah closed down upon the movement, estimated to have 7,000 followers, and arrested some 50 of the leaders. In 1930 and later Rusta, Pishevari, Ovanessian and others were arrested and remained in prison or enforced residence until 1941 when political prisoners were released.

These leaders were not slow in renewing their activity. In 1942 the Tudeh party sponsored a Central Committee of Trade Unions which organized chapters in the main industrial centers of the country. The Central Committee made effective use of demonstrations, newspaper publicity, and strikes to gain higher wages for union members; Reza Rusta headed this activity.

In 1946 a cabinet decree authorized the implementation of a comprehensive Labor Law, intended to fill the gap existing in this field in Iran. Some forty-seven articles regulated working hours, wages, holidays and paid vacations, and labor by women and children. Also, the terms of contracts between employers and employees, safeguards for the health of workers, an unemployment service, unions, boards of conciliation and arbitration, savings societies and social security. In this same year the newly created Ministry of Labor absorbed many of the established unions into the government sponsored Union of Iranian Workers.

However, it was not until after the Tudeh party was banned in 1949 that Soviet and communist domination of the unions was broken: Rusta was arrested, surrendered bail, and fled the country. Since that time the government has taken definite steps to improve working conditions, while maintaining a considerable measure of control over the unions. Cooperatives have been encouraged. The first of these, called the Workers' Consumers Society, was established in 1948 and by 1954 some 25 additional groups with the same name had been formed. These and other similar societies benefited from the advice of United Nations personnel.

In January 1953 a law provided for workers' insurance and in August 1955 it was superseded by a more comprehensive Workers' Insurance Law, detailed in at least 75 articles. In 1957 it appeared certain that the government favored equitable treatment of industrial workers but was not ready to permit unrestricted union activity. It was not at all certain how many workers were members of trade unions; a semi-official estimate of 50,000 seemed rather high.

The largest organization was the Iranian Trade Union Congress, founded in 1951 when the Federation of Iranian Workers and the Central Federation of Trade Unions of Workers and Peasants of Iran were urged by the government to consolidate. Other active elements include the Central Council of Syndicates of Workers and Farmers; the General Federation of Unions and Syndicates of Workers of Khorasan; and the United Front of Workers. In addition, there are over one hundred guilds of non-industrial artisans.

Foreign Trade

The foreign trade of Iran is a monopoly of the state. According to a bill passed in July 1953 the government has very broad powers in this field, including the right to establish import quotas on items which private concerns may bring into the country. The current pattern continues that in effect prior to World War II when measures of control introduced and conducted by the Iranian government enabled the country to maintain a rather precarious but favorable balance of trade. In years when the value of imports tended to exceed that of exports foreign exchange received from the operations of the oil concession was diverted to purchases abroad, and serious repercussions on the economic system of the country were avoided. This balance was upset during the war years and those which followed: unfavorable trade balances were influenced by the difficulty of reentering the competitive world markets and by the situation prevailing within Iran following the nationalization of the oil industry in 1951. Probably balances would have been even more unfavorable had not Iran executed a number of clearing agreements with European countries.

Prior to the beginning of each Persian calendar year the Ministry of National Economy releases the contingents for that year. Under appropriate headings, such as machinery, electrical equipment, automobiles, chemicals, textiles, etc., are listed the value of those items which may be brought into the country by Iranian merchants. In certain categories the contingents are taken up very rapidly. The objective of arriving at a favorable balance of trade may be hampered by the amount of goods which enter the country free of duty. In 1958 some 40% by value of the total imports were brought in by some 22 agencies of the government and charitable organizations. This number included the Plan Organization, the Iranian National Oil Company, and the Iranian State Railways. The number of such organizations and the total value of goods imported free of duty increases with each passing year.

The figures given in the following table, which represent the total value of Iran's foreign trade over a number of years, originated in publications of the Iranian customs administration. Converted from rials, these figures may or may not agree with other published statements. During the last decade the price of the rial in relation to foreign currencies has fluctuated as a number of rates have been available at the same time for various types of transactions. For the table conversion has been made at the rate of 32.5 rials to the American dollar up until 1955 when it was established at 75 rials to the dollar.

	Exports	Imports	Total Trade
1964	$153,133,000	$757,173,000	$910,306,000
1963	128,220,000	523,757,000	651,977,000
1962	114,704,000	558,742,000	673,446,000
1961	127,906,000	496,766,000	624,666,000
1960	111,300,000	702,090,000	813,390,000
1959	101,700,000	552,000,000	653,700,000
1958	104,800,000	443,200,000	548,000,000
1957	110,300,000	333,000,000	443,300,000
1956	106,000,000	268,000,000	374,000,000
1955	105,700,000	251,000,000	356,700,000
1954	316,500,000	232,000,000	548,500,000
1953	260,000,000	166,250,000	426,250,000
1952	182,500,000	162,700,000	345,200,000
1951	131,900,000	215,700,000	347,600,000
1950	107,500,000	189,100,000	296,600,000
1949	52,600,000	207,400,000	260,000,000

The figures for imports include purchases of gold and silver but not the value of goods which were exempt from customs duties. The export figures do not include the value of oil products exported from Iran, nor the exports of the Iranian Fisheries Company, nor the value of trade conducted under barter agreements.

The major imports of Iran are machinery, motor vehicles, railway equipment, construction materials, cotton piece goods, sugar, and tea. Fairly comprehensive lists of the country's imports and exports follow:

Imports: Passenger cars, buses, trucks, motorcycles, bicycles, and their spare parts; tires and tubes; railway equipment and rails; structural and industrial iron and steel; industrial chemicals; pharmaceutical and toilet goods; paper and cardboard; electrical communication and lighting equipment; light bulbs and wire of all types; telephones; radios; electric motors and transformers; storage batteries; Diesel motors; mechanical refrigerators and stoves; hand and motor water pumps; china and glassware; second hand clothing; office equipment and drawing supplies; dyestuffs; agricultural machinery; sugar, tea, coffee, cocoa, and spices; machine tools; cotton piece goods and woolen and silk fabrics, haberdashery and millinery.

Exports: Sheep, goat, and lambskins; skins of wild animals; gums, resins, natural balsams and juices; cotton and wool; hides; rice; sheep intestines for sausage casings; hand woven rugs and carpets; dried fruit and raisins, caviar; minerals; oil and oil products.

The table below indicates the relative shares of certain foreign countries trading with Iran.

Between 1935 and 1940 trade between Iran and the USSR, and Iran and Germany increased steadily because of barter agreements with Russia and special payment clearing agreements with Germany. During World War II India rose to first place in Iran's foreign trade because of its ability to supply vital items which were then unobtainable from other sources.

After the war the United Kingdom made a serious effort to take and hold a large percentage of the market but other countries of Europe made heavy inroads under clearing agreements. Agreements were reached with West Germany and France in 1949, with the USSR in 1950, and with Czechoslovakia, Italy, Poland, and Hungary in 1952. Such agreements for extensions of the agreements. However, in more recent years the trend has been toward the gradual termination of such agreements.

Percentage of Total Dutiable Foreign Trade of Iran*

	1962	1961	1960	1959	1958	1956	1950	1940
U.S.A.	10.05	6.03	15.33	15.05	13.69	15.19	20.34	10.50
United Kingdom	11.47	13.00	11.37	12.35	12.20	9.52	24.85	4.00
U.S.S.R.	2.07	4.05	11.18	13.90	12.43	12.08	3.63	11.00
Germany	17.73	29.06	18.31	19.13	19.04	16.71	8.07	45.00
Japan	7.26	5.44	5.99	6.92	5.22	4.72	2.37	3.00
France	3.29	3.25	3.35	5.61	6.27	8.46	2.64	0.50
India	7.61	5.57	2.67	2.52	3.62	4.19	6.96	7.50
Other countries	40.52	33.50	31.70	24.57	28.53	37.13	27.18	18.00

* excluding exports of petroleum products

The table illustrates the importance of the trade between Iran and the United States. Converting Persian figures at the rate of 75 rials to the dollar, in 1960 the United States shipped $91,500,000 in dutiable goods to Iran and imported items valued at $14,500,000 from Iran. The United States is the largest purchaser of Persian lambskins, and buys quantities of carpets, gums, and sausage casings. The United States used to supply nearly all the automobiles to Iran and in 1962 shipped about one-third the passenger cars, jeeps, and trucks purchased by Iran. Jeeps led in sales, followed in order by Chevrolet, Buick, Dodge, Ford, and Plymouth; in 1962 a Chevrolet cost the equivalent of $4,000 at Tehran. The United States also supplies electrical equipment, motors and transformers, water pumps, china and glassware, and chemicals.

Banking

Before the opening of the twentieth century Iran had no adequate system of government finances. The national revenues had always been the personal property of the rulers, who made their own decisions as to what amounts they would pass on for the upkeep of the army or to their personal favorites. Because ready cash was always wanting, loans were obtained from European powers under terms which assigned customs revenues or granted concessions to the creditor nation making the loans.

As soon as the Constitution was in force, leaders of the country realized that foreign specialists must be called in to help in the creation of a stable financial system. At first Belgians and French were employed, and in 1911 came an American, Morgan Shuster, whose disinterested devotion won the hearts of the Iranians before he was forced out by foreign pressure on the Iranian government. Chaos reigned until the period of Reza Shah. Then a request was again made for American advice, and in 1922 A. C. Millspaugh arrived, at the head of a mission which in the next five years succeeded in establishing a balanced budget and in assuring the efficient collection of fair taxes. After the departure of the mission in 1927 the government maintained a balanced budget for several years, but was finally compelled to take over the control of trade and industry in an attempt to cope with the problems of the general world depression.

Mr. Millspaugh returned to Iran by government invitation in 1943, and requested and was granted very broad powers. His staff of Americans, numbering as many as fifty at one time, made a serious attempt to reform the entire financial structure.

The comprehensive program of the Millspaugh Mission was complicated and slowed by the emergency conditions of the war, which also made it difficult for the Iranians to observe what progress was being made. Parliament began to limit the powers of the Mission, and as a result Millspaugh resigned and left Iran in 1945. His experiences during these two hectic missions are described in books published in 1925 and 1946.

Long the most important bank in the country, the Imperial Bank of Persia (later Iran), was founded near the end of the nineteenth century, operating under a sixty-year concession. In 1949 the concession ended and following negotiations with the Iranian government its directors agreed to carry on business under new, somewhat stringent regulations, and under the name of the British Bank of Iran and the Middle East. These regulations proved too restrictive and in 1952 the bank withdrew from Iran. This left the field of foreign banking to the long active Soviet-owned Russian Bank in Iran which operated under these same regulations and which employed its capital of 100,000,000 rials to promote trade between Iran and the USSR.

The Iranian constitution had envisaged the creation of a state bank, but it was not until 1927 that the *Bank Melli Iran,* or the National Bank of Iran, was established. It grew very rapidly and in 1932 took over the privilege of note issue from the Imperial Bank. In 1957 this institution had a capital of 2,000,000,000 rials, some 222 branches or agencies throughout Iran, and correspondents in many foreign countries.

In 1960 the Bank Melli Iran was reorganized into two banks: the Bank Melli Iran, the National Bank of Iran, and the Bank Markazi Iran, the Central Bank of Iran.

The National Bank maintains the backing for the paper currency in the form of gold, foreign exchange, crown jewels, and debts of the government guaranteed by the excess value of the crown jewels and by excess foreign exchange. A law of 1954 provides that the bank must hold in gold the equivalent of 35% of the notes in circulation, and a law of May 1957 fixed the value of a gram of gold at 85.2 rials: by this latter action the value of the rial was stabilized at about 75 to the dollar rather than 32 to the dollar. The profit was to be made available for productive loans, and the possibility of increasing the note circulation was established.

The National Bank did much to promote the concept of savings accounts in Iran. In 1940 the bank had 55,153 accounts with a value of $1,165,000 and in 1965 the Central Bank held accounts amounting to over $321,000,000. At Tehran one of every four persons in the city had a savings account.

The headquarters of the National Bank at Tehran is one of the showplaces of the city. The central building is an impressive modern structure, and within its extensive grounds is a club for its employees with a good restaurant; sports facilities including tennis courts, swimming pool, and squash courts; a zur khaneh, a hospital, and the best equipped printing plant in the country. The fabulous crown jewels of Iran, a splendid national heritage assembled by the rulers of the country from the eighteenth century to the present day, are beautifully displayed in a special strong room.

Most of the other banks in Iran are owned by branches of the government and have been established within recent years. The Agricultural Bank, founded in 1933 and with a present capital of 5,061,000,000 rials, makes loans to farms and rural industries. The Bank Sepah, with a capital of 685,000,000 rials, was originally set up to afford banking and credit facilities to the Iranian army and later entered the general banking field. The Mortgage Bank, founded in 1939, has a capital of 1,720,000 rials to finance building construction and for making loans against property. The Plan Bank was brought into being after 1950 and took over the assets of the former Bank of Industry and Mines: it has a capital of 150,000,000 rials. The Commercial Bank of Iran is a private institution which was established in 1953 and purchased the premises of the former Imperial Bank of Iran. It has a capital of 200,000,000 rials. In 1953 the National Bank, the Plan Organization, and the Iran Insurance Company provided 275,000,000 rials of capital to establish a Bank for the Expansion of Exports. The Construction Bank has a capital of 150,000,000 rials, the Commercial Insurance Bank 110,000,000 rials in capital, and the Bank for Mining Exports 150,000,000 rials capital. Several private banks specialize in mortgages and in making loans. These banks charge 8, 9, and 10% for 30, 60, and 90 day loans. Currently there are twenty-seven active banks, with those established in more recent years specializing in financing land reforms and workers credit.

Public Finance

The state of the finances of Iran are clearly depicted in a table of balance of payments, with figures in millions of dollars:

	1964		1963	
	Credit	Debit	Credit	Debit
A. Goods and Services	1,219.9	1,341.5	1,095.2	1,043.0
1. Merchandise	1,151.1	736.2	1,035.3	508.5
1.1 Oil sector	811.2	82.1	897.1	36.3
1.2 Other	153.1	666.7	138.2	472.2
2. Non-monetary gold	......	0.4	......	0.2
3. Freight and merchandise insurance	1.0	......	1.0	......
4. Other transportation	6.8	9.6	4.9	8.3
4.1 Passenger fares	6.1	7.1	3.9	7.0
4.2 Time charters	......	2.5	......	1.3
4.3 Bunker fuel	0.7	......	1.0	......
5. Travel	8.0	40.0	14.0	48.0
6. Investment income	2.7	458.7	3.1	404.1
6.1 Oil consortium	......	440.2	......	388.0
6.2 Other	2.7	18.5	3.1	16.1
7. Government, not included elsewhere	18.5	46.0	22.6	40.3
8. Other services	25.8	42.6	20.3	41.6
8.1 Oil consortium	......	21.8	......	20.5
8.2 Other	25.8	20.8	20.3	21.1
Net goods and services	......	121.6	52.2	......
Trade balance (1 and 2)	414.5	......	526.6	......
Net services	......	536.1	......	474.4
B. Transfer payments	12.5	0.1	17.0	0.1
9. Private	1.1	0.1	1.1	0.1
10. Central government	11.4	......	15.9	......
Net total (1 through 9)	......	120.6	53.2	......
Net total (1 through 10)	......	109.2	69.1	......
C. Capital and monetary gold	322.6	210.8	88.7	109.3
11. Private long term direct investment	263.5	......	48.4	......
11.1 Oil sector	261.9	......	44.2	......
11.2 Other	1.6	......	4.2	......
12. Other private long term	1.0	......	1.0	0.4
13. Private short term	......	......	......	......
13.1 Changes in dollar assets	......	......	......	......
14. Central Government	34.1	74.7	19.1	65.0
14.1 Long term loans	12.8	36.1	19.1	31.8
14.2 U.S. government rial holdings	2.6	......	......	6.0
14.3 Supplier's credits	18.7	38.5	......	26.3
14.4 Subscription to non-monetary international organizations	......	0.1	......	0.9
15. Central monetary institutions	17.8	121.9	14.5	26.8
15.1 IMF rial holdings	17.5	......	......	......
15.2 IBRD and IDA rial holdings	......	......	0.8	0.1
15.3 Marketable assets	......	1.0	7.1	......
15.4 Exchange deposits	......	118.7	......	10.9
15.5 Other short terms assets and liabilities	......	2.2	6.6	3.5
15.6 Gold	0.3	......	......	12.3
16. Other monetary institutions	6.2	14.2	5.7	17.1
16.1 Marketable assets	......	6.3	......	6.0
16.2 Exchange deposits	6.2	......	......	11.0
16.3 Rial deposits	......	7.9	5.7	......
16.4 Gold (Bank Melli Iran)	......	......	......	0.1
Net errors and omissions	......	2.6	......	48.5

In this table the key figures are represented by the favorable transactions of the Oil Sector and the unfavorable balance of Other Goods and Services, specifically, by the heavy excess values of imports over exports. Periodically, different governments announce financial stabilization programs and ban the import of nonessential items of trade, but sooner or later such restrictions are lifted.

In 1965 the government was a heavy debtor to the National Bank of Iran. Some 4,561 million rials represented government liabilities secured by the value of the crown jewels, while 36,139 million rials represented debts of the government that were guaranteed by the Ministry of Finance. This total of 40,700 million rials, or $542,666,000, also included loans made by the National Bank to the Plan Organization which, in 1965, totaled 24,100 million rials.

Roads

The history of roads and trade and travel in Iran goes back into remote antiquity. In the Achaemenid period the famous "Royal Road" ran from the city of Susa through Mesopotamia and Asia Minor to the city of Sardis, just inland from the Aegean coast, for a total length of about fifteen hundred miles. The post system introduced in this period and carried on in one form or another into the twentieth century is based on a series of rest houses, located at convenient intervals, where official messengers or travelers can obtain lodging, food, and fresh horses.

By the beginning of the Christian era the great east-west highway from China to the Mediterranean was heavily traveled, and was known as the "silk route." Over it not only silk but quantities of pottery, spices, and other wares were transported from the Far East to the markets of the western world. The camel caravan, immortalized in the famous reliefs at Persepolis, was the main method of transport through many long centuries until a network of trade routes grew and covered Iran. The lines of some of these routes are paralleled by modern roads, while others are marked only by deserted caravanserais and ruined villages. The security of caravans traveling them was always a major consideration; for example, in the early fourteenth century guards were stationed along all important routes, and local officials were compelled to make good any losses caused by attacks on caravans passing through their districts.

Caravanserais may be seen at intervals of about twenty miles along every road. Many were erected by Shah 'Abbas in the early seventeenth century; according to legend the number reached nine hundred and ninety-nine. Others are far older than his time, while those of quite recent date were built by local governors, by pious wealthy men, or by the innkeepers themselves. Constructed of baked brick or stone, they are rectangular in plan with a large, open central court and a well in the center, and around the court are rooms for the men and stables for the beasts. Welcome as the sight of a caravanserai must have been at the end of the day, one early traveler was not too well satisfied with them, for he wrote: "Coming to our Inns, we have no Host, or Young Damosels to bid us welcome, nor other furniture than bare walls; only an open house with no enlivening glass of wine to encourage the badness of the march, but after the fragments of yesterday's provisions we betake ourselves to rest with much eagerness amid the noise of carrier bells, feeding, neighing, braying and with the singing, chatting and din of the servants and muleteers."

Across the level stretches these early routes were mere tracks, but in the mountain passes wide, ladder-like steps were cut out of the bare rock. Shah 'Abbas fostered a better type of road, called the *sang-i-farsh* or "stone carpet"—a stone pavement laid upon a high embankment of earth, sections of which may still be seen south of Tehran and along the Caspian shore.

Today the camel caravans are less frequently seen along the many motor roads, but they are still common in the eastern part of the country where the age-old trails cross desert wastes impassable to motor traffic.

The camel himself is one of the major curiosities of nature;

as an old Arab story has it, God created him last of all the animals, out of all the ill-matching odds and ends that were left over. An observant European who traveled in Iran some two centuries ago has this to say: "Camels, a beast abounding in Persia, and of great use, esteem and value in those Oriental parts; long-lived they are, oft-times exceeding three score years, of disposition very gentle, patient in travel, and of great strength, well enduring a burden of towards a 1000 pound weight; content with little food and that of the meanest sort, as tops of trees, thistles, weeds and the like, and less drink, in those dry countries, usually abstaining little less than four days."

When setting out on a long journey the caravans usually get under way in the late afternoon and travel only about three miles, so that after the first camp has been made and the equipment checked, someone can be sent back to collect those items which have been left behind. Road distances are measured in *farsakhs*, which are not always of uniform length: a farsakh on level ground is just under four miles while in hilly country it is about three miles. The caravan covers about half a farsakh an hour; an average day's travel is between four and five farsakhs.

In hot weather or on very long trips, the caravan starts after sunset and travels all night. The lead camel and the one at the end of the long procession carry great bells hung to their necks, and as long as the bells sound the line keeps moving. Each stage of the journey is marked by a caravanserai, where the loads are removed and the camels sent out to graze during the day while the men sleep.

Throughout the country the single-humped Arabian camel, or dromedary, predominates, while toward the northeast the two-hump Bactrian camel is much more frequently found.

More modern roads became a necessity after the introduction, in the nineteenth century, of wheeled vehicles. The first modern road built may have been that from Tehran to Qum, constructed in 1883. By 1899 a new road was open from Rasht, on the Caspian, to Tehran, one section of which was built by a Russian company and the rest by the Iranian government. Other early roads connecting Russia with points in northern Iran were usually treated as concessions, and the builders permitted to charge for the use of the roads and for the horses and lodging supplied along the way. The concessions were held by a Russian company and a British company called the Iranian Road and Transport Company. By 1914 there was a network of these carriage roads, one branch of which extended to the Persian Gulf from Tehran. But motor traffic was still very limited, and when in 1919 a British task force traveling in Ford cars attempted to reach Qazvin from Baghdad they were forced to do a great deal of engineering work along the highway.

Modern road construction, after 1925, begun by order of Reza Shah was pushed until 1941, and additional work has been undertaken since the end of the recent war. The early roads were neither wide enough nor built with a solid enough base to carry heavy truck traffic, and have been entirely rebuilt of gravel on a base of crushed stone.

There are 170,000 motor vehicles in Iran, including 36,500 trucks and 10,500 buses, and nearly half are owned at Tehran. Iran has three automobile assembly plants, but the added costs of shipment and of customs duty make prices quite high. American cars range from $4,000 and up, while the lighter European cars, such as Morris, Fiat and Volkswagen, are about $2,400. Soviet autos are also available, the Pobioda for about $2,600 and the Moscovitch for about $2,100. An annual operating tax is very high, as are insurance rates.

Within Tehran transportation is almost exclusively by bus and taxi, and is inexpensive. The usual taxi fare for a trip of moderate length is 20 cents. Only in the older, southern part of the city are there a few of the *droshkas*, horsedrawn carriages, which were so common just a decade ago. From Tehran bus routes radiate to all parts of Iran. Many of the bus bodies are built at Tehran on imported chassis. Prices for long trips are very modest and the service usually reliable.

The main routes in the country, of which there are at present about 9,000 miles, may be traced out on the map. Every route of any length crosses high mountain passes, and in winter hundreds of villagers are employed in keeping the passes open. Maximum grades are not over six per cent; and turns in the road have an average radius of 27 yards. Stations with gasoline pumps are found not more than fifty miles apart and in many villages gasoline is obtainable in five gallon tins. In 1957 gasoline sold at the fixed price of twenty-one cents a gallon.

There are probably 15,000 miles of second- and third-class roads. Second-class roads carry less traffic than main routes and are narrower and more lightly graveled. The third-class roads, which lead from main routes to isolated towns and villages, usually are only a cleared roadbed with neither foundation nor top dressing and are often impassable after the spring rains. The animal trails which wind from village to village and are wide enough for a car make it possible to travel by automobile into many areas where no motor roads have been built. In the summer and fall the only real difficulties are presented by irrigation ditches cutting across the track, and by the necessity of circling around villages whose streets are too narrow for a motor vehicle.

Before 1941 stretches of the three main routes leading out of Tehran had been asphalted. During the war, when the constant pounding of the truck convoys carrying supplies from the Persian Gulf to Russia made necessary a more permanent and resistant surface than gravel, the British, American, and Russian engineering units either executed or supervised the asphalting of long stretches of the supply route. At the end of the war the road from Khanaqin, on the frontier of Iraq, to Qazvin; the long route from Khorramshahr through Ahwaz, Khorramabad, and Malayer to Hamadan; and a part of the road from Rasht, on the Caspian Sea, to Qazvin had been asphalted—a total length of just over nine hundred miles. Another long stretch of asphalt runs from Tehran to Baghdad, and then on across the Syrian desert to Damascus and Beirut.

For the last several years the Plan Organization and the Ministry of Roads have cooperated on far reaching plans for the expansion and improvement of the road network. A British firm, John Mowlem, Ltd., received contracts to repair and construct some 6,000 kilometers of highways and has brought quantities of the latest road building machinery into the country. Through the efforts of this concern and other contractors, within a few years many thousands of miles of first- and second-class roads should be soundly constructed and asphalt coated. Concrete highways will not be built in Iran; asphalt is obtainable from the local petroleum industry, while cement is expensive to transport and in long stretches of the country the water essential for concrete-mixing is lacking.

Railways

Throughout the nineteenth and early twentieth centuries both Great Britain and Russia were interested in the construction of rail lines through Iran as a means of furthering the economic and commercial interests of the two powers. The line proposed by the British would have crossed southern Mesopotamia, south and southeast Iran, and Baluchistan to link India and the Mediterranean. Russia planned a line across the northern breadth of Iran which would link the Caucasus with Turkestan, and would also serve to strengthen Russian economic penetration in her chosen sphere of influence.

In the end neither country was able to carry through its plans, and they constructed only a few short lines of very little value to Iran. The first was a narrow-gauge line built in 1892 to connect Tehran with the shrine village of Shah Abdul Azim, some six miles to the south. This line is still in service, and every Friday a tiny train of a small locomotive and several open cars makes the trip carrying crowds of picknickers and pilgrims. In 1914 a Russian company began the construction of a ninety mile line from Julfa to Tabriz, which, together with a thirty mile branch to the shore of Lake Rezaieh, was completed in 1916. The track is of the Russian broad gauge and connects directly with a main Russian line by means of a bridge over the Aras River on the frontier. Ownership of this line came to the Iranian government through one of the clauses in the Irano-Soviet Treaty of 1921. A short narrow-gauge rail line once ran from the town of Rasht to the shore of the Caspian, and a narrow-gauge line was built by the

Anglo-Iranian Oil Company in 1923 for the movement of supplies and equipment within the area of the oil fields. During the first World War the government of India extended its Trans-Baluchistan railway from Mirjaveh, on the Iran-Baluchistan frontier, to Zahidan, some fifty-two miles inside Iran. The line was the very wide Indian 5'6" gauge, and after the war the tracks inside Iran were taken up. After 1941 they were relaid as standard-gauge, and the line is now in service from Zahidan to Pakistan.

Even before Reza Shah became ruler of the country, steps had been taken toward the building of a Trans-Iranian railway which would serve less as a mere link with railroads in adjacent countries than as a means of promoting Iran's own interests. The route selected, from the Persian Gulf to the Caspian, offered several advantages. It would enable the central government to maintain closer liaison with the provinces and provide for rapid troop movements necessary to maintain internal security. It would provide for a better distribution of the country's natural resources; food products of the fertile Caspian littoral could easily be transported to the arid south, and minerals and raw materials could reach the newly established industrial enterprises. It would also, by establishing an Iranian port of access on the Gulf, help to reduce Iran's dependence upon Great Britain and Russia for her commerce.

As early as 1925 Parliament enacted a law which gave the government a monopoly on sugar and tea and a bill providing for a tax on the transport of merchandise by road: funds from these sources were allocated exclusively to railway construction. A bill providing for survey work was passed in 1926, and in 1927 another law authorized construction of the railway from the Persian Gulf to the Caspian Sea. In 1928 a syndicate of American and German engineering firms was awarded a contract for the survey of the entire line and the construction of sections south from the Caspian terminus and north from the Persian Gulf, at a fee of 10 per cent of the costs. In 1931 this contract was canceled by the Iranian government, and the job was turned over in 1933 to Kampsax, a syndicate of

Swedish and Danish firms, who proceeded to let various stretches of the line to local and foreign contractors.

In 1938 the single track, standard-gauge line was in operation from the newly built port of Bandar Shapur on the Gulf through Tehran to the new port of Bandar Shah at the southeast corner of the Caspian, for a total distance of 865 miles.

Probably the construction of no other railway line in the world has met with more natural difficulties than did that of the Trans-Iranian, much of which is through very mountainous country. The southern section, from the Persian Gulf to Tehran, runs for miles on ledges blasted out of the precipitous walls of deep gorges, and finally climbs to the plateau through a pass 7,253 feet above sea level. Hundreds of bridges had to be built, and in this section there are 125 tunnels with a total length of 35 miles. The northern section makes the ascent from the Caspian shore to the plateau in a much shorter distance, with a gradient as high as one in thirty-six. The final pass is traversed by a tunnel more than two miles long, at an altitude of 6,924 feet. In this section, on which forty to fifty thousand workmen were employed, the length of the 65 tunnels total 12 miles, and in one stretch the line winds for 33 miles to cover a distance of only 18 miles as the crow flies.

Stations, warehouses, sidings, and water tanks were erected along the entire line at intervals of not more than twenty miles. Many special problems, such as the necessity for water-softening equipment in many areas, were met and solved. Rails, locomotives, cars, structural materials, and machinery were all brought in from abroad; only the wooden ties were domestically produced. The final cost of this line has been estimated at between $150,000,000 and $200,000,000, all of which was raised within the country and represented a serious drain on the national income.

Railway construction did not end with the completion of the main Trans-Iranian line, for work had already been started on two other long lines which would connect eventually with systems already in operation in neighboring countries. One of these was to cross the north of the country, and by 1942 trains were running on its western section from Tehran to Mianeh, about two-thirds of the way to Tabriz. The eastern section, branching off from the main line to the Caspian at a point some sixty miles east of Tehran, was surveyed as far as Mashhad. By 1941 trains were running on this line as far as Shahrud, nearly half way from Tehran to Mashhad.

The other new line took off from the Trans-Iranian at Qum and was to run southeastward through Kashan and Yazd to Kerman. By 1941 the roadbed had been built almost to Yazd.

During the war the operation of the Iranian railway was taken over by the Allies in order to expedite the movement of supplies to Russia. The Iranian government was to receive payment for the use of the system according to the volume of freight carried and England paid some £20,000,000. British, American, and Russian forces were responsible for the operation of different sections of the line; scores of locomotives were shipped far across dangerous seas into the Persian Gulf to be brought into the country, and hundreds of cars and several million tons of supplies were carried over the line. The Americans and British did some additional construction work, the British building a new line from Ahwaz to Khorramshahr, on the Persian Gulf, and a spur from this line to Basra in Iraq.

In 1947 work was resumed on the two northern arms of the line. In January 1957 the first train to cover the eastern arm arrived at Mashhad from Tehran, a distance of 578 miles. The western arm of the cross country line from Tehran to Tabriz came into operation in 1959. The total length of all the lines has grown steadily so that at present it is about 2,500 miles.

Serious consideration is being given to the extension of the present system. First priority would go to the extension of the line west from Tabriz to the frontier and to a junction with the Turkish railway system. Other plans envisage the extension of the Qum to Kashan line to Yazd, Kerman, Bam, and, finally, to Zahidan where it would link up with the line from Pakistan. Also, a branch to run north from Mashhad and join the Soviet Trans-Caspian line, and a line that would link Shiraz, Isfahan, and Yazd.

On the main line from the Persian Gulf to Tehran traffic

is hauled largely by Diesel mountain locomotives; the daily traffic is reported at about 4,000 tons, 1,000 tons above rated capacity. Oil products make up 2,000 tons and sugar 1,000 tons of the daily movement of freight.

Air Services

Mehrabad International Airport, some six miles west of Tehran, is served by some twenty foreign and local airlines. Its facilities include a concrete runway capable of handling the heaviest jet transports, and a modern terminal structure which houses a hotel. Abadan is also the site of an international airport.

Iranian Airways began operations in 1946 as a privately owned company. In recent years it has had a management contract with Pan-American International Airways, and, still more recently, has been taken over by the government of Iran. Daily flights serve fifteen towns within the country, while its international service connects Tehran with Kabul, Qandahar, Karachi, Kuwait, Baghdad, Damascus, and Beirut.

As concerns facilities for passenger flights within the country, the hard-packed earth or gravel surfaces of the fields adjacent to the larger towns have been replaced with permanent surfaces at such communications centers as Mashhad, Isfahan, Shiraz, Yazd, and Kerman, and facilities for communications and weather reporting have been greatly improved.

Navigation

Passengers and freight on the Caspian Sea are carried in Soviet Russian ships. Iranian ports along the Caspian coast are Bandar Pahlavi, Naushahr, Mashhad-i-Sar, Bandar Gaz, and Bandar Shah, of which Pahlavi and Bandar Shah are the most important. At Bandar Pahlavi ships of small tonnage may dock within the harbor, while at Bandar Shah there is a long jetty capable of serving ships of up to 1,000 tons.

The principal ports along the northern shore of the Persian Gulf, served by steamship lines of several foreign countries, are Khorramshahr, Bandar Shapur, Abadan, Bushire, Jask,

Bandar 'Abbas, and Lingueh, but only at the first three are ships able to tie up at docks. Abadan has extensive facilities for loading vast quantities of both crude and refined oil, while Bandar Shapur, a dreary site situated on mud flats, handles 400,000 tons of cargo annually. It originally loaded crude oil, but this function has been taken over by Bandar Mashur, a few miles to the east. Still more recently Kharg Island, 20 miles offshore in the Persian Gulf, has been developed as a major crude oil port: its development was undertaken because the adjacent water depths are suitable for the largest super-tankers. From the oil fields pipelines run 99 miles to the island, with 23 miles of pipe laid under water.

Khorramshahr, the principal port of the country, lies just upstream from Abadan on the Shatt al-Arab, the confluent stream of the Tigris and Euphrates Rivers. Docking facilities were expanded during World War II, and since that date more docks and many warehouses have been erected. However, traffic is so heavy at the port that there are frequently delays in unloading ships and in moving goods to the interior.

Navigation of Lake Rezaieh in the northwest of Iran is limited to small steamers and barges which make a circuit of the lake, calling at several points along its shores. Since the level of this large body of salt water is slowly sinking, this traffic may decrease. Of the many rivers of Iran only the Karun, which discharges into the Persian Gulf near Khorramshahr, is navigable for any distance. Barges and launches ply this river between the Persian Gulf and Ahwaz.

Iran has its own government-owned National Society of Oil Tankers and the National Navigation Company. The former operates two large oil tankers and plans a substantial increase in the fleet; these vessels carry Iran's direct share of the oil production. The latter company plans to obtain ships to carry Persian pilgrims to Jidda.

IRAN'S FUTURE

IX. TRENDS TOWARD TOMORROW

EARLY in 1955 the present writer summarized three important trends in this same section of a previous edition of this book. This summary, in two sentences, follows. In the political field no major, local political party will emerge and government support will come from uncoordinated public opinion. In the economic field significant progress will be made in development programs and in related social reforms, and in the field of foreign relations subversive, foreign-directed elements will be kept under control and Iran will move closer to the noncommunist world.

As recently as the opening months of 1963 these prophetic sentences remained valid. However, a number of significant events and decisions of recent date must be regarded as working to modify familiar currents in the political, social, and economic fields, and in this section attention will be concentrated upon the probable nature of these modifications as they relate to the future of Iran.

On the political scene the Shah himself remains the dominant figure. His autobiography, *Mission for My Country*, published in 1961, reveals his mystical conviction that God is guiding him and that he can rely upon God's support. In stating his belief that he is the first Shah of Iran who ever fully exercised his constitutional powers, Muhammad Reza Pahlavi touches briefly upon possible patterns for the use of these powers. As the present writer would define these possibilities, they are three in number. First, to rule, rather than reign; second, to reign; and, third, to combine these approaches, outlining major policies and programs to a responsible cabinet which he retains in office as long as it makes substantive progress toward these goals. In his long years on the throne he has experimented with each of these patterns, and even some variants. Related to the choice of patterns is his conviction that the progressive goals of his governments deserve a public consensus of understanding and popular support; how to create such a consensus is one of his major concerns.

After his appointment of Dr. Manuchehr Eqbal as Prime Minister in 1957, the Shah moved toward a posture of ruling. Although the constitution stresses the nonaccountability of the ruler and states that imperial decrees must be countersigned by a member of the cabinet, in practice few officials are prepared to resist the expressed wishes of the Shah. Dr. Eqbal was not so inclined, and was particularly responsive to the ruler's decision to bring two competing political parties into being.

The new parties were to support the foreign policies of the government, but the Mardum party was to advocate more liberal internal policies, such as the distribution of land to peasants, raising the living standards of industrial workers and others, and equal rights for women. Dr. Eqbal and Asadullah Alam, party leaders, were in active competition in urging members of the intellectual elite of the country to join their parties. It may be assumed that the establishment of these parties by the Shah was regarded by him as one facet of his newly articulated program of "positive nationalism," described as maximum political and economic freedom consistent with national interests. The ruler recognized the artificial aspect present in the creation of these parties, but appeared convinced that in time they would strike deep roots and evolve into broadly based, democratically oriented parties. It was believed that the Shah expected the Mardum party to win out over the more conservatively inclined Melliyun party. Also, in establishing these parties the Shah hoped to attract supporters of the National Front through their advocacy of similar aims.

The elections of August 1960 and January 1961 proved the experiment unsuccessful. Forces which had so long participated in the arrangement of elections—including members of the Melliyun and Mardum parties—seem to have insisted that complete freedom might bring into the Majlis unreliable individuals, even subversive elements. The results of a hidden competition between entrenched forces and advocates of popular rights were reflected in the different outcomes of the two elections. In the first round the Melliyun party came out far ahead of the Mardum party, while only a few independents were successful: in the second round the official parties came out on nearly even terms, while a score of independents were elected.

On May 5 and 9 the Shah took actions which marked the beginning of a new pattern of his sovereignty. In the first instance, in naming Dr. 'Ali Amini as Prime Minister he chose an individual of competence who had no close relations with him and who, he knew, would not be subservient to royal manipulation. In the second instance, by dissolving the Parliament without, as legally required, giving a reason for his action, the ruler seemed to abandon the experiment with a two party system. Through these actions he seemed to be moving to a position of reigning and to be withdrawing from his exposed position in which widespread dissatisfaction with the shortcomings of the government found outlet in criticism of the ruler himself.

Dr. Amini was delighted with the opportunity to move against targets specifically designed by the Shah—the large landowners, the so-called ruling class, and corruption in public life—for there their views coincided. However, the National Front and other opponents of the government insisted that elections must be held at once in order to satisfy the legal requirement that a new Majlis must be convened within three months after the dissolution of the preceding one. The Prime Minister, earlier an advocate of free elections, stated that in the present circumstances the Majlis was a luxury which the country could not afford: this statement compelled him to abandon his initial goal of drawing moderate leaders of the National Front into the government.

Indications that the Shah had determined upon a new method of winning popular enthusiasm and support for the monarchy and the government appeared in January 1962 when he signed a cabinet decree providing for the distribution of agricultural villages among the landless peasants, and several months later when he announced that the owners of industries and factories must share their profits with their employees. Then, early in 1963 he was said to be planning to hold a national referendum to approve or disapprove of his actions in favor of the peasants and industrial workers. Through these actions he seemed to be cutting the traditional mutual ties between the monarchy and the country's elite—the families of property, of business interests and of social status—and to intend to substitute the mass support of the voiceless millions of Iran.

Implications of this new policy may be drawn from the initial results of the program of land distribution. According to the decree, a landowner may retain a single village of his holdings or the equivalent in one-sixth shares, a customary division, of separate villages. Orchards, tea plantations, forests, and farms cultivated with machinery are exempt from the decree. Excess holdings are purchased by the state at figures equal to ten times annual income, with payments in ten annual installments, while the peasants purchase the land they formerly share-cropped in fifteen annual installments. These excess holdings are valued at $950 million. The program of land distribution got underway in March 1962: originally it was estimated that it would take two years to turn over some 10,000 villages, but the program gained such momentum that an earlier date of completion was anticipated.

The distribution of these villages will alter drastically the graded social structure of Iran. Not only will the established landowning families be deprived of their ability to round up votes at times of elections for the Parliament, but countless town-dwelling individuals and families will lose their income from ownership of one-sixth shares in these villages. To fill the void created by the departure of traditional ownership and management, the government places faith in agricultural cooperatives—each new proprietor must join a cooperative and pay for the privilege. Local cooperatives are grouped into regional cooperatives, and the regional organizations will come under the direction of a Central Bank for Cooperatives. Firmly attached to the belief that the purchasing power of the independent farmers will soar, the Ministry of Agriculture will use the mechanism of the new bank and of the cooperatives to manufacture and distribute such basic items as textiles, insecticides, pumps, and canned and packaged products at below normal market prices. The more successful this operation becomes, the greater its harmful impact upon established merchandising patterns, upon wholesalers and retailers alike.

The government has suggested that former landowners invest the sums they receive in local industry, although many of these industries are currently unprofitable. Then too, industrialists and entrepreneurs are bound to react in a negative way—by refraining from expansion—to the concept of profit sharing.

The Third Five-Year Plan was initiated in September 1962 and will run until March 1968—actually five and a half years. Before framing this program the Plan Organization reviewed progress under the previous Second Seven-Year Plan: in that period the Gross National Product had risen at least 6 per cent each year, and the industrial output 11 per cent annually. On the other hand, the inflow of foreign capital fell off, foreign exchange reserves dropped, imports rose stupendously, and inflation set in. Also, too great a share of resources had gone into such fixed capital assets as the 180 meter high Karej River dam, the 103 meter Safid Rud dam, and the 203 meter high Dez River dam.

The Third Plan was envisaged as a unified scheme to integrate all ordinary budgetary and developmental expenditures and programs in order to raise the national income by at least 6 per cent annually. The original draft called for a coordinated attack on both economic and social problems, an attack which would be successful only if understood and supported by the entire nation. This draft included a total development budget of $2.457 billion but prior to September this figure was cut to $1.86 billion. Of this final total, some $533 million will be sought from foreign lenders and most of the balance will come from the nation's oil revenues—the share of these revenues assigned to the Plan Organization was to rise in steps from 55 to 80 per cent.

In July 1962 Asadullah Alam succeeded Dr. Ali Amini as prime minister, and instituted milder measures to cope with an economic recession.

In January 1963 over six million voted in a referendum, approving by about 12 to 1, six reform measures sponsored by the ruler. These were, the Land Reform bill, the sale of state-owned factories to finance land reform, sharing of workers in up to 20 per cent of industrial profits, nationalization of forests, amendment of the election law, and establishment of a Literacy Corps. These measures, and subsequent ones, such as female suffrage, were hailed by the regime as the Shah's White Revolution, or the Shah-People Revolution.

In October the Shah opened the XXIst Majlis: the country had been without a Parliament for 18 months. In December Hasan Ali Mansur presided over the founding meeting of the Iran Novin (New Iran) Party. Pledged to support the Shah-People Revolution, its members soon included a majority of the Majlis and many high officials. On March 7, 1964 Hasan Ali Mansur became prime minister, charged to push forward the reform program. Religious opposition appeared to die down with the exile of an outspoken figure, Ayatullah Khomeini, to Turkey.

On January 21, 1965 prime minister Mansur was shot by a student, alleged to be a member of the Devotees of Islam. When he died on the 26th, his place was taken by Amir Abbas Hoveida, a cabinet minister and second in command of the Iran Novin Party. Early in April a conscript in the royal guard attempted to assassinate the Shah. Although he was killed by other guards, a court found that individuals allied with the Tudeh Party had planned the attempt.

At the end of 1966 political opposition to the regime was disorganized, with the National Front inactive. Only outside Iran was it vocal; among Iranian students abroad, and in the persons of leaders of the Tudeh Party who attended the 23rd Congress of the Communist Party of the Soviet Union and used the occasion to attack the government of Iran. However, the party was already split into pro-Soviet and pro-

Chinese factions. Serious threats to internal security seemed remote.

Land reform, including the distribution of farming villages among the peasants and the formation of cooperatives, continues to move ahead, but the production of food grains falls short of the demand. Indeed, the government states that it is unable to predict when massive annual imports of wheat will come to an end. A most successful aspect of land reform is the work of the Literacy Corps, with over 8,000 village teachers, and the Health Corps, established in 1964. The members are conscripts who volunteer to spend their two years of military service in these corps.

Economic development will continue at an accelerating rate, featuring increased electrical generating capacity, the creation of a petrochemical industry, and the construction of assembly plants for a wide range of products. The remarkable expansion of the petroleum industry underwrites this development, providing funds to offset the perennial unfavorable balance of trade. Highly productive wells brought in by joint Iranian-foreign companies near the head of the Persian Gulf led to competitive bidding for offshore sites down the Gulf, and in the Middle East Iran is now second only to Kuwait in annual production. Natural gas, long wasted, is increasingly valuable. In October 1965 Iran achieved a long cherished ambition by concluding an agreement with the Soviet Union which provides for Soviet construction of a steel mill and machine tool plant near Isfahan. Soviet credits of $284 million will be refunded through the sale of natural gas piped to the USSR.

The Shah will continue to dominate internal affairs and foreign relations. His trips abroad are frequent and productive: itineraries include the United States, the USSR, and countries of Western and Eastern Europe. Providing the Iranian army with the most modern planes, missiles and equipment will remain his continuing concern. Iran sees potential danger in the alleged expansionist policies of certain Arab states, typified by their renaming the Persian Gulf the Arabian Gulf and Khuzistan as Arabistan, and moves to strengthen the defense of the petroleum installations. Relations with the United Arab Republic, severed in 1960, and with Syria, broken off in 1965, may not soon be renewed, while displeasure with the government of Iraq has been, in part, reflected by extending support to the Kurdish revolt.

While maintaining its alliances with the West, Iran will continue efforts to strengthen relations with the Communist bloc. Confidence placed in CENTO as a source of military aid in case of aggression against Iran has declined. Relations with the United States will remain good, but less close than formerly as Iran, weaned from dependence on American budgetary support, grants, and loans, diversifies its trade relations and sources of industrial equipment and supply. The USSR, recognizing the stability of the regime, offers friendship and technical assistance, while maintaining the nuisance value of the Tudeh Party and of radio stations under Soviet control which insult the Shah and attack the government. Regionally, some of the non-military activities of CENTO have been assumed by the Regional Cooperation for Development. This promising organization was established in July 1964 by Iran, Turkey, and Pakistan, with its members hopeful of bringing in Afghanistan.

APPENDIX

The Iranian Flag

*T*HE Iranian Constitution designates as the official flag of Iran the insignia of a golden lion and sun upon a field of a green, a red, and a white stripe. The lion, holding a sword in one raised paw with the sun appearing over his back, is placed upon the central white stripe.

This insignia has a very ancient history. Firdawsi, in his story of Sohrab and Rustam, has a description of the banners of famous commanders among which was one bearing the figure of a lion, and another bearing a yellow sun. The combination of the lion and sun as a sign of the Zodiac appears on objects of Iranian art, but the earliest known use of the form as the heraldic device of Iran is on a silver coin of Ghayath ad-din Kaykhusraw, minted not long after A.D. 1200. A star tile of the thirteenth century bears the same device.

Miniature paintings of later periods show Iranian soldiers carrying a banner decorated with the lion and sun, and Safavid coins bear the same device. The lion received his sword during the Qajar period when many of the coins bore the insignia.

The Iranian Calendar

The first six months of the year have thirty-one days each, the next five months have thirty days, and the last month has twenty-nine days, or thirty if the year is a leap year. The year begins with the first day of spring, on March 21 or 22. The names of the months, in order, are: *Farvardin, Ordibehesht, Khordad, Tir, Mordad, Shahrivar, Mehr, Aban, Azar, Dey, Bahman,* and *Esfand.* This solar calendar was adopted by law in 1925 to replace the Arab lunar calendar, and the names of the solar months used in ancient times were then revived.

Iranian Currency
COINS

Gold coins

One Pahlavi
One-half Pahlavi

The gold Pahlavi contains 7.322 grams of fine gold and thus corresponds to the gold content of the British sovereign.

Silver coins

Ten rials
Five rials
Two rials
One rial

From 1943 through 1954 the official rate of exchange for the rial stood at 32.5 to the American dollar. In February 1955 the buying rate was fixed by law at 75 rials to the dollar and the selling rate at 76.5 rials.
The rial is also popularly referred to as the kran. Ten rials are referred to as one toman.

Other coins

Copper 50 dinar pieces,
Bronze-Aluminum 50,
   10, and 5 dinar pieces

The rial is worth 100 dinars. It is also popularly divided into shahis so that the 50 dinar piece is called 10 shahis, the 10 dinar piece 2 shahis, and the 5 dinar piece 1 shahi.

Banknotes

Paper currency is issued
   in 10, 20, 50, 100,
   200, 500, and 1,000
   rial notes.

The bills of high denominations are larger in size, and bear watermark portraits of Reza Shah or of Muhammad Shah, or scenes of the Iranian landscape, of the Trans-Iranian railway or of historical monuments of Iran.

Iranian Weights and Measures

A number of years ago Iran adopted the metric system. However, the earlier local system is still widely used, and certain common units are here defined in relation to the metric system.

Weights

1	sir	75	grams
10	sir	1	charak
1	charak	750	grams
4	charak	1	(Tabriz) man
1	man	3	kilograms
100	man	1	kharvar
1	kharvar	300	kilograms

Measures

1	zar	104	centimeters
6000	zar	1	farsakh
1	farsakh	6240	meters
1	farsakh		approximately 6 kilometers and approximately 4 miles.

SELECTED BIBLIOGRAPHY

* Titles so marked are recommended to the readers on the basis of their general interest and of their availability.

THE HISTORY AND CULTURE OF IRAN

Browne, E. G., *A Literary History of Persia*, Cambridge, 1928. 4 vols. 2180 pp.

Christensen, Arthur, *L'Iran sous les Sassanides*, Paris, 1944.

Edwards, C. A., *The Persian Carpet. Survey of the Rug Weaving Industry of Persia*, London, 1953. 384 pp. and 419 ill.

*Ghirshman, R., *Iran from the Earliest Times to the Islamic Conquest*, Penguin Books, 1954. 367 pp.

Ghirshman, R., *The Parthians and Sassanians*, London, 1962.

Herzfeld, Ernst, *Iran in the Ancient East*, New York, 1941.

*Lockhart, Laurence, *Persian Cities*, London, 1960. 188 pp.

Olmstead, Albert T. E., *The History of the Persian Empire, Achaemenid Period*, Chicago, 1948. 576 pp.

Pope, Arthur U. [Ed.] *A Survey of Persian Art from Prehistoric Times to the Present*, London and New York, 1938-39. 6 vols. 2817 pp. and 1482 plates.

*Pope, Arthur U., *Masterpieces of Persian Art*, New York, 1945.

Schmidt, Erich, *Persepolis I*, Chicago, 1953. 297 pp.

Sykes, Percy, *History of Persia*, London, 1930. 2 vols. 1179 pp.

Vanden Berghe, L., *Archéologie de l'Iran Ancien*, Leiden, 1959. 285 pp. and 173 plates.

Wilber, Donald, *The Architecture of Islamic Iran: The Il Khanid Period*, Princeton, 1955. 208 pp.

Wilber, Donald, *Persian Gardens and Garden Pavilions*, Tokyo, 1962. 239 pp.

THE CHARACTER OF THE CIVILIZATION OF EARLIER IRAN

*Arberry, A. J. [Ed.], *The Legacy of Persia*, Oxford, 1953.

*Arberry, A. J., *Classical Persian Literature*, London, 1958. 464 pp.

Beroukhim, Moussa, *La pensée iranienne à travers l'histoire*, Paris, 1938. 244 pp.

Bowen, J. C. E., *Poems from the Persian*, Oxford, 1948. 105 pp.

Donaldson, Dwight M., *The Shi'ite Religion*, London, 1933. 393 pp.

Elgood, Cyril, *A Medical History of Persia and the Eastern Caliphate from the Earliest Times until the year* A.D. *1932*, Cambridge, 1951. 617 pp.

Field, Henry, *Contributions to the Anthropology of Iran*, Chicago, 1939. 2 vols. 706 pp.

Frye, Richard N., *The Heritage of Persia*, London, 1962.

Hafiz. Fifty Poems. Introduction and annotations by A. J. Arberry, London, 1947. 187 pp.

*Herbert, Sir Thomas, *Travels in Persia, 1627-1629. Abridged and edited by Sir William Foster*, London, 1928. 352 pp. (If obtainable, the original London edition of 1638 is preferable.)

Lambton, A. K. S., *Landlord and Peasant in Persia*, London, 1953. 459 pp.

Levy, Reuben, *A Mirror for Princes. The Qabus Nama by Kai Ka'us ibn Iskandar, Prince of Gurgan*, London, 1951. 265 pp.

Levy, Reuben, *The Persian Language*, London, 1951. 125 pp.

Massé, Henri, *Persian Beliefs and Customs*, New Haven, 1954. 516 pp.

*Morier, James, *The Adventures of Hajji Baba of Isfahan*. (Many editions of this marvelous tale are available.)

Nizam al-Mulk. Siasset Nameh, traité de gouvernement composé pour le Sultan Melik-Chah par le vizir Nizam oul-Moulk. Traduit par Charles Schefer, Paris, 1893. 312 pp.

*Stevens, R., *The Land of the Great Sophy*, London, 1962. 307 pp.

ʿUmar Khayyam. (Any of the numerous editions of his poems, as translated by Fitzgerald or others.)

Virolleaud, Charles, *Le theatre persan ou le drame de Kerbéla*, Paris, 1950. 141 pp.

Voyages du chevalier Chardin en Perse, et autres lieux d'Orient . . . , Amsterdam, 1711. 3 vols. 987 pp.

COUNTRY AND PEOPLE AS SEEN BY CONTEMPORARY OBSERVERS

Barth, Fredrik, *Nomads of South Persia*, Oslo, 1961. 159 pp.

Blunt, Wilfred, *A Persian Spring*, London, 1957. 252 pp.

*Browne, E. G., *A Year amongst the Persians*, Cambridge, 1927.

Costa, A. and Lockhart, L., *Persia*, New York, 1958. 45 pp. and 110 plates.

Cronin, Vincent, *The Last Migration*, London, 1957. 343 pp.

Donaldson, Bess A., *The Wild Rue. A Study of Muhammadan Magic and Folklore in Iran*, London, 1938. 216 pp.

Filmer, Henry, *The Pageant of Persia*, Indianapolis, 1936.

Isfandiary, F., *The Day of Sacrifice*, London, 1960.

Ishaque, Mohammad, *Modern Persian Poetry*, Calcutta, 1943.

Mazda, Maideh, *In A Persian Kitchen*, Tokyo, 1960.

Mehdevi, Anne S., *Persian Adventure*, New York, 1953. 320 pp.

Merritt-Hawkes, O. A., *Persia: Romance and Reality*, London, 1935. 322 pp.

Monteil, Vincent, *Iran*, Paris, 1957. 191 pp.

Najafi, Najmeh, *Persia is my Heart*, New York, 1957.

Najafi, Najmeh and Hinckley, H., *Reveille for a Persian Village*, New York, 1958.

Smith, Anthony, *Blind White Fish in Persia*, London, 1953.

Stark, Freya, *The Valleys of the Assassins . . .* , London, 1934.

Suratgar, Olive, *I Sing in the Wilderness*, London, 1951, 222 pp.

Sykes, P. M. and Khan Bahadur Ahmad Din Khan, *The Glory of the Shia World. The Tale of a Pilgrimage*, London, 1910.

Ullens de Schotten, M. T., *Lords of the Mountains. Southern Persia and the Kashkai Tribe*, London, 1956. 128 pp.

Material on Contemporary Iran

Afschar, M., *La politique europiénne en Perse*, Berlin, 1921.

Agabekov, G., *Ogpu, the Russian Secret Terror*, New York, 1931. 277 pp.

Arasteh, R., *Education and Social Awakening in Iran, 1850-1960*, Leiden, 1962. 144 pp.

*Banani, Amin, *The Modernization of Iran, 1921-1941*, Stanford, 1961. 191 pp.

Binder, Leonard, *Iran. Political Development in a Changing Society*, Berkeley, 1962. 362 pp.

Elwell-Sutton, L. P., *Persian Oil: A Study in Power Politics*, London, 1955. 343 pp.

Fatemi, N. S., *Diplomatic History of Persia, 1917-1923; Anglo-Russian Power Politics in Iran*, New York, 1952. 331 pp.

Fatemi, N. S., *Oil Diplomacy. Powder Keg in Iran*, New York, 1954. 405 pp.

Ford, Alan W., *The Anglo-Iranian Oil Dispute of 1951-1952*, Berkeley, 1954. 348 pp.

Frye, Richard N., *Iran*, London, 1960. 126 pp.

Haas, William S., *Iran*, New York, 1946. 273 pp.

Hamzavi, A. H., *Persia and the Powers*, London, 1946, 125 pp.

*Lenczowski, George, *Russia and the West in Iran, 1918-1948*, Ithaca, 1949. 383 pp.

Millspaugh, Arthur C., *The American Task in Persia*, New York, 1925. 322 pp.

*Millspaugh, Arthur C., *Americans in Persia*, Washington, 1946. 293 pp.

*Mohammed Reza Shah Pahlavi, *Mission for My Country*, London and New York, 1961. 336 pp.

Motter, T. H. Vail, *The Persian Corridor and Aid to Russia*, Washington, 1952. 545 pp.

Skrine, C., *World War in Iran*, London, 1962. 330 pp.

*Upton, Joseph M., *The History of Modern Iran An Interpretation*, Cambridge, 1960. 163 pp.

Vreeland, H. H. [Ed.], *Iran*, New Haven, 1957. 429 pp.

Warne, William E., *Mission for Peace: Point Four in Iran*, New York, 1956. 320 pp.

Weaver, Paul E., *Soviet Strategy in Iran 1941-1957*, Washington, 1958. 277 pp.

*Wilber, Donald, *Contemporary Iran*, New York, 1963.

Yeselson, Abrahim, *U.S.-Persian Diplomatic Relations, 1883-1921*, New Brunswick, 1956. 252 pp.

DOCUMENTARY SOURCES

Ebtehaj, G. H., *A Guide to Iran*, Tehran, 1956. 4th ed. 318 pp.

Echo Almanac and Book of Facts. 1962. Tehran, 1962. 879 pp.

Echo Reports, Tehran (daily press digest, in English)

Elwell-Sutton, L. P., *A Guide to Iranian Area Study*, Ann Arbor, Michigan, 1952. 235 pp.

Farman, Hafez F., *Iran; A Selected and Annotated Bibliography*, Washington, 1951. 100 pp.

Guide Bleu. Moyen Orient: Liban, Syrie, Jordanie, Iraq, Iran, Paris, 1956. (Iran, pp. 657-921)

Iran-Presse, Tehran (daily press digest, in French)

Middle Eastern Affairs, New York (monthly)

Saba, Mohsen, *Bibliographie Française de l'Iran*, Tehran, 1951, 297 pp.

The Middle East Journal, Washington (quarterly)

Wilson, Arnold T., *A Bibliography of Persia*, Oxford, 1930. 253 pp.

INDEX

Abadan Island, refinery at, 222; air-field at, 276; port, 277; riot at, 112

Abadeh, town, 181

Abaqa, Il Khan ruler, 51, 53, 56

'Abbas, Shah, Safavid ruler, 67-70, 73, 163, 164, 191-194

'Abbas II, Safavid ruler, 70

'Abbas III, Safavid ruler, 74

'Abbas Effendi, Bahai leader, 77

Abbasid Caliphate, 38, 40, 51

'Abdullah ibn Fazlullah (Wassaf), historian, 54

Abhar River, 49

Ab-i-Diz River, 234

Abu 'Ali ibn Sina (Avicenna), phi-losopher, 39, 72

Abu Bekr, Caliph, 36

Abu Sa'id, Il Khan ruler, 54, 58

Achaemenid Empire, 20f.; establish-ment, 20; military campaigns, 20, 21; administration, 22, 23; army, 22; roads, 22, 140; language, 23; religion, 23, 24; architecture, 24, 25; art, 25, 26

'Adud ad-dawla, Buvayhid ruler, 40

Afghanistan, Helmand River in, 8; in Islamic times, 40; war with, 74, 78; relations with, 283

Afshar period, 74, 75

Agricultural Bank, 265

agriculture, 227f.; in prehistoric times, 14; technical offices and in-stitutes for, 154; research program for, 155

Agriculture, Ministry of, 154, 155

Ahmad, Buvayhid ruler, 40

Ahmad, Il Khan ruler, 51

Ahmad Shah, Qajar ruler, 81, 97

Ahriman, deity, 89

Ahura Mazda, deity, 23, 32, 33, 35

Ahwaz, town, 8, 163

air force, strength, 148

air service, 276

Akhal, Treaty of, 79

'Ala' ad-din, "world incendiary," 41

'Ala, Husein, 112, 119, 128, 130

al-Biruni, author, 41, 57

Alam, Asadullah, 128, 132, 282, 283, 286

Alborz College, 207, 208

Aleppo in Syria, 52, 59

Alexander the Great, Persepolis burned by, 26; campaigns of, 27; marries Roxana, 27; at tomb of Cyrus, 27; plans a new world state, 27; marries daughter of Da-rius III, 27; death of, 27

Alexander Severus, Emperor, 31

al-Ghazali, philosopher, 42, 47

'Ali, Shi'a Caliph, 53, 89

'Ali ibn Buvayh, ruler, 40

'Ali Shir Nawa'i, poet, 62, 64, 66

Allies, in World War I, 82; in World War II, 102f.

Alp Arslan, Seljuq ruler, 45

Alptegin, Ghaznavid ruler, 40

American Legation, 79

American missions, financial, 263; military, 148; to Security Guard, 151

American schools, 207, 208

Amini, Dr. 'Ali, 125, 126, 128, 132

Amiranian Oil Company, 223

Amir Hamza, Sultan, Safavid ruler, 67

Amr ibn Layth, Saffarid ruler, 38

Anahita, temple of, 31

Anarak, mines, 220

ancient mounds, 16

Anglo-Iranian Oil Company, 222, 223; terms of concessions, 222; production, 222; employees, 222; nationalization of, 114; negotia-tions with, 112-126; member of consortium, 126, 224; becomes British Petroleum Co., 224

Anglo-Russian agreement of 1907, 81

animals, domestic, 242-245

animals, wild, 243, 244

annual rainfall, 11

[297]